S0-BUF-956

DEMOGRAPHIC CHANGE
IN SUB-SAHARAN AFRICA

DEMOGRAPHIC EFFECTS OF ECONOMIC REVERSALS
IN SUB-SAHARAN AFRICA

EFFECTS OF HEALTH PROGRAMS ON CHILD MORTALITY
IN SUB-SAHARAN AFRICA

FACTORS AFFECTING CONTRACEPTIVE USE
IN SUB-SAHARAN AFRICA

POPULATION DYNAMICS OF KENYA

POPULATION DYNAMICS OF SENEGAL

SOCIAL DYNAMICS OF ADOLESCENT FERTILITY
IN SUB-SAHARAN AFRICA

NOTE: This map, which has been prepared solely for the convenience of readers, does not purport to express political boundaries or relationships. The scale is a composite of several forms of projection.

FACTORS AFFECTING

CONTRACEPTIVE USE

IN SUB-SAHARAN AFRICA

• • • • • • • • • • • • • • • • •

Working Group on Factors Affecting Contraceptive Use

Panel on the Population Dynamics of Sub-Saharan Africa

Committee on Population

Commission on Behavioral and Social Sciences and Education

National Research Council

HQ
766.5
.A357
F33
1993
West

*A15045 869163

NATIONAL ACADEMY PRESS
Washington, D.C.   1993

NATIONAL ACADEMY PRESS • 2101 Constitution Avenue, N.W. • Washington, D.C. 20418

NOTICE: The project that is the subject of this report was approved by the Governing Board of the National Research Council, whose members are drawn from the councils of the National Academy of Sciences, the National Academy of Engineering, and the Institute of Medicine. The members of the committee responsible for the report were chosen for their special competences and with regard for appropriate balance.

This report has been reviewed by a group other than the authors according to procedures approved by a Report Review Committee consisting of members of the National Academy of Sciences, the National Academy of Engineering, and the Institute of Medicine.

The National Academy of Sciences is a private, nonprofit, self-perpetuating society of distinguished scholars engaged in scientific and engineering research, dedicated to the further-ance of science and technology and to their use for the general welfare. Upon the authority of the charter granted to it by the Congress in 1863, the Academy has a mandate that requires it to advise the federal government on scientific and technical matters. Dr. Bruce M. Alberts is president of the National Academy of Sciences.

The National Academy of Engineering was established in 1964, under the charter of the National Academy of Sciences, as a parallel organization of outstanding engineers. It is autonomous in its administration and in the selection of its members, sharing with the National Academy of Sciences the responsibility for advising the federal government. The National Academy of Engineering also sponsors engineering programs aimed at meeting national needs, encourages education and research, and recognizes the superior achievements of engineers. Dr. Robert M. White is president of the National Academy of Engineering.

The Institute of Medicine was established in 1970 by the National Academy of Sciences to secure the services of eminent members of appropriate professions in the examination of policy matters pertaining to the health of the public. The Institute acts under the responsibility given to the National Academy of Sciences by its congressional charter to be an adviser to the federal government and, upon its own initiative, to identify issues of medical care, research, and education. Dr. Kenneth I. Shine is president of the Institute of Medicine.

The National Research Council was organized by the National Academy of Sciences in 1916 to associate the broad community of science and technology with the Academy's pur-poses of furthering knowledge and advising the federal government. Functioning in accor-dance with general policies determined by the Academy, the Council has become the principal operating agency of both the National Academy of Sciences and the National Academy of Engineering in providing services to the government, the public, and the scientific and engi-neering communities. The Council is administered jointly by both Academies and the Institute of Medicine. Dr. Bruce M. Alberts and Dr. Robert M. White are chairman and vice chairman, respectively, of the National Research Council.

Library of Congress Catalog Card No. 93-85134
International Standard Book Number 0-309-04944-X

Additional copies of this report are available from: National Academy Press, 2101 Constitu-tion Avenue, N.W., Box 285, Washington, D.C. 20418. Call 800-624-6242 or 202-334-3313 (in the Washington Metropolitan Area).

B168
Copyright 1993 by the National Academy of Sciences. All rights reserved.

Printed in the United States of America

WORKING GROUP ON FACTORS AFFECTING CONTRACEPTIVE USE

JANE T. BERTRAND (*Chair*), School of Public Health and Tropical Medicine, Tulane University
EVASIUS K. BAUNI, Department of Geography, Kenyatta University, Kenya
RON J. LESTHAEGHE, Faculteit van de Economische, Sociale en Politieke Wetenschappen, Vrije Universiteit Brussel, Belgium
MARK R. MONTGOMERY, Department of Economics, State University of New York at Stony Brook
OLEKO TAMBASHE, Faculté d'Economiques, Département de Démographie, Université de Kinshasa, Zaire
MARIA J. WAWER, Center for Population and Family Health, Columbia University

CAROLE L. JOLLY, *Staff Officer*
SUSAN M. COKE, *Senior Project Assistant*
DIANE L. GOLDMAN, *Administrative Assistant**
JOAN MONTGOMERY HALFORD, *Senior Project Assistant***
PAULA J. MELVILLE, *Senior Project Assistant*

---

* through December 1991
**through July 1992

PANEL ON THE
POPULATION DYNAMICS OF SUB-SAHARAN AFRICA

KENNETH H. HILL (*Chair*), Department of Population Dynamics, Johns Hopkins University

ADERANTI ADEPOJU, Institut de Développement Economique et de la Planification (IDEP), Dakar, Senegal

JANE T. BERTRAND, School of Public Health and Tropical Medicine, Tulane University

CAROLINE H. BLEDSOE, Department of Anthropology, Northwestern University

WILLIAM BRASS, Centre for Population Studies, London School of Hygiene and Tropical Medicine, England

DOUGLAS C. EWBANK, Population Studies Center, University of Pennsylvania

PHILIPPE FARGUES, Centre d'Etudes et de Documentation Economique, Sociale et Juridique (CEDEJ), Cairo, Egypt

RON J. LESTHAEGHE, Faculteit van de Economische, Sociale en Politieke Wetenschappen, Vrije Universiteit Brussel, Belgium

PATRICK O. OHADIKE, Regional Institute for Population Studies (RIPS), Accra, Ghana

ANNE R. PEBLEY, The RAND Corporation, Santa Monica, California

DANIEL M. SALA-DIAKANDA, Institut de Formation et de Recherche Démographiques (IFORD), Yaoundé, Cameroon

COMMITTEE ON POPULATION

SAMUEL H. PRESTON (*Chair*), Population Studies Center, University of
  Pennsylvania
JOSE-LUIS BOBADILLA, World Bank, Washington, D.C.
JOHN B. CASTERLINE, Department of Sociology, Brown University
KENNETH H. HILL, Department of Population Dynamics, Johns Hopkins
  University
DEAN T. JAMISON, School of Public Health, University of California,
  Los Angeles
ANNE R. PEBLEY, The RAND Corporation, Santa Monica, California
RONALD R. RINDFUSS, Department of Sociology, University of North
  Carolina, Chapel Hill
T. PAUL SCHULTZ, Department of Economics, Yale University
SUSAN C.M. SCRIMSHAW, School of Public Health, University of
  California, Los Angeles
BETH J. SOLDO, Department of Demography, Georgetown University
MARTA TIENDA, Population Research Center, University of Chicago
BARBARA BOYLE TORREY, Population Reference Bureau, Washington,
  D.C.
JAMES TRUSSELL, Office of Population Research, Princeton University
AMY O. TSUI, Carolina Population Center, University of North Carolina,
  Chapel Hill

LINDA G. MARTIN, *Director*
BARNEY COHEN, *Research Associate*
SUSAN M. COKE, *Senior Project Assistant*
KAREN A. FOOTE, *Research Associate*
DIANE L. GOLDMAN, *Administrative Assistant**
JAMES N. GRIBBLE, *Program Officer*
JOAN MONTGOMERY HALFORD, *Senior Project Assistant***
CAROLE L. JOLLY, *Program Officer*
DOMINIQUE MEEKERS, *Research Associate**
PAULA J. MELVILLE, *Senior Project Assistant*

---

* through December 1991
** through July 1992

Preface

This report is one in a series of studies that have been carried out under the auspices of the Panel on the Population Dynamics of Sub-Saharan Africa of the National Research Council's Committee on Population. The Research Council has a long history of examining population issues in developing countries. In 1971 it issued the report *Rapid Population Growth: Consequences and Policy Implications.* In 1977, the predecessor Committee on Population and Demography began a major study of levels and trends of fertility and mortality in the developing world that resulted in 13 country reports and 6 reports on demographic methods. Then, in the early 1980s, it undertook a study of the determinants of fertility in the developing world, which resulted in 10 reports. In the mid- and late-1980s, the Committee on Population assessed the economic consequences of population growth and the health consequences of contraceptive use and controlled fertility, among many other activities.

No publication on the demography of sub-Saharan Africa emerged from the early work of the committee, largely because of the paucity of data and the poor quality of what was available. However, censuses, ethnographic studies, and surveys of recent years, such as those under the auspices of the World Fertility Survey and the Demographic and Health Survey Programs, have made available data on the demography of sub-Saharan Africa. The data collection has no doubt been stimulated by the increasing interest of both scholars and policymakers in the demographic development of Africa and the relations between demographic change and socioeconomic developments. In response to this interest, the Committee on Population held a meeting in 1989 to ascertain the feasibility and desirability of a major study of the demography of Africa, and decided to set up a Panel on the Population Dynamics of Sub-Saharan Africa.

The panel, which is chaired by Kenneth Hill and includes members from Africa, Europe, and the United States, met for the first time in February 1990 in Washington, D.C. At that meeting the panel decided to set up six working groups, composed of its own members and other experts on the demography of Africa, to carry out specific studies. Four working groups focused on cross-national studies of substantive issues: the social dynamics of adolescent fertility, factors affecting contraceptive use, the effects on mortality of child survival and general health programs, and the demographic effects of economic reversals. The two other working groups were charged with in-depth studies of Kenya and Senegal, with the objective of studying linkages between demographic variables and between those variables and socioeconomic changes. The panel also decided to publish a volume of papers reviewing levels and trends of fertility, nuptiality, the proximate determinants of fertility, child mortality, adult mortality, internal migration, and international migration, as well as the demographic consequences of the AIDS epidemic.

This report, one of the four cross-national studies, analyzes the factors affecting contraceptive use. The study was initiated because of interest in recent survey results that indicated increases in contraceptive use in several sub-Saharan African countries. Because of historically high fertility levels and low contraceptive use in the region, it was debated whether these changes heralded a new era for Africa or were anomalies.

This report examines the literature on the socioeconomic, social organizational, and family planning program factors that are related to contraceptive use. Multivariate analysis is employed to assess the relative importance of those factors that can be measured and for which data are available from surveys. In Chapter 7, the relative importance of contraceptive use versus postpartum practices in inhibiting fertility in Africa is assessed.

As is the case for all of the panel's work, this report would not have been possible without the cooperation and assistance of the Demographic and Health Survey (DHS) Program of the Institute for Resource Development/Macro Systems. We are grateful to the DHS staff for responding to our inquiries and facilitating our early access to the survey data.

We are also grateful to the organizations that provided financial support for the work of the panel: the Office of Population and the Africa Bureau of the Agency for International Development, the Andrew W. Mellon Foundation, the William and Flora Hewlett Foundation, and the Rockefeller Foundation. Besides providing funding, the representatives of these organizations were a source of information and advice in the development of the panel's overall work plan.

This report results from the joint efforts of the working group members and staff, and represents a consensus of the members' views on the issues addressed. The Committee on Population and the Panel on the Population Dynamics of Sub-Saharan Africa appreciate the time and energy that all the working group members devoted to the study. The following people deserve recognition for their special contributions: Mark Montgomery analyzed the socioeconomic and social organizational factors affecting contraceptive use and wrote the first drafts of Chapters 3 and 4. He also developed the framework of the factors affecting contraceptive use (described in Chapter 1 and Appendix A), which guided the working group's research, and carried out the individual-level bivariate analysis of contraceptive use discussed in Chapter 2.

Maria Wawer explored the development of family planning policies and programs, and their effect on contraceptive use. Her research is the basis for Chapter 5, which she first drafted. Ron Lesthaeghe performed the regional multivariate analysis of contraceptive use based on a data set developed by Carole Jolly. Chapters 6 and 7 reflect this effort. Ron Lesthaeghe was also instrumental in documenting the historical context of contraceptive use in sub-Saharan Africa and graciously hosted the second of the three meetings of the working group in Brussels. Oleko Tambashe pulled together the evidence on levels, trends, and differentials in contraceptive use to write, with Jane Bertrand, the first draft of Chapter 2. Evasius Bauni contributed to the sections on knowledge of contraceptive use. Both Oleko Tambashe and Evasius Bauni played important roles in promoting the working group's understanding of the experiences of their respective countries.

Jane Bertrand, as the working group's chair, was instrumental in directing the research of the group during the last two years and wrote the first drafts of Chapters 1 and 8. She and Carole Jolly served as the principal editors and coordinators for the report. Linda Martin provided substantive comments on numerous drafts of the report, as well as participating in all the group's meetings and contributing substantially to the review process. Jay Gribble took care of innumerable details in the final drafting stages. As noted above, however, this report reflects the views of the working group as a whole, and considerable effort by all the members and staff has gone into its production.

The working group was assisted in its efforts by several commissioned background papers. Lisa Brecker and Regina McNamara coauthored a paper on family planning programs in Africa. Thérèse Locoh wrote a paper on the socioeconomic context of contraceptive use. Maria Messina authored a paper on household decision making, reproductive roles, and local social organization as they affect contraceptive use and fertility. G. Verleye assisted in the regional analysis of contraceptive use.

Special thanks are also due Susan Coke, Joan Montgomery Halford, Diane Goldman, and Paula Melville for providing superb administrative and logistical support to the working group, to Florence Poillon for her skillful editing of the report, and to Elaine McGarraugh for meticulous production assistance. Joan Montgomery Halford and Paulette Vallière Korazemo provided excellent French to English translation of a draft chapter and a background paper. Eugenia Grohman and Elaine McGarraugh were instrumental in guiding the report through the review and production processes.

SAMUEL H. PRESTON, *Chair*
Committee on Population

Contents

Executive Summary

This report stems from interest in recent survey results indicating increases in contraceptive use in several countries in sub-Saharan Africa. Because Africa is the only region of the world yet to undergo a contraceptive revolution resulting in fertility decline, there has been substantial debate about the implications of these increases for the rest of Africa. The task of the working group was to examine the factors affecting contraceptive use, with special attention to why use has risen in some areas and not in others.

KEY ISSUES

To fulfill the task, the report focuses on identifying the key factors that affect the demand for children and the supply of contraception. On the demand side, the conditions under which people in sub-Saharan Africa can be expected to desire smaller family sizes are examined. There is much debate surrounding this issue. On one hand, fertility decline is seen as the result of economic development; as elsewhere in the world, improvements in socioeconomic conditions will stimulate the desire for family limitation. Africa's sustained high fertility is therefore explained in terms of factors that inhibit economic development more generally. From the other perspective, sub-Saharan Africa is described as being different from the rest of the world in its supports for high fertility, which stem from unique features of social organization that are not easily modified by economic development.

1

Are the past structures so deeply embedded and immutable that high fertility will persist? Or might pronatalist values and constraints give way in the face of new socioeconomic influences, as they have elsewhere in the world?

On the supply side, the report examines the effects of family planning policies and programs on the provision of contraceptives. A central question concerns the conditions under which family planning activities have affected contraceptive use in Africa. Are there particular regions where family planning programs have been particularly successful?

Finally, multivariate analysis is undertaken to determine empirically the factors that are associated with observed increases in contraceptive use. The analysis also examines the relative importance of contraceptive use compared to postpartum nonsusceptibility in inhibiting fertility in Africa.

FINDINGS

In exploring the linkages between economic development and fertility, the report focuses on levels of per capita income, child mortality, educational attainment among adults, and the costs and benefits of having children. Although the associations between these factors and fertility are not always strong in Africa, especially relative to the experience of Latin America, they are nonetheless important and indicate a receptivity to smaller family sizes among particular groups. The distinct socioeconomic experiences of Botswana, Kenya, and Zimbabwe have contributed to their substantial increases in contraception. In particular, the sustained improvements in, and resulting low levels of, mortality in these countries are unique within Africa. However, the diverse nature of these socioeconomic linkages in Africa suggests that features of African social structure remain important determinants of the demand for children.

The long-standing forms of African social organization—the high value attached to the perpetuation of the lineage; the importance of children as a means of gaining access to resources, particularly land; the use of kinship networks to share the costs and benefits of children, primarily through child fostering; and the weak nature of conjugal bonds—clearly inhibit contraceptive adoption and fertility decline. However, the working group believes that these features are not immutable and are being affected by changing economic conditions in some settings. In particular, there is evidence to suggest that changes in childrearing costs and educational aspirations, as well as deteriorating economic conditions, are resulting in increased conjugal closeness and shared decision making. Many of these changes are particularly notable in urban areas and among the educated—populations that exhibit higher contraceptive prevalence.

Our review of family planning programs indicates a clear link between program implementation and contraceptive use. In Botswana, Kenya, and

Zimbabwe, political commitment and the development of population policies supportive of family planning have created environments for the successful implementation of programs. Private organizations have been instrumental in demonstrating the acceptability of contraception in Africa and inducing further investments in this sector. However, those countries that show substantial increases in national prevalence all have well-developed public sector service delivery programs.

In the empirical examination of the factors affecting modern contraceptive use, female education emerges as an important determinant of prevalence at the individual, regional, and national levels. Urbanization and the proportion Muslim are shown to affect schooling levels and thus contraceptive use.

Polygyny, a proxy for aspects of the high-fertility rationale, negatively affects contraceptive use at the regional level, providing support for the view that African social organization continues to influence the demand for children.

Only in regions in the higher use countries does contraceptive use play a more important role in inhibiting fertility than postpartum nonsusceptibility. If no additional declines in the period of postpartum nonsusceptibility occur, future increases in contraceptive use should directly result in lower fertility.

Several primary factors are essential to these future increases in contraceptive use: continued improvements in female education, reductions in infant and child mortality, and strengthening of family planning programs. Continued progress in these areas should provide the impetus for the uptake of contraception in other regions of Africa. Thus, the central conclusion of the report is that, although the high-fertility rationale has not disappeared, Africa may be entering a new era of increased contraceptive use.

1

Introduction

THE CONTRACEPTIVE REVOLUTION IN
THE DEVELOPING WORLD

Over the past 25 years the world has experienced a contraceptive revolution (Donaldson and Tsui, 1990). Contraceptive prevalence—the percentage of women of reproductive age, married or living in union, that use some type of contraceptive method—has risen from less than 10 percent around the world in the early 1960s to an estimated 55 percent in the late 1980s and early 1990s (Bongaarts et al., 1990; Population Reference Bureau, 1992). This increase is by no means limited to the developed countries. Although prevalence levels are higher in the industrial than in the developing world (72 versus 51 percent), it is noteworthy that more than half the women of reproductive age in developing countries currently use some form of contraception (Population Reference Bureau, 1992).

The importance of this phenomenon lies in the close relationship between contraceptive prevalence and fertility (Mauldin and Segal, 1988). Contraceptive use is one of four key factors that determine fertility, the other three being involvement in sexual union, postpartum nonsusceptibility, and induced abortion (Bongaarts, 1978). Of the four, contraception has the strongest effect on fertility in most developing countries (Donaldson and Tsui, 1990). Africa[1] is different, in that in the past the duration of postpar-

---

[1]Throughout this volume, the terms sub-Saharan Africa and Africa are used interchangeably. The countries north of the Sahara (Egypt, Libya, Algeria, Tunisia, and Morocco) are labeled as

tum nonsusceptibility has been the key determinant of fertility levels. However, with an increase in the use of modern contraception, the relative importance of the two factors is changing (Chapter 7; Jolly and Gribble, 1993). In short, for those interested in current and future fertility rates, it is essential to examine the issue of contraceptive prevalence.

Even so, the contraceptive use rate in Africa, 13 percent, is low relative to other regions of the developing world (Population Reference Bureau, 1992; United Nations, 1993). The prevalence rates for Asia and Latin America are surprisingly similar and much higher, namely, 56 and 57 percent, respectively. However, these regional figures mask considerable variation among countries of a given continent: for example, Thailand (66 percent) versus Pakistan (12 percent); Costa Rica (70 percent) versus Bolivia (30 percent); and Zimbabwe (43 percent) versus Mali (3 percent) (Population Reference Bureau, 1992; Demographic and Health Survey data tapes). No doubt there are also marked differences within each country.

The moderate to high levels of contraceptive use found in most Asian and Latin American countries generally reflect both existing social conditions (as measured by literacy, female education, life expectancy, infant mortality, and related indicators) and access to family planning services through the public or private sector (Mauldin and Ross, 1991). The country-by-country differences in contraceptive prevalence notwithstanding, family planning has become a widely practiced, culturally acceptable behavior throughout many countries in Asia and Latin America.

CONTRACEPTIVE USE IN SUB-SAHARAN AFRICA

The situation is markedly different in sub-Saharan Africa, where high birth rates have been the norm, and access to modern contraception was extremely limited (except in pilot program areas) prior to 1980.

Among the factors that have contributed to sustained high fertility in Africa are a large percentage of the population living in rural areas, low levels of socioeconomic development, high rates of infant and child mortality, and patterns of social organization and deeply ingrained cultural values that maintain the demand for large families. Moreover, until recently, the majority of African government officials expressed little support for "popu-

---

North Africa. The Sudan, listed by the United Nations as North Africa, is nonetheless included in our analysis. Except where noted, discussion is limited to the 39 mainland sub-Saharan countries plus the large island-nation of Madagascar. Mauritius, which has a relatively high modern contraceptive prevalence rate of 46 percent, is excluded, given its unique sociohistorical background and the ethnic composition of its population (Mauritius Ministry of Health et al., 1992).

lation control," as enunciated at the World Population Conference in Bucharest in 1974; their position then was that "development is the best contraceptive" (Donaldson and Tsui, 1990). African governments questioned the motivation of Western nations concerned with limiting the population growth of African nations, and they viewed foreign assistance for population programs as a poor use of resources, given the other development needs of their countries. The successful implementation of family planning programs seemed so unlikely in most African countries that prior to the 1980s, most international agencies working in family planning chose to invest their financial and human resources in the more promising areas of Asia and Latin America. This allocation served as an additional constraint to contraceptive use: the lack of access to family planning services.

Historical Factors Leading to High Fertility

In virtually all societies, even those where contraception is not practiced, human fertility falls considerably short of its biological maximum as a consequence of cultural practices or physical impairments that curb reproduction. Such constraints were certainly in place in sub-Saharan Africa during the colonial and precolonial periods; prolonged breastfeeding coupled with long periods of postpartum abstinence supported a marked pattern of birth spacing. In some areas, there prevailed high levels of sterility, which further reduced fertility.

Although there was considerable regional variation, the mean length of the nonsusceptible period in western Africa before the 1950s following each live birth was commonly on the order of 2.5 years, due primarily to postpartum taboos on sexual relations (Page and Lesthaeghe, 1981). Where there was such a taboo, other practices worked in support of this prolonged abstinence (e.g., a woman's returning to her native village at the time of the baby's birth and remaining there until the child was 1 to 2 years old). Similarly, the practice of polygyny (having more than one wife) provided males with alternate sexual partners during the postpartum abstinence period.

In several regions where Islam was prevalent, birth spacing was more a function of lactational amenorrhea (i.e., nonsusceptibility to conception due to breastfeeding) because the accompanying period of postpartum abstinence followed the direction of the 40-day rule, common to Islamic custom. In eastern Africa, periods of postpartum abstinence were also shorter than in western Africa, but the overall nonsusceptible period was still on the order of 1.5 to 2.0 years as a consequence of prolonged lactation (Page and Lesthaeghe, 1981). Very few African societies had no postpartum taboo at all. Historically, the basic pattern of fertility limitation hinged on these birth-spacing practices.

Birth spacing continues to be widely accepted and practiced in many African societies. Even today, one can go to remote villages throughout the continent and find women with little or no education who recognize the importance of birth spacing for the health of their children. In fact, women who fail to observe this practice in some societies may find themselves the target of scorn or ridicule by other members of the community (Caldwell and Caldwell, 1981). Although birth spacing results in a delay in pregnancy, the motivation has not been one of achieving a smaller family size. To the contrary, spacing may have arisen to enhance the probability that each child would survive through childhood and beyond. Thus, although Westerners tend to view family planning as a means of achieving a small family norm, birth spacing in Africa has been used to attain what many Africans consider the ideal: a large number of healthy children.

Reports from the early 1980s indicated that the practice of postpartum abstinence was on the wane throughout Africa (Page and Lesthaeghe, 1981). Increased female education and urbanization have affected patterns of union in a number of countries, making prolonged periods of sexual abstinence more difficult to observe. For example, with urbanization, returning to one's village for childbirth may be logistically or economically difficult. Some women reduce the abstinence period in an effort to keep their husbands closer to home. However, available data suggest no further decline in the components of the nonsusceptible period during the decade of the 1980s (Lesthaeghe et al., 1992). If postpartum practices remain fairly stable in the coming years, any decrease in fertility will necessarily result from increased contraceptive use.

In many instances, women have moved from postpartum abstinence to modern contraception as a means of achieving the desired spacing without the inconvenience of abstinence. For example, Hill and Bledsoe (1992) cite the case of The Gambia, where women appear to be using Western contraceptive technologies to achieve a characteristically African goal: long birth intervals between children. By contrast, traditional methods of birth spacing and modern contraceptive use are viewed by many Africans as being two very distinct practices: The former is perceived to be highly beneficial to the health and welfare of the family; the latter has been less readily embraced.

In addition to postpartum practices, pathological sterility (the inability to bear a first birth caused mainly by sexually transmitted diseases (STDs), particularly gonorrhea) resulted in diminished levels of fertility in a variety of populations from the coast of the Indian Ocean to the western Sahel. The eastern coastal zones of Kenya and Tanzania were particularly affected, together with several lake regions. Also, nomadic populations in the western and central Sahel exhibited higher than normal levels of sterility. However, the zone with the most severe sterility was unquestionably Central

Africa, including southern Sudan, northern Zaire, the Central African Republic, Gabon, and parts of Cameroon (Page and Coale, 1972; Frank 1983a,b).

Because of these factors, fertility levels in sub-Saharan Africa in the 1950s were low compared to many other developing countries. This picture started to change in the following decades as a result of declining levels of pathological sterility (in part due to the introduction of antibiotics) and especially the reduction in the durations of both breastfeeding and postpartum abstinence. Increased education, urbanization, and access to baby-milk formulas were typically associated with reduction of the postpartum nonsusceptible period. In many areas the resulting rise in fertility, in tandem with declining mortality, yielded record rates of population growth (e.g., Kenya had an annual population growth rate of 4.0 percent in the late 1970s).

Family Planning Initiatives

In the 1980s, major economic and political crises occurred that dramatically changed the climate for population policies and family planning programs. Government leaders and other policymakers in some African countries became increasingly concerned that rapid population growth would have a detrimental effect on socioeconomic development. Moreover, government officials recognized the potential health benefits of birth spacing and were willing to support family planning service delivery as a maternal and child health (MCH) intervention. In an unprecedented move, African leaders collectively endorsed family planning and the necessity of integrating it into MCH programs in the 1984 Kilimanjaro Action Program (Economic Commission for Africa, 1984). The same year they joined with leaders from developing countries around the world at the World Population Conference in Mexico to advocate increased support for family planning service delivery by donor nations.

This shift in position was reflected in the results of a recent United Nations (UN) survey on population issues: 27 of the 45 governments in the region estimated their country's level of fertility to be too high, 15 judged the level to be satisfactory, and only 3 judged the level to be too low (United Nations, 1989a). A number of countries—Ghana, Kenya, Nigeria, Rwanda, and Senegal—currently have explicit population policies with precise demographic objectives. Even governments not supportive of population policies have tended recently to turn a blind eye to private family planning initiatives. Laws in some francophone countries forbidding all publicity and distribution of contraceptive products are rarely enforced.

This change in political climate was coupled with significant increases in the quantity of resources allocated to developing and strengthening family planning service delivery in Africa. The population budget dedicated to Africa by the U.S. Agency for International Development, the primary funder of family planning programs worldwide, increased from $21.6 million in 1983 to $128 million in 1991 (U.S. Agency for International Development, Africa Bureau and Office of Population, personal communication, 1992). Over the same period, the United Nations Population Fund's support for population activities in Africa increased from $16.9 to $55 million (R. Cornelius, U.S. Agency for International Development, Office of Population, personal communication, 1993). Other bilateral, multilateral, and nongovernmental programs also contributed to this effort.

This dramatic increase in inputs to family planning activities is reflected in the Family Planning Program Effort Index, developed originally by Lapham and Mauldin (1984) and revised by Mauldin and Ross (1991). Between 1982 and 1989, the program effort score for Africa improved from 15 to 36 (of a possible score of 120), representing the largest increase for any of the regions examined. However, even with this increase, Africa lagged well behind Asia and Latin America.

By the late 1980s, the results of population-based surveys showed that family planning was gaining acceptance in at least three countries: Zimbabwe, Botswana, and Kenya (with prevalence levels for all methods combined of 43, 31, and 27 percent, respectively). Although low by the standards of Asia and Latin America, the prevalence data from these few countries have led population experts to reconsider their views regarding the potential acceptance of contraceptive use in sub-Saharan Africa.

Potential Effect of AIDS on Contraceptive Use

The potential effect of acquired immune deficiency syndrome (AIDS) must be considered in any examination of trends in contraceptive use and fertility in African populations. AIDS may affect contraceptive use in two ways. In regions where mortality from AIDS is high, couples may decide to have more children than they otherwise would in order to increase the likelihood of a certain number of surviving children. This resulting increase in the demand for births would lower the likelihood of couples adopting a contraceptive method to control their fertility. On the other hand, efforts to prevent the spread of AIDS may result in increased condom use.

Data necessary to elucidate such effects are not yet available. Preliminary findings from several African settings suggest increasing use of condoms for AIDS prevention (Plummer et al., 1988; Mony-Lobe et al., 1989; Musagara et al., 1991), a trend that may also reduce birth rates. One study found that serotesting and counseling of couples, where one partner was HIV-positive, resulted in increased condom use. Condoms were used more consistently when the man was the HIV-negative partner (Allen et al., 1992). However, the rise in condom use has been small or limited to very specific populations (such as commercial sex workers and their clients), so that effects on fertility have likely been minimal to date.

In the Rakai district of southwestern Uganda, a high seroprevalence area, there has been some resistance to condom use, because it reduces fertility at a time when entire populations are worried about their long-term survival as a result of AIDS (Musagara et al., 1991). Resistance to condom distribution has been found even among trained community health workers, who see childbearing as an essential countermeasure to the perceived effect of the epidemic on the survival of the clan and the tribe. Qualitative information from Rakai indicates that older men are seeking to have sexual relations with younger women as a means of avoiding HIV infection (Serwadda et al., 1989). Consistent with this trend is the finding that 25 percent of girls aged 13 to 14 in Rakai trading centers were found to be HIV positive in a 1989 serological survey, whereas the boys in this age group were all seronegative (Serwadda et al., 1990). The trend of much lower HIV seroprevalence among males persists up to age 20 and for all geographic strata of the district, from the trading centers to the most rural villages (Wawer et al., 1991a). Bledsoe (1989) reports that some parents may become reluctant to send their daughters to school for fear of their beginning relationships with older, wealthier, married men who may be HIV positive. Instead, they may encourage their daughters to marry early, increasing their exposure to pregnancy (which may lead to higher fertility) and possibly reducing their interest in contraception.

Implications of the Rise in Contraceptive Use

Is Africa on the brink of a contraceptive revolution that would mark the onset of widespread fertility decline? Or is the experience of a few countries unlikely to be repeated elsewhere, making them an exception to the reluctance to use modern contraceptives that has characterized much of Africa? Will the current economic crisis in many parts of Africa bring on a "crisis-driven" reconsideration of the desired number of children at the individual level or simply reinforce the demand for many children that accompanies high levels of infant and child mortality?

This volume addresses these key questions by exploring the determinants of contraceptive use and how they operate in sub-Saharan Africa. The multiple levels of socioeconomic organization that influence fertility decision making are spelled out in the next section, and these form the basis of the chapters that follow.

LEVELS OF SOCIOECONOMIC ORGANIZATION AFFECTING CONTRACEPTIVE USE

Although fertility decision making is sometimes viewed as an individual matter, it is strongly influenced by factors at several levels. As illustrated in the top box of Figure 1-1, factors that affect contraceptive use can be organized into four main categories:

- national;
- regional;
- community, kinship, and household; and
- individual.

The different factors at each level (shown in boxes in Figure 1-1) are described in the sections that follow, with an indication of the chapters in which each topic is more fully developed. In our framework, these factors influence contraceptive use (bottom box of Figure 1-1) via their effects on the demand for and supply of births (middle box of Figure 1-1). A more thorough discussion of the links among demand, supply, and contraceptive use, based on the synthesis model of Easterlin and Crimmins (1985), can be found in Appendix A.

National Level

The *social policy environment* of a country has direct implications for reproductive practices. For example, policies regarding education and, more specifically, female education are likely to influence contraceptive use and fertility. Similarly, policies regarding age of marriage may affect the potential reproductive span for childbearing.

A second major factor at the national level is the *economic situation*. The demographic literature is replete with examples of the links between low levels of socioeconomic development and sustained high fertility. It is not coincidental that industrialized countries have low birth rates, whereas much of the developing world—and sub-Saharan Africa in particular—has a much higher level of fertility. It has been argued that without improvements in standards of living, little change in fertility can be expected. However, others have argued that deteriorating economic conditions could in fact diminish the demand for children (Lesthaeghe, 1989a; Caldwell et al., 1992; Working Group on Demographic Effects of Economic and Social Reversals, 1993). In Chapter 3 we examine this question with respect to Africa.

A third significant factor at the national level is *government and donor support for family planning*. Over the past decade there has been a growing recognition of the importance of political will in determining the success of family planning efforts (Keller et al., 1989; Donaldson and Tsui, 1990). Private family planning associations have played a pioneering role in pro-

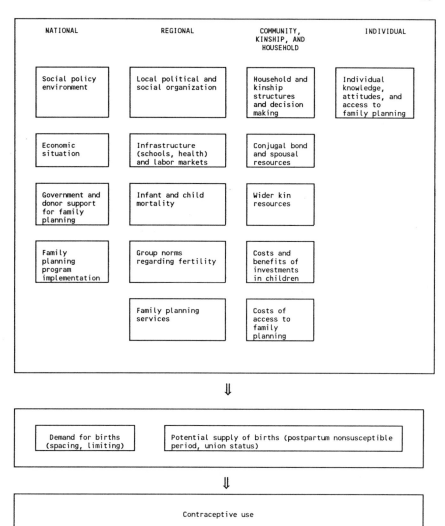

FIGURE 1-1 Factors affecting contraceptive use.

moting family planning worldwide, but strong government support has been an important element in most developing countries with high levels of contraceptive use. This political will is often reflected both explicitly, in the form of a national population policy with demographic goals, and implicitly, through policies affecting female education and occupational opportunities, legal restrictions on the importation of contraceptives, and policies governing access to specific contraceptive methods.

A fourth national-level factor is *family planning program implementation*. For a successful program, the political will cited above cannot be limited to verbal support. Rather, it must consist of a concerted effort to diffuse this support throughout the government bureaucracy and, moreover, to harness the available infrastructure for the delivery of services. Those involved in international family planning programs argue that access to services is a major determinant of contraceptive use and that the resources needed to ensure access are controlled at the national level. These two interrelated issues of political will and program implementation are the focus of Chapter 5.

Regional Level[2]

Countries are used as the unit of analysis in many demographic studies for obvious reasons. Yet there may be substantial variation across regions within a country. The socioeconomic conditions and social policies that are influential at the national level by no means wield uniform influence at the regional level. Differences in economic activity, standards of living, transportation and communications infrastructure, and ethnic composition contribute to regional variation. Although the situation at the national level will determine in part what occurs at the regional level, there are other factors that influence regional outcomes.

Local political and social organization comes into play in a variety of distinctive ways in sub-Saharan Africa. Most African countries are characterized by relatively centralized systems of government. Nonetheless, much of the power at the local level often lies outside the government in more traditional patterns of social organization. Especially in matters related to fertility decision making, the village chief whose power is bestowed by locally sanctioned means may have far greater influence than government officials who may not be from the region.

There are certain aspects of social organization at the regional level that may work to the benefit of family planning. Community networks may serve as channels for the dissemination of information about contraception, thereby providing a vehicle for the diffusion of fertility control (Lesthaeghe, 1989a; Watkins, 1991). These networks, which often precede public sector service provision, operate at the grass-roots level enabling them to reach people in remote areas. This quality is especially important given research

---

[2]Many of the variables we identify as operating at the regional level can also operate at the national or community level. Our purpose in assigning variables to different levels is to point out very general levels of disaggregation of the factors affecting contraceptive use.

questioning the ability of the public sector to provide adequate services at the local level, particularly in rural areas.

Differences in *infrastructure* at the regional level may also influence contraceptive prevalence rates. These differences are manifested in the degree of urbanization, the density of roads, and the quantity and quality of schools and health services. Urbanization and the density of roads reflect the level of economic development, which in turn affects desired family size. Access to education affects the literacy level of the population and the costs of children. Access to health services is associated with lower infant and child mortality, thereby increasing the proportion of children surviving and decreasing the number of children couples need to bear to meet their fertility goals. The nature of *labor markets* may also vary greatly by region, depending on the type of economic activity, proximity to major lines of transportation, female participation in the labor force, and so on.

Both the standard of living and the infrastructure for health and social services at the regional level are reflected in the level of *child and infant mortality*. Where parents fear that one or more of their children may not survive to adulthood, the response may be to have a large number of children to ensure that some will reach adulthood.

The political, social, and economic organization of a region has a direct bearing on the *group norms regarding fertility*. The demand for a large number of children is likely to be sustained in regions where children are needed as a source of labor, where infant mortality is high, and where women's sole means of gaining status and economic security is by having a large number of children. The strong influence of religions (Islam in particular) in parts of western Africa supports the widespread practice of polygyny and early entry into marriage, which may be both a cause and an effect of low levels of female education. Until the recent past, these diverse economic and social factors have tended to reinforce pronatalist norms.

An important factor that counterbalances prevailing high fertility norms is *access to family planning services* at the regional level. It is generally the case that services are far more accessible in urban than in rural areas of Africa. Also, they tend to be more accessible in those regions with a higher standard of living, because of improved infrastructure for health and social services, higher levels of female education, a greater degree of westernization, and thus greater receptivity to birth limitation.

Community, Kinship, and Household

The factors affecting contraceptive use outlined in Figure 1-1 are by no means unique to sub-Saharan Africa. Indeed, much of the above narrative relating to national- and regional-level factors could be applied equally well to Asia or Latin America. Similarly, factors operating at the community, kinship, and household level play a role in fertility decision making in societies around the world. Yet it is the nature of the familial relations and their overriding influence on fertility decision making in sub-Saharan Africa that is often cited as the defining characteristic of Africa's demographic experience. Chapter 4 is devoted to exploring ways in which the household, kinship, and community context of fertility in Africa is different and how its influences on fertility may be changing.

To understand reproductive decisions in sub-Saharan Africa, it is important to understand the relation of individual couples to broader *household and kinship structures*. A number of studies have emphasized the interests of kin in the reproduction of an individual couple. A wife and husband may be under pressure from other relevant decision makers in the wider family who have a stake in maintaining the couple's continued fertility. Furthermore, the couple may distribute some of the costs of childrearing among its kin through the mechanism of child fostering, particularly where educational costs are concerned. Some authors (notably Caldwell and Caldwell, 1987) suggest that a primary source of pronatalist pressure is from kinship structures, which have their roots in traditional African religions, as discussed in Chapter 4.

Similarly, the weak *conjugal bond* that is evident throughout most of sub-Saharan Africa has direct implications for fertility decision making. In the conventional economic-demographic view of the household, the individual couple is implicitly regarded as a well-defined decision-making unit, within which all economic resources are pooled and from which emanate well-defined reproductive demands. Three aspects of social organization in sub-Saharan Africa undermine the applicability of this model: high rates of marital dissolution, polygyny, and an unusually sharp separation of male and female budgets and childrearing responsibilities. It has been argued (see among others, Caldwell and Caldwell, 1987; Frank and McNicoll, 1987) that wives and husbands in sub-Saharan Africa hold sharply differing views regarding the costs and benefits of childbearing, with the net consequences being pronatalist. Differences in views give rise to the possibility of intrahousehold conflicts of interest and implicit bargaining strategies.

Another determining factor of contraceptive use at the level of communities and households involves the *costs and benefits of investments in children*, particularly with respect to schooling. In societies that have undergone rapid transitions in fertility and contraceptive use, changes in the perceived benefits and costs of schooling have played an important role (see Knodel et al., 1987, 1990, for Thailand). As economists have noted, parents may think in terms of a "quantity-quality trade-off," where quantity refers to the number of children and quality to the level of human capital investment per child. The scope for a quantity-quality transition in Africa is not yet known, but some researchers (Kelley and Nobbe, 1990) argue that the trade-off will prove to be a key to future fertility decline in Kenya and elsewhere.

The *cost of access to family planning services* is also a factor at this level. On one hand, there are financial costs for clinic visits, contraceptive supplies, transport to and from the site, child care, and so forth. On the other, there may be opportunity costs such as losing time from one's other occupations. In addition, where contraceptive use remains controversial, there may be high psychological costs: fear of rejection or reproach by one's spouse, in-laws, and friends, and self-doubt over the wisdom of the decision.

Individual Level

When all is said and done, it is the individual who must make the decision to use or not to use a means of pregnancy prevention. Three categories of factors come into play here.

First, does the individual want more births and, if so, when? The personal preferences of the individual, as well as group norms regarding family size and appropriate spacing, will have a bearing on the *demand for births*.

Second, is the individual or the individual's partner at risk of pregnancy? Contraceptive prevalence rates estimated from the Demographic and Health Surveys are generally based on all women of reproductive age, married or living in union. Such measures are very useful for cross-national comparisons, but they do not necessarily focus precisely on the populations at risk of conceiving, as discussed in Appendix A. For example, women in the postpartum period who are amenorrheic or abstaining from sexual relations are at little or no risk of pregnancy. Likewise, women who are infecund as a consequence of STDs find their *supply of births* compromised and would be less likely to consider contraception.

Third, does the individual know of contraception and want to use it? This issue is examined in Chapter 2. *Knowledge of modern contraception* is by no means universal in sub-Saharan Africa, though it is increasing quickly with the expansion of family planning programs. *Attitudes toward family planning* are closely linked with the demand for births. That is, contraception is valued and sought after in those situations in which the individual wants to prevent a pregnancy; it is rebuked by those who believe that pregnancy prevention is undesirable if not immoral.

Collectively, these factors at the national, regional, community, household, and individual levels determine rates of contraceptive use in a given country. Generally, conditions and policies at the national and regional levels have repercussions at the community, household, and individual levels, though the flow may occur in the opposite direction (e.g., government leaders may be reluctant to take a strong stance on family planning, fearing the backlash of a strongly pronatalist population).

ORGANIZATION OF REPORT

In this report we begin by examining the current levels and trends in contraceptive use in Africa (Chapter 2). From there we proceed to explore the factors that explain these levels and trends in terms of the socioeconomic context (Chapter 3) and of community, kinship, and household structure (Chapter 4). Together, Chapters 3 and 4 describe numerous factors that affect (either sustaining or reducing) the demand for large families. Chapter 5 on population policies and family planning programs indicates how improvements in the family planning supply environment affect fertility decision making. In Chapter 6 we present the results of multivariate analyses of the relative importance of sociodemographic and economic factors in contraceptive use at the regional level. In Chapter 7 we analyze the importance of contraceptive use relative to the traditional methods of birth spacing in determining fertility levels in selected African countries. Finally, in Chapter 8 we present the conclusions that emerge from this examination of contraceptive use in Africa.

2

Levels and Trends
in Contraceptive Use

This chapter describes the extent to which contraception is being practiced in sub-Saharan Africa. We first review sources of data on and definitions of contraceptive use. We then discuss what these data show regarding levels and trends in prevalence and differentials in current use by women. Next, we look at indicators related to contraceptive use: ever use, discontinuation, contraceptive knowledge, knowledge of sources, of supply and fertility preferences. Finally, we briefly present evidence of use from the perspective of men. Information on contraceptive use is far from complete, given that contraceptive prevalence data based on nationwide surveys are not available for all African countries.[1]

SOURCES OF DATA ON CONTRACEPTIVE USE

There are three main sources of data on contraceptive use in Africa based on representative samples at the national level: the World Fertility Surveys (WFS), the Contraceptive Prevalence Surveys (CPS), and the Demographic and Health Surveys (DHS). Studies to date in Africa for which

---

[1]However, most countries that have initiated active family planning programs have also conducted surveys; thus, if data from the existing surveys were used to obtain a regional average, it would tend to overstate the actual use of modern contraception in Africa.

data are available include nine WFS (from 1977-1982), seven CPS (1982-1984), and 12 DHS (1986-1990) (Kendall, 1979; Rutstein et al., 1992).

Six populations were included in both the WFS and the DHS programs: Cameroon, Ghana, Kenya, Nigeria, Northern Sudan, and Senegal.[2] For Benin, Côte d'Ivoire, Lesotho, and Mauritania, data are available from the WFS only. Populations with only DHS data include Botswana, Burundi, Liberia, Mali, Togo, Uganda, Zimbabwe, and the state of Ondo in Nigeria. Surveys using the CPS questionnaires have been conducted in selected sites in Zaire (four urban and two rural areas in 1982-1984) and in selected regions of Somalia (1983), but they do not provide national-level estimates and thus are omitted from most of the tables in this chapter.

There are also numerous small-scale studies that have been conducted in the capital cities and/or selected regions of countries. (For a review of studies of fertility and knowledge, attitudes, and practice of contraception for Africa from 1960 to 1973, see Baum et al., 1974. For the period after 1983, see Gelbard et al., 1988.) However, no data from these have been included in the tables below, because it is doubtful that the results are representative or that the data collection techniques are comparable.

Details on the year of data collection and of data included in this chapter are listed in Table 2-1. As the table indicates, despite the three major data collection efforts, for large parts of sub-Saharan Africa neither fertility (except from occasional censuses) nor contraceptive use data are available. This situation is most notable in Central Africa; with the exception of the Cameroon study and the 1982-1984 contraceptive prevalence survey in Zaire (subnational in scope), there is very little demographic information for this region of Africa.

DEFINITION OF CONTRACEPTIVE USE

In the DHS studies conducted in sub-Saharan countries between 1986 and 1990, at least half the current users of contraception in 5 of the 12 countries were relying on traditional methods, such as withdrawal and rhythm. There is little literature on the effectiveness of such methods, but they are considered much less effective than modern methods; thus the convention has emerged of differentiating between modern and traditional (or modern versus all methods) in reporting contraceptive prevalence results, especially in the context of Africa.

In the three main types of studies conducted to date (WFS, CPS, DHS), methods defined as "modern" include oral contraceptives, intrauterine de-

---

[2]Data for Cameroon were not available during the writing of this report. Some data were available for Nigeria (from the DHS country report) and are included in relevant tables.

TABLE 2-1 Data Sources on Contraceptive Use in Sub-Saharan Africa

Country	Survey Program and Date			
	WFS[a]	CPS[b]	DHS[c]	Others
Western Africa				
Benin	1981-1982			
Côte d'Ivoire	1980-1981			
Ghana	1979-1980		1988	
Liberia			1986	
Mali			1987	
Mauritania	1981			
Nigeria (Ondo State)			1986-1987	
Nigeria	1981-1982		1990	
Senegal	1978		1986	
Togo			1986	
Eastern Africa				
Burundi			1987	
Ethiopia				1990
Kenya	1977-1987	1984	1988-1989	
Malawi				1984
Rwanda				1983
Sudan (northern)	1978-1979		1989-1990	
Somalia[d]		1983		
Uganda			1988-1989	
Zimbabwe		1984	1988-1989	
Central Africa				
Cameroon[e]	1978		1991	
Zaire[d]		1982-1984		
Southern Africa				
Botswana		1984	1988	
Lesotho	1977			
South Africa				1975-1976
				1981
Swaziland[f]				1988

[a]World Fertility Survey.

[b]Contraceptive Prevalence Survey.

[c]Demographic and Health Survey.

[d]The data for the CPS in Zaire and in Somalia are not national. In Somalia, the survey was conducted for urban areas. In Zaire, the survey covered four cities and two rural areas.

[e]The DHS data for Cameroon are not available as of the writing of this report.

[f]The data for Swaziland are not presented in the tables. As noted in this chapter, Swaziland is not discussed in this report because of its small population size, estimated at under one million people.

vices (IUDs), female and male sterilizations, injections, condoms, diaphragms, and spermicides. The standard questionnaires explicitly mention two types of traditional methods: periodic abstinence (also called rhythm or the calendar method) and withdrawal. Any other method that the respondent considers to be a means of preventing pregnancy is recorded as "other." Other traditional methods include douche, herbs, and "gris-gris" (amulets, charms, or spells to prevent conception). Many of the country-specific questionnaires list the traditional methods common to their populations.

As discussed in Chapter 1, two postpartum practices observed in much of sub-Saharan Africa are sexual abstinence and breastfeeding. Although these practices may result in lower fertility, in Africa they are generally motivated by the desire to ensure the survival of the youngest child and allow the mother to recuperate between births. Accordingly, neither is considered a contraceptive method in this report (see Appendix A for a discussion of the rationale). However, a high proportion of women in the African WFS and DHS did respond that they were using abstinence as a contraceptive method, although many were in fact practicing postpartum abstinence. For example, much of Togo's high level of traditional contraceptive use is due to a large proportion of women who reported using abstinence as a method (72.5 percent of these women were also in postpartum abstinence). In addition, more than half of the DHS did not include abstinence as a possible contraceptive, so we could not consider the use of abstinence as a method for all countries.[3] Although postpartum abstinence and abstinence are not considered contraceptive methods in this report, periodic abstinence (i.e., rhythm) is.

In sum, throughout this volume, the proportion currently using contraceptives refers to the proportion of women currently married or in union, aged 15-49 years, who are using a contraceptive method at the time of the survey (unless otherwise stated).[4] The data are based on all women fulfilling these criteria, regardless of whether or not they are breastfeeding or postpartum abstinent.

---

[3]For those surveys that did include abstinence as a method, the proportion of women who reported practicing abstinence are given in a note to Table 2-2.

[4]There is evidence that contraceptive use is rising among women who are sexually active and unmarried. This topic is addressed for adolescents in a report by the Working Group on the Social Dynamics of Adolescent Fertility (1993) of the Panel on the Population Dynamics of Sub-Sarahan Africa.

PREVALENCE OF CURRENT CONTRACEPTIVE USE IN SELECTED COUNTRIES

Results from Demographic and Health Surveys Conducted from 1986 to 1990

Table 2-2 presents contraceptive prevalence rates (CPRs) for both current use and ever use of all methods combined,[5] of modern and traditional methods separately, and of specific methods listed in the 12 DHS studies conducted in African countries between 1986 and 1990 for which data are available.[6] Of the 12 countries, only two show a modern contraceptive prevalence rate of more than 30 percent: Zimbabwe (36 percent modern, 43 percent all methods combined) and Botswana (32 percent modern, 33 percent all methods combined). Kenya shows the next highest rate with 18 percent modern use (27 percent all methods combined). No other DHS country in Africa has even 6 percent of women of reproductive age using a modern contraceptive, although in Ghana and Togo the percentage currently using any method is greater than 10. The U.S. Agency for International Development denotes populations with 0 to 7 percent modern usage as having emergent family planning programs, and clearly the majority of the countries in Table 2-2 fall into that category (Destler et al., 1990).

Data from these 12 countries also reflect regional differences. The three higher use countries (Zimbabwe, Botswana, and Kenya) are all anglophone countries in eastern or southern Africa. In the four francophone countries surveyed, three of which are in western Africa (Mali, Senegal, and Togo), less than 3 percent of the women use modern contraceptive methods. These differences may reflect a growing divergence between southern and East Africa and West Africa. For example, data from the Swaziland Family Health Survey show prevalence rates for modern methods of almost 14 percent, suggesting that this nation may be following the path of the three high-use countries (Warren et al., 1992).[7] However, there are still too few high-prevalence countries in sub-Saharan Africa to be able to attribute differentials to geographical factors or different colonial histories. Moreover, these geographical or historical distinctions may be proxies for other determinants of demand for children and use of contraception discussed in Chapters 3 to 5, including socioeconomic factors, infant and child mortality rates, levels of female education, and the strength of family planning programs.

---

[5]The ever-use rates are discussed later in this chapter.

[6]Data for Ondo State are excluded when later data for Nigeria as a whole are available.

[7]Swaziland is not discussed in this report because of its small population size, estimated at under one million people.

TABLE 2-2   Women in Union Age 15-49 Who Currently Use or Have
Ever Used a Contraceptive Method, DHS, 1986-1990 (percent)

| Country | Any Method | Modern Methods | | | | | |
		Any Modern	Pill	IUD	Injection	Vaginal Method	Condom
Current Use							
Botswana[a]	32.5	31.7	14.8	5.6	5.4	0.0	1.3
Burundi[a]	6.7	1.2	0.2	0.3	0.5	0.0	0.1
Ghana	12.9	5.2	1.8	0.5	0.3	0.3	0.3
Kenya	26.9	17.9	5.2	3.7	3.3	0.4	0.5
Liberia	6.4	5.5	3.3	0.6	0.3	0.2	0.0
Mali[a]	3.2	1.3	0.9	0.1	0.1	0.1	0.0
Nigeria	6.0	3.5	1.2	0.8	0.7	0.1	0.4
Senegal[a]	4.6	2.4	1.2	0.7	0.1	0.1	0.1
Sudan							
(northern)	8.6	5.5	3.9	0.7	0.1	0.0	0.1
Togo[a]	12.1	3.1	0.4	0.8	0.2	0.6	0.4
Uganda	4.9	2.5	1.1	0.2	0.4	0.0	0.0
Zimbabwe	43.1	36.1	31.0	1.1	0.3	0.0	1.2
Ever Use							
Botswana[a]	61.7	60.1	49.4	17.4	15.0	1.3	10.1
Burundi[a]	23.8	2.3	0.8	0.6	0.9	0.1	0.3
Ghana	37.0	22.5	14.9	1.3	1.0	8.3	4.5
Kenya	45.0	29.0	18.0	8.4	6.7	2.1	4.3
Liberia	18.8	15.9	13.5	2.8	1.7	1.0	1.7
Mali[a]	7.6	3.4	2.7	0.5	0.2	0.4	0.4
Nigeria	14.0	8.4	4.8	1.7	1.9	0.6	2.0
Senegal[a]	11.9	5.7	3.5	1.5	0.4	0.8	1.4
Sudan							
(northern)	25.2	18.6	17.3	1.6	1.1	0.3	1.9
Togo[a]	33.0	10.1	3.8	1.6	1.1	3.7	3.3
Uganda	21.5	7.0	5.0	0.5	1.3	0.2	0.7
Zimbabwe	79.0	63.0	57.1	3.4	14.5	0.3	17.0

[a]Although abstinence is included as a traditional contraceptive method in these country surveys, it is not included as a method in this report (see this chapter for rationale). For the information of the reader, rates of abstinence for these countries follow. Current use: Botswana, 0.5; Burundi, 2.0; Mali, 1.5; Senegal, 6.7; and Togo, 21.8. Ever use: Botswana, 7.9; Burundi, 14.6; Mali, 12.7; Senegal, 23.5; and Togo, 59.0.

SOURCE: Rutenberg et al. (1991) and different national DHS survey reports and data tapes.

| Sterilization | | Traditional Methods | | | |
Female	Male	Any Traditional	Periodic Abstinence	Withdrawal	Other Method
4.3	0.3	0.8	0.2	0.3	0.3
0.1	0.0	5.5	4.8	0.7	0.0
1.0	0.0	7.7	6.2	0.9	1.6
4.7	0.0	9.0	7.5	0.2	1.3
1.1	0.0	0.9	0.6	0.1	0.2
0.1	0.0	1.9	1.3	0.1	0.5
0.3	0.0	2.5	1.4	0.5	0.6
0.2	0.0	2.2	0.9	0.1	1.2
0.8	0.0	3.1	2.2	0.3	0.6
0.6	0.0	9.0	6.4	2.3	0.3
0.8	0.0	2.4	1.6	0.3	0.4
2.3	0.2	7.0	0.3	5.1	1.6
4.3	0.3	9.4	5.1	5.8	0.6
0.1	0.0	22.6	18.8	8.2	0.5
1.0	0.0	25.1	19.7	8.3	3.0
5.0	0.1	24.2	20.9	3.0	3.2
1.1	0.0	6.7	3.3	3.4	1.2
0.1	0.0	5.7	2.8	0.8	2.1
0.3	0.0	8.1	4.3	2.8	2.3
0.2	0.0	8.6	3.4	1.2	8.7
0.8	0.0	14.9	12.1	4.0	1.9
0.6	0.0	29.4	20.2	13.1	1.0
0.8	0.0	17.4	13.5	4.8	3.0
2.3	0.2	48.7	7.2	41.1	10.9

In the three higher use countries, the pill is the most widely used modern method, followed by the IUD, injection, and female sterilization (though the rank ordering of these other methods varies by country). Of note is the fact that 5 percent of women in Kenya and 4 percent in Botswana have undergone sterilization, contradicting the frequent assumption that this method is totally unacceptable in any sub-Saharan African country (see Chapter 4 for discussion). Only two countries report any use of vasectomy: Zimbabwe (0.2 percent) and Botswana (0.3 percent). Chapter 5 provides further discussion of the use of modern methods in specific countries.

Among traditional methods, rhythm is most commonly used, except in Zimbabwe and Botswana where the main traditional method is withdrawal. In no country is the current use of traditional methods greater than 10 percent.

Trends in method mix to date suggest that as countries move from low contraceptive prevalence to higher levels, the use of traditional methods gives way to an increase in oral contraception (particularly in the 10-45 percent CPR range) followed by a rapid rise in female sterilization in countries above the 45 percent level (Destler et al., 1990). Quality issues change as the mix changes, particularly because the more permanent and effective methods (the IUD, NORPLANT[R], voluntary surgical contraception) require clinical settings.

National contraceptive prevalence rates tend to mask the substantial regional diversity that exists within countries. These differences are shown in Table 2-3. The national-level data for each country refer to the percentage of women married or in union currently using a modern contraceptive method. The regional data that follow indicate the number of percentage points by which each region differs from the national average. The range between regions within a given country (i.e., the number of percentage points between the lowest and highest prevalence) varies from 5 percentage points (in Burundi and Senegal) to 30 percentage points (in Zimbabwe). In fact, the countries with the greatest interregional variations are those with higher than average national levels of prevalence, which result from the high levels of use (by African standards) in selected regions. For example, two of the regions with high positive deviations—Harare and Chitungwiza, Zimbabwe, with 48.0 percent modern use, and the Central province of Kenya with 30.8 percent—are in countries with the highest prevalence. However, Kampala, Uganda, shows the greatest positive deviation of all the regions (15.4 percentage points above the national level) with a prevalence rate of 17.9 percent.

TABLE 2-3   Regional Variations in Modern Contraceptive
Prevalence Rates, DHS, 1986-1990 (average prevalence)

Country and Region/Province	Prevalence Rate
Burundi	(1.2)
Imbo	4.9
Mumirwra/Mugamba	0.4
Plateau	-0.4
Lowlands	-1.2
Range	5.1
Ghana	5.2
Western	-2.0
Central	-0.3
Greater Accra	5.4
Eastern	0.6
Volta	-1.3
Ashanti	1.3
Brong Ahafo	0.0
Other regions	-4.5
Range	9.9
Kenya	(17.9)
Nairobi	10.0
Central	12.9
Coast	-3.1
Eastern	1.6
Nyanza	-7.7
Rift Valley	0.2
Western	-7.9
Range	20.8
Liberia	(5.5)
Sinoe	-1.6
Grand Gedeh	-2.6
Montserrado	4.2
Rest of country	-1.1
Range	6.8
Mali	(1.3)
Kayes, Koulikoro	-0.5
Sikasso, Segou	-0.7
Mpoti, Gao, Tombouctou	-0.5
Bamako	4.7
Range	6.8
Nigeria	6.0
Northeast	-4.0
Northwest	-4.8
Southeast	2.8
Southwest	9.0
Range	13.0

TABLE 2-3   *continued*

Country and Region/Province	Prevalence Rate
Senegal	(2.4)
West	3.1
Central	-1.8
Northeast	-1.8
South	0.0
Range	4.9
Sudan (northern)	(5.5)
Khartoum	9.8
Northern	2.8
Eastern	-3.4
Central	-1.4
Kordofan	-4.1
Darfur	-5.3
Range	15.1
Togo	(3.1)
Coast	1.5
Plateau	-0.7
Central	-1.2
Kara	0.2
Savana	-2.8
Range	4.3
Uganda	(2.5)
West Nile	-2.5
East	-0.5
Central	-0.1
West	0.9
Southwest	-1.6
Kampala	15.4
Range	17.9
Zimbabwe	(36.1)
Manicaland	-10.5
Mashonaland Central	4.0
Mashonaland East	7.0
Mashonaland West	7.1
Matabeleland North	-18.1
Matabeleland South	-14.9
Midlands	-0.9
Masvingo	-0.8
Harare/Chitungwiza	11.9
Bulawayo	5.6
Range	30.3

NOTE: Shown in parentheses for each country is the average prevalence. The figures for each region represent percentage point deviations from the national average. The range indicates the difference between the highest and the lowest regional rates.

SOURCE: DHS national survey reports.

Results of WFS, CPS, and Other Surveys, 1975-1990

Data on contraceptive use by method are presented in Table 2-4 for African countries participating in the WFS, CPS, and other national-level fertility or family planning surveys from 1975 to 1990. The countries that have had at least two surveys are discussed under the section on trends below. For the ten countries that have not had a subsequent DHS (Benin, Cameroon, Côte d'Ivoire, Ethiopia, Lesotho, Mauritania, Rwanda, Somalia, South Africa, and Zaire), these are the only available national-level data on contraceptive prevalence.

Several findings merit comment. First, contraceptive prevalence was less than 6 percent at the time of the survey in all but two of these ten countries (the exceptions being South Africa with 48 percent in 1981 and Rwanda with 11 percent in 1983). Although some change may have taken place since that time, the available data do not indicate any significant use of contraception (apart from South Africa, which is by no means typical of the region) among this group of countries. Second, even at these very low levels of prevalence, there was greater use of traditional than modern methods in all countries except Ethiopia and South Africa. For example, Rwanda reported an overall prevalence of 11 percent, but only 1 percent of women were using a modern method. Third, among the users of modern methods, the most common method was the pill, except in Rwanda, where injection was the most common. This finding parallels the experience in other African countries, as well as numerous other developing countries in other regions (United Nations, 1989a).

Trends in Modern Contraceptive Prevalence

The analysis of trends in contraceptive prevalence in the region is limited by the number of countries for which there are at least two points of observation over time. Apart from Kenya, a veritable demographic laboratory in terms of the number and frequency of surveys conducted to date, only seven other countries have data from two time points: Botswana (1984 and 1988), Ghana (1979-1980 and 1988), Nigeria (1981-1982 and 1990), Senegal (1978 and 1986), South Africa (1975-1976 and 1981), Sudan (1978-1979 and 1989-1990), and Zimbabwe (1984 and 1988-1989).

In Zimbabwe, Botswana, and Kenya as well as in South Africa, there were dramatic increases in the use of modern methods between surveys (shown in Table 2-5), which is evidence of the growing acceptance of family planning in these countries during the 1980s. Modern prevalence rose an average of 1.2 percentage points per year in Kenya, 1.9 points per year in Zimbabwe, and 3.3 points per year in Botswana. In South Africa, it rose an average of 2.0 points per year between the two surveys.

TABLE 2-4 Women in Union Age 15-49 Who Currently Use or Have
Ever Used a Contraceptive Method, WFS, CPS, and Other Surveys,
1977-1990 (percent)

Country	Any Method	Modern Methods					
		Any Modern	Pill	IUD	Injection	Vaginal Method	Condom
Benin	5.9	0.5	0.2	0.1	0.0	0.1	0.1
Botswana	19.3	18.6	10.0	4.8	1.0	0.1	1.2
Cameroon	2.4	0.6	0.2	0.2	0.0	0.0	0.2
Côte d'Ivoire	2.9	1.6	0.4	0.1	0.0	0.0	0.0
Ethiopia	3.1	2.5	1.9	0.3	0.0	0.0	0.1
Ghana	6.4	5.5	2.4	0.3	0.1	1.6	0.6
Kenya							
1977-1978	5.5	4.2	2.0	0.7	0.6	0.0	0.1
1984	14.2	9.6	3.1	3.0	0.5	0.1	0.3
Lesotho	5.1	2.5	1.2	0.1	0.2	0.0	0.1
Malawi	3.5	1.1	0.7	0.3	0.1	a	0.0
Mauritania	0.8	0.3	0.0	0.0	0.0	0.1	0.0
Nigeria	1.0	0.6	0.2	0.1	0.2	0.0	0.0
Rwanda	10.8	0.9	0.2	0.3	0.4	0.0	0.0
Senegal	1.3	0.6	0.3	0.2	0.0	0.0	0.1
Somalia (urban)							
Baydhaba	0.5	0.5	0.3	0.2	0.0	0.0	0.0
Burco	0.3	0.3	0.3	0.0	0.0	0.0	0.0
Hargeisa	2.6	0.8	0.7	0.1	0.0	0.0	0.0
Kismayo	0.5	0.5	0.3	0.0	0.0	0.2	0.0
Mogadishu	0.6	0.5	0.4	0.0	0.0	0.0	0.1
South Africa							
1975-1976	37.0	35.0	11.0	4.0	11.0	0.0	2.0
1981	48.0	45.0	15.0	6.0	14.0	3.0[b]	
Sudan							
(northern)[d]	4.6	3.9	3.1	0.1	0.2	0.1	0.1
Zaire (urban)							
Kananga	11.3	2.6	0.6	0.1	0.3	0.0	0.3
Kinshasa	34.8	4.2	1.3	0.6	1.3	0.2	0.4
Kisangani	18.3	2.3	0.4	0.7	0.5	0.0	0.3
Lubumbashi	35.8	7.6	3.6	1.6	0.8	0.3	0.2
Zaire (rural)							
Nkara	16.9	2.1	1.2	0.0	0.2	0.0	0.0
Vanga	38.1	10.9	1.8	0.9	1.8	0.0	0.3
Zimbabwe	38.4	26.6	22.6	0.7	0.8	0.1	0.7

[a]Method not asked.

[b]Total for vaginal methods and condom.

[c]Total for periodic abstinence and withdrawal.

[d]Numbers are for ever-married women.

Sterilization		Traditional Methods			Other
		Any	Periodic		
Female	Male	Traditional	Abstinence	Withdrawal	Method
0.0	0.0	5.4	1.7	3.1	0.6
1.5	0.0	0.7	0.3	0.3	0.1
0.0	0.0	1.8	1.2	0.4	0.2
0.0	0.0	2.4	1.8	0.1	0.5
0.2	0.0	0.6	0.5	0.1	0.0
0.5	0.0	0.9	0.7	0.2	0.0
0.9	0.0	1.3	1.1	0.2	0.0
2.6	0.0	4.6	3.8	0.6	0.2
0.9	0.0	2.6	0.1	2.5	0.0
a	*a*	2.4	0.1	0.2	2.1
0.2	0.0	0.5	0.0	0.4	0.1
0.1	0.0	0.4	0.3	0.1	0.0
0.0	0.0	9.9	8.4	1.4	0.1
0.0	0.0	0.7	0.4	0.0	0.3
0.0	0.0	0.0	0.0	0.0	0.0
0.0	0.0	1.8	0.1	0.0	1.7
0.0	0.0	0.0	0.0	0.0	0.0
	0.0	0.1	0.0	0.0	0.1
6.0	0.0	3.0	0.0	0.0	3.0
8.0	0.0	3.0	0.3[c]		0.0
0.3	0.0	0.5	0.4	0.1	0.0
1.3	0.0	2.0	1.6	0.4	0.0
0.4	0.0	21.5	13.9	6.9	0.7
0.4	0.0	7.9	4.5	2.5	0.9
1.1	0.0	11.3	8.8	1.4	1.1
0.7	0.0	8.5	8.3	0.2	0.0
6.1	0.0	8.1	3.6	4.5	0.0
1.6	0.1	9.7	0.6	6.5	2.6

TABLE 2-5   Change in Modern Contraceptive Use Over Time in Sub-Saharan Regions

Country and Region	WFS/Other	DHS/Other
Botswana (1984, 1988)	18.6	31.7
Urban	37.1	40.8
Rural	24.9	27.5
Ghana (1979-1980, 1988)	3.3	5.2
Central, Western	5.3	4.1
Greater Accra, Eastern	11.3	7.9
Volta	6.0	3.9
Ashanti, Brong Ahafo	8.5	6.0
Northern, Upper	1.1	0.7
Kenya (1978, 1988-1989)	4.3	17.9
Nairobi	18.8	27.9
Central, Eastern	9.0	24.5
Rift Valley	4.7	18.1
Coast	5.1	14.8
Western, Nyanza	2.6	10.1
Nigeria (1981-1982, 1990)	1.0	3.5
Northeast	0.0	1.3
Northwest	0.3	0.7
Southeast	1.4	3.9
Southwest	1.5	10.5
Senegal (1978, 1986)	0.6	2.4
Central	0.4	0.5
Northeast (Fleuve, Oriental)	0.0	0.6
South (Casamance)	0.0	2.4
West (Dakar, Thiès)	2.3	5.5
South Africa (1975-1976, 1981)	35.0	45.0
Sudan (northern) (1978-1979, 1989-1990)	3.7	5.5
Khartoum	17.6	15.8
Northern, Eastern	2.9	4.4
Central	7.1	4.1
Kordofan, Darfur	1.5	0.8
Zimbabwe (1984, 1988-1989)	26.6	36.1
Bulawayo		41.2
Harare/Chitungwiza		48.0
Manicaland	17.1	25.6
Mashonaland	37.7[a]	40.1
Mashonaland East (except Harare/Chitungwiza)		43.1
Mashonaland West		43.2
Masving	14.5	35.3
Matabeleland North (except Bulawayo)	20.8[b]	18.0
Matabeleland South		21.2
Midlands	24.2	35.2

[a]Includes Mashonaland East, West, and Harare/Chitungwiza.
[b]Includes Matabeleland South.

By contrast, there was relatively little increase in the use of modern methods in the four other countries that had data for at least two points: Ghana (increased from 3 to 5 percent in eight years), Nigeria (from 1 to 4 percent in eight years), Senegal (from 1 to 2 percent in eight years), and Sudan (from 4 to 6 percent in eleven years).

Where modern contraceptive use has increased, one might expect a decrease in the reliance on traditional methods, perhaps due to substitution between the two. However, evidence from the three higher use countries is mixed. Data from Zimbabwe tend to support this substitution hypothesis: Between 1984 and 1988 the use of modern methods increased by almost 10 points, while the use of traditional methods decreased by about 3 points. However, in Botswana, modern use increased 13 points in the four years between surveys, while traditional use remained at slightly less than 1 percent in both surveys. In Kenya, the 12-point increase in modern method use was accompanied by an 8-point increase in the use of traditional methods (from 1 to 9 percent over 11 years).

Differentials in Use

At the individual level, a number of socioeconomic factors are associated with current modern contraceptive use. We use DHS data to investigate these relationships, as illustrated in Figures 2-1 to 2-3 (see Table 2A-1 for percentages presented in these figures). The main findings are as follows (see Chapter 3 for additional discussion):

• *The use of modern contraceptives is higher in urban than rural areas.* Without exception, prevalence rates for modern methods are higher in urban than rural areas (see Figure 2-1), though in Ghana and Ondo State, Nigeria, the difference is not statistically significant.[8] The difference ranges from a few percentage points in those countries where modern use is low even in urban areas to as much as 18 points in Zimbabwe.

---

[8]The bivariate comparisons presented in Figures 2-1 to 2-3 and Tables 2-7 and 2-8 were checked against multivariate results derived from logit models (the latter using unweighted data). In the logit models, the explanatory variables included the woman's age, urban or rural residence, her level of education, and also the region of residence. All of the covariates were treated as categorical in nature and were entered into the logit models as main effects (i.e., no interactions between covariates were explored). (The omitted categories were (1) residence = urban, (2) education = none, and (3) age = 15-19.) The aim was to determine if the bivariate contrasts displayed in the figures and tables provide a reliable guide to the direction and significance of effects in the presence of multivariate controls. Generally they do, except where noted in the text. See Table 2A-1 to this chapter for the significance of the effects in the multivariate model.

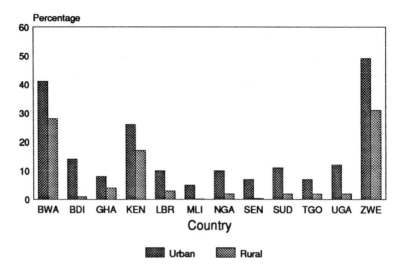

FIGURE 2-1 Modern contraceptive use by residence of women currently in union (age 15-49). NOTE: BWA=Botswana; BDI=Burundi; GHA=Ghana; KEN=Kenya; LBR=Liberia; MLI=Mali; NGA=Nigeria; SEN=Senegal; SUD=Sudan; TGO=Togo; UGA=Uganda; ZWE=Zimbabwe.

Except in Botswana, Kenya, and Zimbabwe, the use of modern methods remains an essentially urban and periurban phenomenon in the region. Elsewhere in the western and eastern African countries studied, less than 5 percent of married women in rural areas report modern contraceptive use. Analyses of the earlier WFS data revealed similar tendencies (Lightbourne, 1980; Sathar and Chidambaram, 1984).

With urbanization comes greater exposure to Western ideas and greater access to family planning and health services. Except in Zimbabwe where the community-based distribution of contraceptives is strongly developed in rural areas (London et al., 1985; Zimbabwe National Family Planning Council, 1985), family planning services are far more likely to reach urban than rural residents.

• *The use of modern contraceptives varies markedly by region within a given country.* As mentioned above and shown in Table 2-3, there are marked differences between the national average and region-specific prevalence rates. The greatest use of modern methods is observed in regions that are very urban. For example, in the Kampala region in Uganda, the region of Nairobi and the Central province in Kenya, and the region of Harare and Chitungwiza in Zimbabwe, the proportion of married women using a mod-

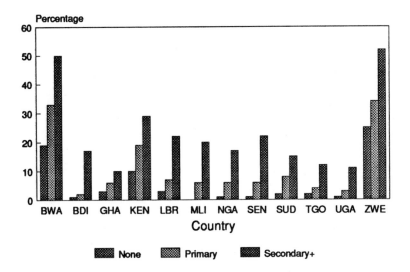

FIGURE 2-2 Current use of modern contraception by level of education of women in union (age 15-49), selected countries of sub-Saharan Africa. NOTE: BWA=Botswana; BDI=Burundi; GHA=Ghana; KEN=Kenya; LBR=Liberia; MLI=Mali; NGA=Nigeria; SEN=Senegal; SUD=Sudan; TGO=Togo; UGA=Uganda; ZWE=Zimbabwe.

ern contraceptive method is at least 10 points higher than for the country as a whole. Conversely, in the less urbanized regions, modern contraceptive use is lower than the national averages. Examples include Matabeleland North and South and to a lesser degree Manicaland in Zimbabwe; the Nyanza and Western provinces in Kenya; and the regions of Darfur and Kordofan in Sudan. Other explanations for these regional differences in modern contraceptive use are explored in Chapter 6.

For traditional methods, there is less regional variation than is the case with modern methods (data not shown), which may suggest that traditional methods are part of a set of culturally prescribed practices that are less affected by forces of modernization or access to family planning services.

• *The use of modern contraception increases with education.* Female education is an important determinant of demographic behavior in general and of family planning behavior in particular. The African data yield results similar to those obtained from DHS studies worldwide: The use of modern contraceptives increases with the educational level of the woman (see Figure 2-2).

Surprisingly, this same positive relationship between education and use is seen for traditional methods in at least half of the DHS countries in

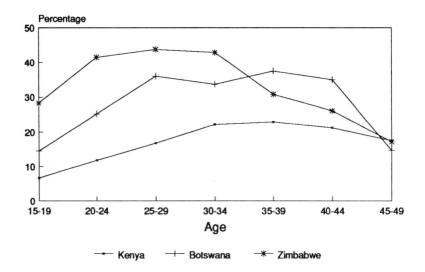

FIGURE 2-3 Current use of modern contraception by age of women (15-49 years) for the vanguard countries.

Africa (data not shown). However, it is not the case in Zimbabwe and Botswana, where the better-educated women are generally using a modern method, or in Togo where the use of traditional methods is high across all categories of education.

•   *The use of modern contraception generally increases, then decreases, with age.*[9] The variation in contraceptive prevalence by age is similar in the higher prevalence countries: The use of a modern method among married women is lowest among women aged 15-19, gradually increases, and then decreases again toward the end of the reproductive years. The peak in the curve differs somewhat by country. In Zimbabwe, use is highest among women aged 20-34 compared to Botswana and Kenya where it tends to be highest among women aged 25-40 (see Figure 2-3).

In summary, modern contraceptive prevalence increases with the education of the woman and is higher in urban areas and among women aged 20-39.

---

[9]For several countries, particularly Burundi, Mali, and Togo, the changes in use do not vary significantly by 5-year age group. See Appendix Table 2-1 for the significance of the age effects.

Reason for Use: Spacing Versus Limiting

It is important to understand the motivations for contraceptive use, that is, to what extent is use motivated by a desire to limit family size versus the desire to space births?   In the WFS, CPS, and DHS conducted to date, there is no direct question regarding the reason for contraceptive use. Rather, respondents are asked if they desire more children and, in the case of the DHS, when they would like their next birth. This information, when combined with contraceptive use data, allows researchers to infer the motive for use. Those users who desire no more children are classified as limiters; those users who want more children eventually but not for at least two years, are considered spacers. (For more information on this indirect means of defining motivation, see Mauldin and Segal, 1986; Westoff, 1991; Westoff and Ochoa, 1991).

At first glance the data in Figure 2-4 suggest that in at least half of the DHS countries, modern contraceptives are used for limiting rather than spacing. However, it is important to note that in the five of the six coun-

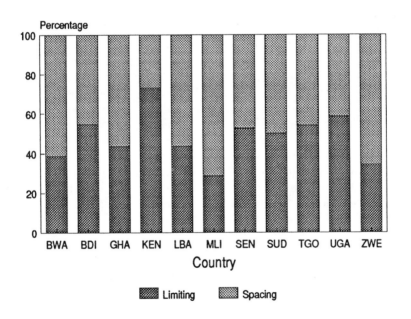

FIGURE 2-4 Use of modern contraception for spacing versus limiting, women in union (age 15-49), selected countries of sub-Saharan Africa. NOTE: BWA=Botswana; BDI=Burundi; GHA=Ghana; KEN=Kenya; LBR=Liberia; MLI=Mali; SEN=Senegal; SUD=Sudan; TGO=Togo; UGA=Uganda; ZWE=Zimbabwe.

TABLE 2-6   Proportion of Women Using a Modern Method by Number of Living Children for the Higher Prevalence Countries

Country	Number of Children					
	0	1	2	3	4	5+
Botswana	13.6	30.4	37.2	41.2	33.4	31.2
Kenya	0.9	10.1	18.6	19.6	22.5	21.0
Zimbabwe	1.4	36.5	42.4	42.2	43.6	32.3

tries where limiting emerges as the primary motive, modern contraceptive use is low (less than 6 percent). In two of the three higher use countries, Zimbabwe and Botswana, the primary motive is spacing; these findings support the often-heard statement that family planning is used for spacing rather than limiting in sub-Saharan Africa. For example, Westoff (1991) maintains that data from the DHS in Africa on reproductive intentions and desired timing of births reflect the persistence of a double desire: sustained fertility, on the one hand, and appropriate spacing between successive births, on the other. By contrast, Kenya presents an intriguing case in which more than half the users openly state that they want no more children.

Table 2-6 sheds light on the relationship between modern method use and current family size for Botswana, Kenya, and Zimbabwe. Only in Botswana, do a substantial proportion (14 percent) of women with no living children use modern contraception. Among those with one living child, the percentage using contraception increases sharply. Between one and two children, there is a slight additional increase in use, but above parity two, use seems to plateau (and even drops for parities of five or greater in the case of Zimbabwe). In sum, these cross-sectional results imply that most women in these countries probably do not begin using modern contraception until they have at least one to two children.

OTHER INDICATORS RELATED TO
CONTRACEPTIVE PRACTICE

Current use of a modern contraceptive method is the aspect of contraceptive practice that is of greatest interest both to demographers (as a proximate determinant of fertility) and to family planning policymakers (as a measure of the coverage of their programs). However, several other aspects of contraceptive practice are of interest: ever use of a method, discontinuation, knowledge of contraceptive methods, knowledge of sources of contraception, and fertility preferences. Family planning researchers often use these variables as indicators of constraints on use in a population. Ever use of contraception can signal the degree to which contraception is accepted or tried. Low levels of knowledge of contraception may indicate that the population is unaware of fertility-limiting options. Low levels of knowledge of sources of contraception may suggest that access to family planning is limited and program extension is warranted. Fertility preferences indicate the potential demand for children and suggest regions where there is unmet need for family planning.

Ever Use of a Modern Method

Ever use of a modern method refers to the percentage of women ever in union who at some point during their lifetimes have used a modern contraceptive. Ever use by definition must equal or exceed current prevalence. The ever-use measure reflects the extent to which a given population has used contraception (and thus serves as a useful indicator in studies designed to test specific family planning interventions). Moreover, the comparison between ever use and current use gives an indication, admittedly crude, of the perseverance of users and the relative duration of contraceptive use (London et al., 1985; United Nations, 1989a).

In 10 of the 12 African DHS countries, less than 30 percent of women ever in union have used a modern contraceptive method. In sharp contrast, 60 and 63 percent in Botswana and Zimbabwe, respectively, have ever used modern contraception. The rank ordering of countries is similar for ever use and current use. As shown in Table 2-2, the five African countries leading the list on current use of a modern method are (in descending order) Zimbabwe, Botswana, Kenya, Sudan, and Liberia (although in the last two, 6 percent of currently married women use one). These same countries are first in ever use with the same ranking ordering except for Liberia, which is replaced by Ghana, where "experimentation" with contraception would be in line with available information on program activity in that country (described in more detail in Chapter 5).

In Zimbabwe, Botswana, and Kenya, at least half the women who have ever used any method are currently using one. Despite a very low prevalence rate, the data in Table 2-2 suggest that in Burundi, more than half the "ever users" of modern methods are currently using one. The difference between ever and current use is smaller in these countries than in other DHS countries, indicating that a higher percentage who try a method stick with one.

Differentials in ever use of a modern method among different types of women ever in a union are shown in Table 2-7.[10] As with current use of a modern method, ever use is higher in urban than rural areas, and it increases monotonically with education for all countries. Ever use generally reaches its highest level among women aged 25-34.

Discontinuation

It is widely recognized that the rate of contraceptive use at a given time depends not only on having attracted acceptors to adopt contraception in the past but also on maintaining their motivation to continue use for a prolonged period, in accordance with their own reproductive intentions. However, data on this subject are severely lacking in sub-Saharan Africa—an important research gap in understanding prevalence in this region. One promising approach to data collection is the "calendar," which has been developed and tested as part of the DHS. However, to date none of the African surveys has included this instrument, in part because it is thought to be more appropriate to countries with high prevalence.

Information on continuation rates can also be obtained from program-based data; however, these data have several limitations. First, samples represent the users of specific clinic-based services, rather than a cross section of the population who are using the method (including patients of private physicians or clients who obtain methods from pharmacies). Second, there is a serious loss-to-follow-up problem; typically the dropout levels are moderate to high, and one can speculate that those who discontinue their clinic visits are not necessarily similar in education, ethnic group, parity, etc., to those who follow their appointments regularly. Thus, the results of the analysis of such program data are only applicable to those who continue their visits, not the full sample of people who have ever used the clinic services. Third, some countries have their record-keeping systems set up to follow individual clients and thus measure continuation; however, these records are not kept with sufficient accuracy to allow meaningful analysis.

Knowledge of a Modern Contraceptive Method

The DHS surveys report "knowledge of a contraceptive method." This phrase is somewhat of a misnomer, in that the surveys measure re-

---

[10]The denominators of the proportions in Tables 2-7 and 2-8 are women aged 15-49 who have ever been in a union. This denominator is used because ever use and knowledge of contraception attempt to give measures for all women who have been exposed to the risk of becoming pregnant, both now and in the past.

ported awareness of different contraceptive methods. Specifically, the interviewer asks the respondent to name all methods of which she or he has heard ("spontaneous mention"). For each method that is not mentioned, the interviewer names the method, gives a one line description of it, and then asks if the respondent has ever heard of it ("prompted recall"). In the family planning literature, these two questions are combined into a single variable that is conventionally labelled as "knowledge," either of a specific method or of any method.[11] We report knowledge of methods in Table 2-8.

More than two-thirds of the women ever in union have heard of at least one modern method of contraception in almost all of the 12 African DHS countries; the exceptions are Burundi (63 percent) and, more notably, Mali (29 percent). Knowledge is higher in urban than in rural areas, although the gap is small or insignificant in the higher use countries where contraception is known to more than 90 percent of women, whether urban or rural. The data also show a positive and monotonic relationship between knowledge and level of education. However, Zimbabwe is remarkable, because 94 percent of women with no education have heard of at least one modern method, which suggests that family planning programs have reached all segments of the population.

Knowledge of contraception is related to age in a pattern best described as an inverted U, although the differences by age are not significant in Burundi, Mali, and Togo. Generally, women aged 15-19 are less likely to have heard of a modern contraceptive method than are women aged 20-39. However, among women 40 and over, the percentage drops markedly, reflecting perhaps the lower educational attainment and lower need for contraception over the life cycle among this age group. Zimbabwe is again the only exception, where at least 95 percent of women in each age group know of a modern method.

---

[11]Some might question the validity of this self-reported "knowledge," especially when the respondent can qualify for "knowing a method" simply by a nod of the head when the interviewer reads those methods not previously mentioned. However, the results obtained from this series of questions from numerous DHS or DHS-type surveys tend to be highly consistent with other sources of data. For example, the levels of professed knowledge are high for those methods most widely used in a given country, as shown by program service statistics. By contrast, few respondents claim to have heard of vasectomy, a method that is not widely promoted in public programs in developing countries. Also, data on knowledge of methods tend to show a consistent pattern of increase in subsequent surveys in a given country and to correlate predictably with education, urban residence, and economic status. Thus, the problem lies not with the utility of the indicator, but rather with the label "knowledge" when in fact "awareness" is a more accurate term. In this report we have retained the term "knowledge" to be consistent with the family planning literature.

TABLE 2-7   Women Who Have Ever Used a Modern Method (percent)

Country[a]	Total	Residence		Education		
		Urban	Rural	None	Primary	Secondary
Botswana	60.2	71.2	55.1	40.8	65.5	81.7
Burundi	2.5	26.7	1.5	1.4	4.8	28.8
Ghana	23.1	33.2	18.4	11.0	30.9	52.1
Kenya	29.1	44.4	26.1	16.1	31.1	48.1
Liberia	17.8	28.9	10.8	8.4	23.0	62.2
Mali[c]	3.4	11.8	0.4	1.3	12.6	56.3
Ondo	9.4	13.8	6.5	3.3	10.7	23.7
Senegal	6.5	16.7	1.1	2.3	19.5	50.6
Sudan	18.1	34.9	8.2	7.0	29.1	41.8
Togo	10.6	21.0	6.2	5.2	15.6	38.8
Uganda	7.6	34.1	4.6	2.2	7.9	37.4
Zimbabwe	62.7	76.0	56.6	47.2	62.6	76.2

NOTE: The base for the table is all women age 15-49 ever in a union.

[a]The Nigeria DHS of 1990 is not included because the standard recode data tape was not available during the writing of this report.

TABLE 2-8   Women Who Know Any Modern Method (percent)

Country[a]	Total	Residence		Education		
		Urban	Rural	None	Primary	Secondary
Botswana	94.4	99.4	92.1	85.2	98.7	99.5
Burundi	63.3	92.3	62.1	60.1	75.9	94.2
Ghana	76.8	88.4	71.5	60.5	89.8	97.2
Kenya	91.3	95.4	90.6[b]	82.8	94.4	98.5
Liberia	69.5	78.5	63.9	61.5	85.6	96.0
Mali[c]	28.8	56.5	19.2	23.1	60.8	100.0
Ondo	49.4	60.0	42.3	33.2	58.2	79.2
Senegal	68.6	87.9	58.7	64.8	87.7	97.8
Sudan	71.0	91.1	59.1	54.8	91.1	98.3
Togo	81.4	92.4	76.7	75.5	91.7	98.2
Uganda	78.5	93.6	76.9[b]	68.0	85.2	96.3
Zimbabwe	97.9	99.0	97.4[b]	94.0	98.4	99.5

NOTE: The base for the table is all women age 15-49 ever in a union.

[a]The Nigeria DHS of 1990 is not included because the standard recode data tape was not available during the writing of this report.
[b]The contrast is *not* significant at the .05 level in a multivariate logit model.

Age						
15-19	20-24	25-29	30-34	35-39	40-44	45-49
36.6	58.3	67.8	68.3	65.4	54.1	31.2^b
3.8	1.9^b	2.9^b	3.0^b	1.7^b	2.2^b	2.6^b
11.6	19.4	25.6	27.5	24.8	26.4	16.9
10.2	22.6	30.2	35.8	34.8	28.9	26.7
8.1	18.5	20.2	22.4	19.2	15.5	12.5
3.8	3.7^b	4.9^b	4.4^b	2.4^b	1.8^b	0.0
7.9	9.5^b	12.5	9.5	11.7	7.7	5.9
1.9	4.0^b	6. 6^b	9.2^b	10.4	6.3	6.3
5.3	14.1	18.4	23.3	20.2	19.4	18.3
9.1	10.4^b	11.0^b	13.2^b	9.8^b	10.3^b	7.4^b
4.4	5.9^b	8.8	8.5	10.1	10.4	4.7
41.1	67.7	70.5	71.8	63.9	52.4	40.9^b

^{b}The contrast is *not* significant at the .05 level in a multivariate logit model.
^{c}For Mali, logistic regression omits cases in which the woman was age 45-49.

Age						
15-19	20-24	25-29	30-34	35-39	40-44	45-49
92.4	96.7^b	96.9	95.9	95.7^b	90.9^b	84.2^b
61.3	61.4^b	71.0^b	62.9^b	65.0^b	56.8^b	50.6^b
70.5	78.7	81.4	77.8	77.5	73.8	66.9^b
86.9	94.5	94.2	93.1	92.8	85.2	82.8^b
54.2	73.7	72.8	74.4	69.5	67.2	63.2
32.7	33.0^b	34.1^b	30.7^b	24.3^b	22.0^b	14.1
40.9	52.2	57.4	55.5	52.5	46.2	34.2
51.2	72.6	71.1	74.3	71.0	65.3	66.4
67.9	75.0^b	72.7	73.1	69.6	67.6	65.0
76.1	82.4^b	84.1^b	83.5^b	80.6^b	80.5^b	74.9^b
75.3	79.5^b	83.4	77.5	81.2	75.4^b	69.5^b
96.0	98.7	98.4	99.1	98.0	94.9^b	96.5^b

^{c}For Mali, the logistic regression omits cases in which the woman had secondary schooling or more.

Sources of Modern Contraceptive Methods

Information on knowledge of sources of contraception is one indicator of the extent to which contraceptives are accessible in a given country (although the data pertain to perceived availability, not actual availability). As shown in Table 2-9, among women aged 15-49 who know at least one method, a high proportion (78 to 100 percent) also know a source where they can obtain contraception. However, the type of source varies markedly by country, reflecting differences in the configuration of family planning service delivery in these countries. The most frequently mentioned source is a government clinic or pharmacy, except in Senegal where three-quarters of the respondents cited a private clinic or other service delivery point. However, knowledge of a second source is much more limited; only in Ghana can at least 50 percent of the respondents name a second source (data not shown).

The strong influence of government programs is reflected in the data in Table 2-9. Far more women know of government than private sources in 11 of the 12 countries. One can assume that the relatively low levels of knowledge of private sources in Botswana, Kenya, and Zimbabwe simply reflects the extent to which family planning services are delivered through government facilities. In contrast, at least one-third of respondents knowledgeable about at least one source mention a private source (clinic or pharmacy) in the low-prevalence countries of Senegal, Ghana, Togo, and the Sudan.

Given that the pill is the most widely known and used modern method in Africa, it is also of interest to examine knowledge of at least one source of the pill. Not surprisingly, the most widely known sources of the pill are similar to the most widely known sources for any method, although the specific percentages knowing each type of facility tend to be lower (data not shown).

With the growing concern about AIDS, knowledge about condoms takes on a new importance. Table 2-10 provides information on women ages 15-49 currently in a union who have knowledge of condoms. There is a remarkably wide range in awareness of condoms (or willingness to admit this knowledge to the interviewer) among countries: In Burundi, Mali, and Sudan, less than 30 percent of women who know any modern method acknowledged having heard of the condom, in comparison to 92 percent in Botswana.

Among women with knowledge of condoms, most (67 percent or more) also know at least one source from which they believe condoms can be obtained. Government clinics or pharmacies are the most widely cited sources in eight of the eleven countries. By contrast, private pharmacies are most frequently mentioned in the remaining three countries (Ghana, Sudan, and Togo).

Fertility Preferences

Data on reproductive preferences are useful indicators of fertility norms and intentions. Both the WFS and DHS collected data on ideal family size and intentions to have another child.

Data from the DHS on ideal family size among ever-married women show that the preferred number in sub-Saharan Africa averages just under six. The lowest ideal number is 4.7 (Kenya) and the highest is 7.1 (Senegal). The ideal number has declined between the WFS and DHS; for the three countries that conducted both surveys, Kenya showed the greatest decline (35 percent) and Ghana showed the smallest decline (9 percent) (Westoff, 1991). Care should be taken in using these numbers as predictors of change in fertility; they are influenced by the number of children the respondent already has.

The DHS also collected information on whether married women intended to postpone or halt childbearing. In sub-Saharan Africa, more women indicated that they wanted to delay a future birth than avoid one (Westoff, 1991). Between the WFS and DHS, the number of women who wanted no more children increased in the three countries that conducted both surveys. Kenya showed the greatest increase (32 percent), followed by Ghana and Senegal (10 and 9 percent, respectively) (Westoff, 1991). Such data are indicative of changes in fertility in the short run (Westoff, 1990).

Westoff and Ochoa (1991) have used data on reproductive preferences to develop measures of unmet need for family planning. They define unmet need as the proportion who are exposed to the risk of conception, are not using a contraceptive method, and say they want to delay or stop childbearing. The total demand for family planning is the proportion of women with unmet need plus the women who are currently using contraception. Results from Westoff and Ochoa show that most of unmet need is for spacing rather than limiting births in sub-Saharan Africa, in sharp contrast to other regions of the world. Table 2-11 summarizes unmet need, as calculated by Westoff and Ochoa, by subgroup for eight populations in Africa. Unmet need generally increases with number of children; is greater in urban areas than rural areas, except in Botswana and Kenya; and is greatest for women with primary education, except in Botswana, where it is greatest among the uneducated, and in Burundi, Liberia, and Uganda, where it is greatest among those with secondary education. Overall, unmet need is highest in Togo (40.1 percent) and lowest in Mali (22.9 percent), suggesting that there is a substantial demand for family planning in all eight countries. Comparisons of unmet need for limiting births between the DHS and the WFS[12] in Ghana

---

[12]Comparisons are noted only for unmet need for limiting births because the WFS did not collect information on spacing preferences.

TABLE 2-9 Knowledge of Sources of Modern Methods Among Women Knowing at Least One Modern Method

Country[a]	Percentage Knowing a Source	Among Those Knowing Any Source, Percentage Citing[b]					
		Government Clinic or Pharmacy	Government Home or Community	Private Clinic or Delivery	Private Pharmacy	Church, Friends, or Books	Other
Botswana	99.8	99.2	0.0	2.9	1.9	0.0	0.0
Burundi	91.9	97.1	0.0	1.7	3.4	2.0	1.6
Ghana	90.8	88.1	1.4	23.6	52.7	3.5	2.3
Kenya	98.5	95.9	0.0	21.1	5.2	0.9	0.1
Mali	78.0	81.7	0.0	10.6	18.0	0.0	29.2
Ondo	96.8	95.3	1.0	9.4	13.9	0.0	0.8
Senegal	99.6	8.9	29.0	76.8	0.0	40.0	12.8
Sudan	83.5	76.8	0.0	45.4	43.1	1.4	0.5
Togo	96.5	97.7	0.0	3.6	35.9	17.2	3.3
Uganda	92.7	6.8	0.7	6.2	9.0	0.7	0.8
Zimbabwe	98.2	86.5	34.6	1.1	12.4	10.2	4.0

NOTE: The base for the table is all women aged 15-49 who are currently in union. For column one, the base includes only women who know of at least one modern method; for the remaining columns, the base includes only women who know at least one modern method source.

[a]No comparable data on method sources are available for Liberia; the Nigeria DHS of 1990 is not included because the standard recode data tape was not available during the writing of this report.

[b]Because more than one source can be cited, the rows do not sum to 100 percent.

TABLE 2-10 Sources of Condoms: Percentage Knowing of Condoms, Knowing a Source, and Type of Source

Country[a]	Knowledge of Condoms[b]	Knowledge of Source[c]	Among Those Knowing Any Condom Source					
			Government Clinic or Pharmacy	Government Home/ Community Delivery	Private Clinic or Other Service Delivery Point	Private Pharmacy	Church, Friends, or Books	Other
Botswana	92.3	98.9	97.2	0.0	1.0	1.8	0.0	0.0
Burundi	23.3	80.0	80.7	0.0	1.7	14.5	1.3	1.8
Ghana	64.7	78.7	19.9	0.3	11.4	65.4	1.1	1.9
Kenya	61.1	92.9	78.3	0.0	12.7	7.7	1.3	0.0
Mali	28.7	75.6	58.4	0.0	11.1	28.2	0.0	2.3
Ondo	36.4	94.4	65.4	0.2	5.1	28.8	0.0	0.4
Senegal	39.2	99.4	0.8	51.7	9.8	0.0	30.5	7.2
Sudan	25.2	75.4	13.4	0.0	7.2	78.1	1.0	0.4
Togo	44.0	83.3	37.4	0.0	2.5	51.0	6.8	2.3
Uganda	39.9	66.6	78.1	0.6	3.6	16.6	0.1	1.1
Zimbabwe	82.1	90.2	64.3	24.9	0.5	5.6	2.3	2.4

NOTE: The base for the table is all women aged 15-49 who are currently in a union.

[a]No comparable data on method sources are available for Liberia; the Nigeria DHS of 1990 is not included because the standard recode data tape was not available during the writing of this report.
[b]Among those who know a modern method.
[c]Among those who know of the condom.

SOURCE: United Nations (1989a) and other national survey reports. Data for South Africa come from the Population Council population data base.

and Kenya (data not shown) indicate that unmet need has increased, 80 and 129 percent respectively.

RESULTS FROM MALE SURVEYS

The evidence on levels and trends in contraceptive use presented thus far in this chapter comes from data gathered for women. Several DHS also questioned men. In Burundi, Ghana, and Kenya, a subsample of the husbands of the women interviewed were selected to respond to the questionnaire for men. In Mali, a sample of men was selected from the households visited by the interviewers; thus, the sample included single men.

Results from these surveys indicate that men were more likely to report using a contraceptive method than women, except in Ghana, where the reported use of any method was approximately the same. Contraceptive use among men was higher in urban areas; generally decreased with age, except in Kenya, where use increased and then decreased with age; and increased with education.[13]

In all four countries, men were more likely to know of a method than women. In Burundi, Ghana, and Mali, of the men that knew any method, more than half of them had not talked with their wives about family planning in the past year. In Kenya, 36 percent of the husbands had not talked with their wives. More than three-quarters of men in Burundi, Ghana, and Kenya approved of family planning; only 16 percent of men in Mali approved. Except in Burundi[14], more than a third of the wives of husbands who approved of family planning either did not know their husbands' attitudes toward family planning or thought their husbands disapproved.

In Burundi and Kenya, men and women indicated the same ideal family size, 5.5 and 4.8 respectively. In Ghana, men preferred more children than their wives, 7.6 versus 5.5. The DHS report for Mali did not report ideal family size for men.

CONCLUSION

Modern contraceptive use in sub-Saharan Africa remains low except in Botswana, Kenya, and Zimbabwe. In all countries, use of modern methods is associated with urban residence and greater education, perhaps indicating that future changes in the composition of the population might be associated with increased use. The knowledge of modern contraceptives is greater

---

[13]In Kenya, there was little difference in use between men with no education and those with primary education.

[14]Data for Burundi are not presented in the DHS report.

TABLE 2-11 Unmet Need for Family Planning for Currently Married Women, Demographic and Health Surveys (percent)

Country	Number of Children					Residence		Level of Education			Total
	0	1	2	3	4+	Urban	Rural	No Education	Primary	Secondary or More	
Botswana	23.3	16.7	22.5	22.1	33.2	22.2	29.0	31.3	27.1	18.8	26.9
Burundi	17.2	11.9	23.9	21.6	30.6	29.9	25.0	23.4	33.2	36.5	25.1
Ghana	20.3	34.7	30.7	35.4	38.2	35.4	35.1	32.3	39.0	27.8	35.2
Kenya	29.0	24.4	37.0	31.8	41.3	33.6	38.7	36.5	40.8	32.5	38.0
Liberia	19.9	27.2	26.4	29.6	43.0	37.6	30.1	29.8	40.9	45.1	32.8
Mali	17.8	19.1	16.9	20.9	29.3	30.6	20.3	21.8	29.9	28.3	22.9
Togo	31.5	35.3	34.9	36.7	46.4	44.3	38.7	36.9	50.6	39.0	40.1
Uganda	9.6	21.1	21.6	25.6	34.2	30.2	27.0	24.4	28.9	35.5	27.2

SOURCE: Westoff and Ochoa (1991).

TABLE 2A-1   Differentials in the Percentage of Women Who Currently
Use a Modern Method

Country	Total	Residence		Education		
		Urban	Rural	None	Primary	Secondary
Botswana	31.7	40.8	27.5	18.9	32.9	50.3
Burundi	1.2	14.0	0.8	0.6	2.2	16.9
Ghana	5.2	8.1	3.9[a]	3.2	6.5	10.1
Kenya	17.8	25.5	16.4	9.7	19.2	29.3
Liberia	5.5	9.7	3.1	2.5	6.6	22.1
Mali[b]	1.3	4.9	0.1	0.4	5.5	20.3
Ondo	3.8	5.3	2.8[a]	1.9	3.6	9.0
Senegal	2.4	6.7	0.3	1.0	5.9	22.1
Sudan	5.5	11.3	2.2	1.9	7.9	14.9
Togo	3.1	6.5	1.7	1.7	3.9	12.2
Uganda	2.5	12.2	1.5	0.9	2.7	11.3
Zimbabwe	36.1	48.8	30.9	25.0	34.0	52.3

NOTE: The base for the table is all women currently in union.

[a]The contrast is *not* significant at the .05 level in a multivariate logit model.
[b]For Mali, the logistic regression omits cases in which the woman was age 45-49.

than their use, and the knowledge of government sources of supply in the
three higher use countries indicates the importance of government family
planning programs in those countries. Estimates of unmet need indicated
that there is substantial demand for additional family planning services,
especially for spacing births.

Age						
15-19	20-24	25-29	30-34	35-39	40-44	45-49
14.5	25.2[a]	36.0	33.7	37.5	35.0	14.7[a]
0.6	0.7[a]	1.4[a]	1.5[a]	1.3[a]	1.0[a]	1.6[a]
2.3	3.4[a]	4.3[a]	6.9	5.9[a]	9.0	4.2[a]
6.7	11.8	16.8	22.2	22.9	21.2	17.5
2.0	4.9[a]	6.7	6.3	5.1	5.7	7.1
1.4	1.4[a]	1.6[a]	1.6[a]	1.4[a]	0.8[a]	0.0
1.7	2.1[a]	3.0[a]	4.6	5.4	4.2	3.5
0.5	0.8[a]	2.5[a]	4.8[a]	3.8	1.1[a]	2.4[a]
2.2	4.2[a]	5.0[a]	7.9	5.7	7.7	4.4
2.1	1.9[a]	2.5[a]	3.7[a]	4.7[a]	4.2[a]	3.4[a]
1.2	1.1[a]	1.9[a]	2.6	6.0	5.2	2.5
28.3	41.5	43.8	42.9	30.8[a]	26.1[a]	17.2[a]

3

The Socioeconomic Context

Contraceptive use is the expression of individual desires to space or to limit births. Individual demands for birth spacing and limitation are themselves shaped by the surrounding social, economic, and policy environment. If our aim is to understand contraceptive use in sub-Saharan Africa, we must look first to the determinants of the demand for children. This chapter opens the investigation with a consideration of the linkages between economic development and fertility. Our discussion will emphasize levels of income per capita, child mortality, educational attainment among adults, and the costs and benefits of child schooling.

The overriding issue here and in Chapter 4 is whether, and under what conditions, sub-Saharan Africa is likely to join in the process of fertility decline in progress elsewhere. Recent demographic literature on Africa presents no consensus about the prospects for change; indeed, the two views that dominate the literature are strikingly opposed. In one, fertility decline is seen as the natural concomitant of economic development; the demographic-economic linkages are thought to apply in sub-Saharan Africa much as they do elsewhere. Continued high fertility is therefore explained in terms of the factors that continue to inhibit economic development more generally. In the other perspective, however, sub-Saharan Africa is regarded as being uniquely resistant to fertility decline. This resistance is said to be rooted in fundamental and very nearly immutable features of social organization, not easily swept away in the course of development. The two competing perspectives on change are perhaps best exemplified in two publications—a report by the World Bank (1986) and an article by Caldwell and Caldwell (1987).

The World Bank report locates the reasons for high fertility in Africa in a set of conventional indices of economic development: low incomes per capita; high infant and child mortality rates; low levels of adult literacy; high proportions of the work force in agriculture; low percentages of the population living in urban areas; and continuing difficulties across the continent in access to education, health, and family planning services. In none of these dimensions has much of Africa advanced to a threshold sufficient to induce fertility decline, according to the report. Thus, there should be nothing very surprising about high African fertility and low contraceptive use at present, but one should not expect these conditions to persist as the development indicators begin to improve.

The alternative view, exemplified by the article by Caldwell and Caldwell, draws attention to the unique features of African fertility decision making. African societies are viewed as being wholly distinctive in respect to social organization. They are said to differ from the remainder of the developing world not merely in terms of the conventional categories of development, but more fundamentally in the nature of spouse relationships, household structure, kinship, culture, and religion. These elements have combined to provide a powerful and coherent rationale for high fertility, one that is without real counterpart elsewhere. Moreover, according to a later article by Caldwell and Caldwell (1988), the high-fertility rationale remains intact even in modern nation-states. The modern African state exerts only a superficial influence on social organization, due to difficulties in formulating population policies at the national level and to continuing deficiencies in local service delivery. The state commands very few of the tools needed to dismantle the high-fertility rationale.

These two lines of argument, seemingly so divergent, in fact have a common point of origin in the historical record. The economic development of sub-Saharan Africa has been profoundly affected by its distinctive material conditions: principally, the relative abundance of land in comparison to labor; soil that in much of the region yields meager dividends to intensified cultivation; and the very considerable uncertainties surrounding the standard of living and life itself, owing to vagaries of climate and the prevalence of disease (Locoh, 1991). These material conditions are expressed in economic relations and kinship structure, and have shaped aspects of both culture and religion. They explain much of the high value placed on labor and fertility, as well as the importance accorded to networks of mutual support, whether established through children, kin, or social relations. They may also help to explain the comparative recency in Africa of territorially based bureaucratic structures, which provide the foundation for nation-states. Thus, in reconciling the views of the World Bank

(1986) and Caldwell and Caldwell (1987), what is at issue is not so much the historical legacy, which has affected both the level of economic development and social structure, as its relevance to African economies entering the decade of the 1990s.

This chapter explores the view that high fertility in Africa can be explained principally by levels of development. (Chapter 4 will focus on the other view.) In an effort to weigh the evidence, we shall first review the major theoretical linkages between socioeconomic variables and fertility. These linkages are illustrated with cross-national data from developing countries including some in sub-Saharan Africa. We also summarize a body of evidence from household-level research on the socioeconomic determinants of fertility, with the aim of assessing whether fertility levels are indeed less sensitive to economic differentials in Africa than elsewhere. We then consider in more detail the evidence on the relation between fertility and child mortality and the prospects for increased survival, and the evidence on the role of schooling costs and benefits in the demand for children. Finally, we speculate as to the longer-run demographic consequences implicit in the current era of economic stagnation and structural adjustment.

SOCIOECONOMIC DIFFERENTIALS OF FERTILITY

National-Level Relationships

In this section we briefly review the theoretical arguments linking fertility levels to a set of socioeconomic determinants: income per capita, child mortality, educational attainment among adults, and the costs and benefits of child schooling. Where appropriate, we illustrate the theoretical arguments with data drawn from recent cross-national samples of developing countries.[1] In so doing, we take per capita income as a convenient index of the level of economic development.

The relationship between income and fertility has been the subject of much study. Evidence from many regions of the world that have experienced fertility declines shows that income growth is associated with lower fertility in the long run (World Bank, 1984). However, economic theory suggests that fertility may rise with increases in income, because additional resources allow the family to afford more children. In the short term, this

---

[1]The data are taken from the sample of countries covered in the *1991 World Development Indicators* (World Bank, 1991) and limited to countries with an income level per capita of $3,000 or less in 1989. The income cutoff is used because no sub-Saharan country exceeded this level in 1989. Gabon's per capita income in that year was estimated as $2,960; South Africa's was $2,470; and the next highest level of income per capita, $1,600, was in Botswana (estimates in 1989 U.S. dollars.)

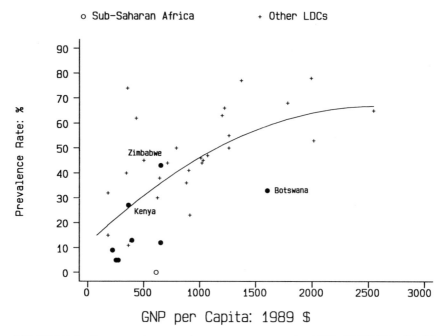

FIGURE 3-1 Contraceptive prevalence versus per capita GNP. SOURCE: World Bank (1991) and Demographic and Health Survey data tapes for sub-Saharan Africa.

positive relationship has been observed many times. The income-fertility relationship is complicated, mainly because changes in income are related to other aspects of economic development, such as educational opportunities, the participation of women in the work force, accessibility of consumer goods, and the value of time. Thus, the effects of income on fertility are both direct and indirect, and income may exhibit both negative and positive associations with fertility (Mueller and Short, 1983). However, it is generally agreed that in the long term, income is negatively associated with fertility, because of the relationship of changes in income with changes in other factors that reduce the demand for children (World Bank, 1984). (See the section in this chapter on economic stagnation and adjustment for further discussion.)

To set the stage for the theoretical discussion, Figure 3-1 shows the positive relationship of contraceptive prevalence (all methods) to gross national product (GNP) per capita for more than 35 developing countries. The data include a small number of sub-Saharan African (SSA) countries with information on contraceptive prevalence as of 1990. In ascending order of incomes, the sub-Saharan group includes Burundi (9 percent prevalence),

Uganda (5), Mali (5), Kenya (27), Ghana (13), Togo (12), Senegal (12), Zimbabwe (43), and Botswana (33).[2] Sub-Saharan countries taken as a whole clearly display lower levels of contraceptive prevalence than would be expected given their levels of development.[3] The African countries compose the majority of countries in the sample with low incomes and prevalence rates. Kenya, Zimbabwe, and Botswana are outliers by comparison with their sub-Saharan counterparts. Kenya and Zimbabwe have the prevalence rates expected given their levels of income, and Botswana, with the highest level of income of the sub-Saharan countries shown here, has a lower than expected prevalence rate (although still higher than all other sub-Saharan countries, except Zimbabwe).

Estimates of total fertility rates[4] are available for a much larger sample of sub-Saharan countries. In what follows, we generally rely on fertility data to provide an indication of the level of demand for births or for surviving children in the populations in question.[5] Figure 3-2 depicts the relationship between total fertility rates (TFRs) and income per capita in 1989. As the figure shows, in comparison to developing countries outside the region, those in sub-Saharan Africa display higher TFRs than their income levels alone would suggest.

---

[2]Income-level data are not available for Liberia.

[3]In Figure 3-1 and several figures that follow, a regression line is used to help guide the eye through the data. In each case the regression was calculated by taking the variable displayed on the vertical axis as the dependent variable and that on the horizontal as the independent variable. Regressions were estimated by using the full sample comprised of all developing countries with per capita incomes of less than $3,000. Linear ($y = a + bX$) and log-linear ($y = a + b\ln X$) specifications were examined in each case; the better-fitting line is shown in the figures.

[4]The total fertility rate (TFR) is a measure of the average number of children that would be born to a woman who survives through her reproductive years. It is usually calculated on a period-specific or calendar-year basis by using the age-specific fertility rates in effect in the period in question.

[5]Fertility may vary for reasons having little to do with the demand for births or for surviving children. In parts of Central Africa, for example, primary and secondary sterility places important constraints on fertility, and in this case, levels of fertility are not easily interpreted in terms of the underlying demands. In other parts of Africa, observed fertility may be higher than desired because there is not perfect control over actual fertility (due to lack of access to efficient contraception, among other reasons). Despite these difficulties in interpretation, we think that fertility rates provide the best approximation of the demand for births.

It is not obvious that the important postpartum proximate determinants, breastfeeding and postpartum abstinence, necessarily cause any difficulties in the interpretation placed on fertility levels. To the degree that these behaviors reflect a demand for surviving children—that is, to the degree that birth spacing is understood to be related to child survival in the populations in question—the level of fertility is a good indicator of the underlying demand. If for some reason the connection between spacing and survival is not recognized, however, the interpretation of fertility levels in terms of demand is more problematic.

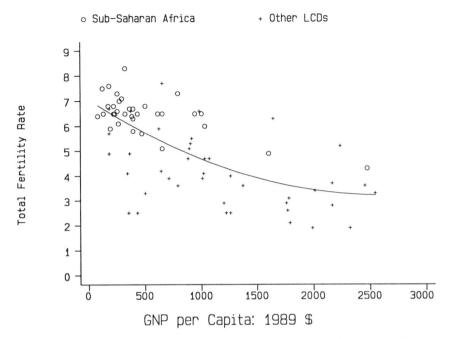

FIGURE 3-2 Total fertility rates by per capita GNP. SOURCE: World Bank (1991).

Figure 3-3 presents fertility rates and income among only the sub-Saharan countries with per capita incomes of less than $1,700 (excluding Gabon and South Africa). Within this group, we should distinguish two sets of countries: the five most populous countries of the region excluding South Africa, that is, Nigeria, Ethiopia, Zaire, Sudan, and Tanzania; and the three countries, Kenya, Zimbabwe, and Botswana, thought to be the forerunners of an African fertility transition.[6] The set of largest countries accounts for some 51 percent of the total sub-Saharan population (as of 1989); Nigeria alone accounts for 23 percent. Simply by virtue of their size, these

---

[6]South Africa's 1989 population, some 35 million, would place it third in terms of size, on a par with Zaire. We have excluded South Africa for consideration here because (1) its per capita income ($2,470 in 1989) is much higher than the norm for the region; and (2) the considerable demographic and economic heterogeneity of its population leads to difficulties of interpretation.

Sudan does not appear in some of our figures because the World Bank data sets that we used did not supply an estimate of its income per capita in 1989. The total fertility rate for Sudan was estimated to be 6.4 as of 1988, and an income estimate per capita for that year was $480 (World Bank, 1990b).

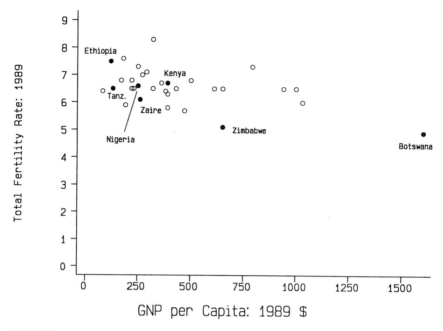

FIGURE 3-3 Total fertility rates in sub-Saharan Africa (countries with GNP per capita less than $1,700). SOURCE: World Bank (1991).

countries must dominate the demographic future of the region. Kenya's population is very nearly the size of Tanzania's. By contrast, Zimbabwe and Botswana collectively comprise only 7 percent of the region's population. Thus, the importance of the higher use countries rests not so much on their contribution to regional totals, as on the lessons they may embody regarding the determinants of change.

Of the countries with higher prevalence, Figure 3-3 shows that both Botswana and Zimbabwe belong in the upper strata of sub-Saharan countries in respect to income per capita. Kenya, by contrast, lies in the middle rank in terms of income and has a TFR comparable to that of Nigeria or Tanzania. Evidently, then, the interest that surrounds the case of Kenya has less to do with the present level of fertility than with its current contraceptive prevalence and the fact of a recent downward change in fertility (Locoh, 1991).

Mortality

The linkages between fertility and mortality consist partly of what has been termed a "physiological effect," whereby a child's death truncates breastfeeding, leaving the woman reexposed to the risk of conception. We expect this physiological effect to be more powerful in societies with longer periods of full breastfeeding, where the contraceptive effect of breastfeeding is itself stronger, and also where postpartum abstinence is linked to breastfeeding. Lloyd and Ivanov (1988), in reviewing Preston's (1975, 1978) work, suggest that in a population with long durations of breastfeeding and postpartum abstinence, a reduction of one infant death would be associated with some 0.25 to 0.30 fewer births over a typical reproductive lifetime. Thus, declines in mortality could be expected to produce declines in fertility, if on something less than a one-to-one basis.[7]

The behavioral linkages[8] between mortality and fertility consist of what are termed insurance and replacement effects, the former having to do with the influence of perceived or anticipated mortality risks on decisions regarding fertility; the latter, with the household's response to an actual child death. The insurance effect is thought to be evident in coefficients that relate community- or area-level indicators of mortality to individual-level information on fertility or contraceptive use.

Very little is known about the relationship between the risks of mortality facing adults and the decisions that adults make regarding fertility. We raise the point here because it will likely become an issue in the regions of Africa suffering from a high prevalence of acquired immune deficiency syndrome (AIDS; see the research agenda laid out in Gribble, 1992). A pronatalist reaction to the threat of AIDS is certainly plausible, especially as infant and child mortality due to mother-child transmission of human immunodeficiency virus (HIV) will increase in these regions. However, the social upheavals associated with an epidemic of the scale anticipated for Central and parts of southern Africa may call into question many previously established behavioral relationships. We see little basis for the extrapolation of existing demographic theory on mortality-fertility linkages to such unprecedented circumstances.

Figure 3-4 shows the relationship between total fertility rates and child mortality rates, with the sub-Saharan countries highlighted. It can be seen that African countries conform to the statistical norm wherein high levels of

---

[7]If the decline in fertility is less than one to one, we expect the net reproduction rate (the average number of daughters born per woman in a cohort given certain mortality rates) to increase as infant survivorship improves.

[8]Although we emphasize only the associations through which mortality affects fertility, it is important to recognize that causation can run in the other direction as well. Higher fertility may imply shorter intervals between births and greater proportions of births occurring in the portions of the maternal age span (under age 20 or over age 35) when children face higher mortality risks (Working Group on the Health Consequences of Contraceptive Use and Controlled Fertility, 1989).

FIGURE 3-4 Total fertility rates versus child mortality rates. SOURCE: World Bank (1991).

fertility are associated with high levels of mortality. Similar correlations are evident across regions within individual African countries. For example, Montgomery and Kouame (1992) find a significant influence of area-level child survival rates on cumulative fertility in Côte d'Ivoire. Kelley and Nobbe (1990) report a high negative correlation between infant mortality and contraceptive use in a set of Kenyan provinces.

Educational Attainment of Adults

Few relationships have been so exhaustively studied as that between a woman's educational attainment and her fertility. Yet the basis of the relationship remains far from understood (Cochrane, 1979, 1983), particularly in settings such as those characteristic of Africa.

Economists have drawn attention to the link between education and labor market earnings. The higher a woman's educational attainment is, the greater is her potential wage. If time spent in work and time in child care are mutually exclusive, then wage measures one of the principal opportunity costs of childrearing. It follows that the higher is the price of time, the lower should be fertility.

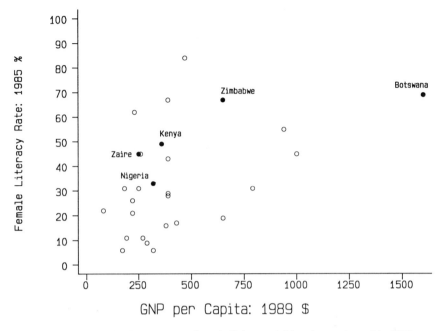

FIGURE 3-5 Female literacy rates in sub-Saharan Africa (countries with GNP per capita less than $1,700). SOURCE: World Bank (1991).

Figure 3-5 shows that higher levels of female literacy are associated with lower total fertility rates in sub-Saharan Africa, as elsewhere. However, it is not at all clear that the chain of reasoning spelled out above can be applied to African economies. For most African women, work need not conflict directly with child care. Where a conflict exists, it may be resolved through the employment of low-cost substitutes for the mother's time in child care, such as care provided by relatives. The link to the opportunity cost argument is therefore likely to be weak.

In an influential paper, Caldwell (1982) envisions a larger role for education than that considered in the simple economic model. In his view, education serves as a vehicle for the adoption of Western ideas regarding the family. It may encourage a more child-centered view of one's parental responsibilities. Education may alter the definition of what constitutes acceptable child care, giving greater weight to the time spent by the mother with her child, compared to time given by mother substitutes. Education may also affect the distribution of authority within the household, so that educated women gain a measure of autonomy vis-à-vis their husbands, and couples vis-à-vis their elders. Little is known in any quantitative sense about these issues (see Chapter 4 on the subject of emotional nucleation), but we suspect that adult educational attainment, and particularly schooling for women, may be a precondition for a decline in the demand for children.

Schooling of Children: The Quantity-Quality Trade-Off

In any number of societies that have gone on to experience fertility decline (for Thailand, see Knodel et al., 1987, 1990), changes in the perceived benefits and costs of child schooling have played a key role in the transition. The impetus for fertility change originates in the economic returns associated with schooling. In the course of modernization, an economy begins to display significant differentials in earnings by schooling level. Parents then come to regard schooling as an avenue to a better life for their children and as a human capital investment that may, over the long term, pay dividends to the parents themselves. Yet education is costly in terms of both direct costs and opportunity costs of forgone child labor; it generally remains too costly for parents to give each child the desired schooling and continue to bear the customary number of children. Some element of household expenditures must give way, and typically fertility falls as household investments in education per child increase. The increase in child schooling, coupled with the decline in fertility, has been termed a quantity-quality demographic transition (Becker and Lewis, 1973; Willis, 1973; Caldwell, 1982).

Figure 3-6 gives an indication of the quantity-quality transition in developing countries. Total fertility rates for 1989 are arrayed on the vertical axis—the quantity dimension. The horizontal axis shows the quality dimension, as expressed in 1988 primary school enrollment ratios. Viewed differently, the vertical axis represents the principal determinant of the future rate of labor force growth, that is, fertility. The horizontal axis indicates the levels of human capital with which future labor market entrants will be equipped (albeit with a shorter time lag). A quantity-quality demographic transition is therefore fundamental to economic development, in that it implies a reduction in future labor force growth and an increase in human capital per worker.

The trade-off should be understood to represent a systematic association between two variables, fertility and child schooling, both of which are determined by the preferences, costs, and financial constraints of the household. Higher fertility does not in itself cause lower school enrollment, nor does greater enrollment cause lower fertility. Rather, each of these variables taken individually reflects the full set of opportunities and constraints facing households. Nothing requires that the relationship between fertility and child schooling have a negative slope. Indeed, Figure 3-6 shows that for sub-Saharan countries, the negative relationship between fertility and primary schooling is far weaker, if it exists at all, than is the case among

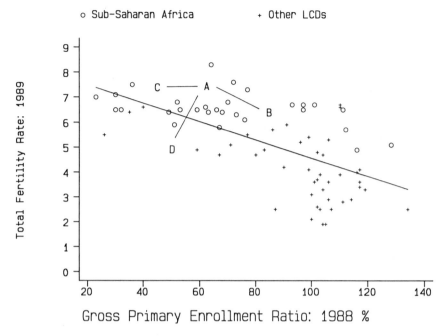

FIGURE 3-6 Total fertility rates versus primary school enrollment ratios. SOURCE: World Bank (1991).

other developing countries. The reason for this difference in slopes must be sought in the socioeconomic background factors that jointly influence fertility and schooling per child.

Among such factors, a good deal of attention has been directed to policy-induced changes in the costs of schooling (discussed below). In some accounts, the magnitude of private schooling costs (tuition, fees, capital levies, etc.) is said to be integral to the quantity-quality transition. These cost increases could conceivably induce a quantity-quality transition, such that an African country previously in position A of Figure 3-6 would move to position B of higher enrollment and lower fertility, but this response is unlikely. More plausible responses to an increase in the price of education are represented in an enrollment reduction accompanied by little change in fertility (a movement from position A to position C), or perhaps a decrease in both fertility and child schooling (movement from A to D).[9] These various responses to changing school costs have profoundly different implications for future demographic and economic development. In short, it is

_____

[9]One would certainly expect an increase in the price of schooling to have a direct negative effect on enrollment. In addition, if quantity and quality are complements, an increase in the price would cause fertility to decline; otherwise it would increase.

far from clear that changes in the costs of schooling alone can engender a quantity-quality transition.

The origins of the transition in Africa are likely to be found not simply in educational costs, but rather in a changing configuration of benefits and costs. The private benefits[10] accruing from an extra year of schooling consist of the extra earnings that year is expected to generate over a working lifetime, suitably discounted and adjusted for unemployment and earnings variability (World Bank, 1988). If parents perceive little improvement in their children's earning potential with the level of schooling, they may be quite sensitive to marginal changes in the price of schooling. Faced with an increase in tuition or fees, they may simply respond by reducing human capital investments, as indicated in movement from point A to point C in Figure 3-6. If the earnings gradient is steep, on the other hand, parents may choose to respond to cost changes in part by making sacrifices in other dimensions of behavior, including that of fertility, as shown in the A to D response. However, one would not expect to observe a quantity-quality transition (A to B) unless the benefits of schooling themselves improve.

In a sense, therefore, the benefits of schooling are critical. They serve as a fulcrum, giving the costs of schooling effective leverage against fertility. If one wishes to make predictions about fertility change, the costs of educational investments cannot be considered in isolation from the anticipated returns.[11]

The Combined Relation of Per Capita Income, Mortality, Education, and Fertility

Above we considered the bivariate relationships between fertility and per capita income, child mortality, and education, using national-level data. Here we investigate the relations in a multivariate regression framework. Two points are at issue in framing such a regression. First, is the level of

---

[10]We emphasize here the private benefits of schooling, recognizing the distinction between private and social returns, because the former are more likely to influence the investment decisions of parents. (Additional social benefits consist, for instance, in the well-documented effects of adult schooling on fertility and child mortality. Private benefits would also be calculated net of taxes on earnings. Social benefits consider pretax effects on productivity; a key issue in their calculation is the extent to which earnings differentials associated with education represent true differentials in productivity, as opposed to credentialism effects.) We do not discuss who in the African household makes such decisions regarding investments in child schooling, nor are we concerned in this chapter with mechanisms for spreading the costs of schooling among kin (see Chapter 4).

[11]Note that schooling costs exert their leverage in large part because of the liquidity constraints facing African households. The possibility of borrowing to finance educational investments in children is available to very few households. Chapter 4 discusses the role of transfers among kin, including child fostering, in this regard.

TABLE 3-1 Regression Analysis of 1989 Total Fertility Rate

Parameter	Model 1	Model 2
Constant	4.569	3.206
(t-statistic)	(3.61)	(1.90)
Income per capita,	–0.85	.206
1965 (log)	(0.47)	(0.89)
Infant mortality	.011	.015
rate, 1965	(2.78)	(3.04)
Primary enrollment	–.008	-.025
ratio, 1965	(1.52)	(2.63)
Secondary enrollment	–.025	–.006
ratio, 1965	(1.99)	(0.44)
Sub-Saharan Africa	1.310	5.037
dummy variable	(4.98)	(1.97)
SSA • income per		–.553
capita		(1.39)
SSA • infant mortality		–.011
rate		(1.34)
SSA • primary		.021
enrollment ratio		(1.74)
SSA • secondary		–.009
enrollment ratio		(0.13)
R-squared	.77	.80
F-statistic	41.98	25.75

NOTE: Number of observations = 68.

fertility in sub-Saharan Africa indeed higher than would be expected given its level of development? Second, is there any statistical support for the proposition of greater African resistance to fertility decline, as evidenced in distinctive regression coefficients on socioeconomic determinants of fertility?

Table 3-1 presents the results of two regression equations based on data from 68 developing countries around the world with per capita incomes in 1989 of less than $3,000. Model 1, shown in column 1, indicates that total fertility rates in sub-Saharan Africa are significantly higher than elsewhere, net of levels of income, infant mortality, and adult enrollment ratios attainment.[12] This difference in levels of fertility is evident in the positive coefficient on the SSA dummy variable, which distinguishes between sub-Sa-

---

[12]The specification employs 1965 infant mortality rates, because more recent mortality figures could as easily be the result of high fertility as its cause, as indicated in footnote 8. (The *1991 World Development Indicators* data (World Bank, 1991) provide information at only two time points: 1965 and the most recent available date.) Lagged school enrollment levels are

haran countries and other developing countries; it amounts to some 1.3 children. Model 2, shown in column 2 of the table, considers whether the response to socioeconomic determinants is systematically different in sub-Saharan Africa by interacting the dummy variable for sub-Saharan Africa with the other explanatory variables. We see no evidence here that fertility rates in the region are any less responsive to incomes, mortality rates, or schooling, by comparison with other developing countries outside Africa. Among all regression coefficients on interactions between the SSA dummy variable and socioeconomic determinants, none achieves statistical significance. At least in the cross section, then, there is little to support the hypothesis that fertility levels in sub-Saharan Africa are unusually resistant to socioeconomic change. Admittedly, the *1991 World Development Indicators* data (World Bank, 1991) are less than adequate for exploring models of change, so the definitive answer to the question of resistance to fertility decline remains to be given.[13]

---

used to explore the distinction between primary and secondary school attainment, a distinction that is not measured by current levels of adult literacy. Various alternative specifications were considered for the regressions, including some that employed 1989 per capita incomes and 1985 literacy levels, and other specifications that used averages of 1965 and the most recent values. These results differed in details, but not in terms of the conclusions that we emphasize in the text.

[13]The difficulties in drawing time-series inferences from cross-sectional data are well known. If in the cross section for country i, time t, we have

$$\text{TFR}_{it} = X_{it}\beta + u_i + \varepsilon_{it}, \tag{1}$$

then change over time (denoted as Δ) in country i can be represented as

$$\Delta\text{TFR}_i = \Delta X_i \beta + \Delta\varepsilon_i, \tag{2}$$

if the relationship between X and TFR did not change over time. The distinction between the cross-sectional model (equation 1) and the differences model (equation 2) does not consist in the parameters beta (β) themselves, but rather in the ability to estimate these coefficients. Suppose that unmeasured country-specific factors embedded in u_i are correlated with socioeconomic variables X_{it}. If the u_i are so correlated, they would invalidate estimation of the cross-sectional equation (1) and so would render suspect any of its implications about the magnitude of fertility change attributable to changes in socioeconomic circumstances X. (In other words, the regressions of Table 3-1 would be invalid, even as a guide to cross-sectional differentials.) The differences model (equation 2) is not vulnerable on this score, but requires much more data.

Even if a full first-differences modeling exercise is beyond the capacities of the *1991 World Development Indicators* data, simple correlations of ΔTFR with ΔX can shed some light on the proposition of resistance. Among all less developed countries, the 1965-1989 ΔTFR is correlated at: −.47 with the change in (the log of) per capita income; .16 with the change in infant mortality; −.15 with the change in primary enrollment; and -.56 with the change in secondary enrollment. (The signs of these correlations give an indication of the signs of the corresponding regression coefficients γ.) Within sub-Saharan Africa, the correlations are −.30 with the change in per capita income; .26 with the change in mortality; −.28 with the change in primary enrollments; and -.63 with the change in secondary enrollments.

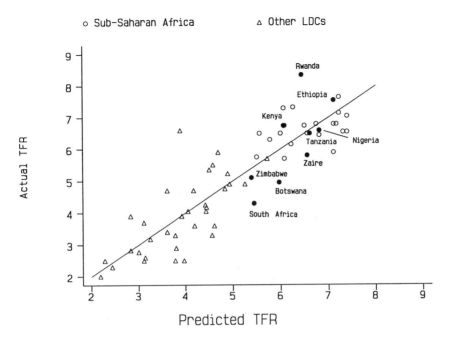

FIGURE 3-7 Predicted and actual total fertility rates, 1989, regression results of Table 3-1, model 1.

Figure 3-7 employs the regression results from column 1 to identify the sub-Saharan countries with pronounced differentials between their expected total fertility rates, given socioeconomic determinants, and their actual TFRs. As can be seen, the largest sub-Saharan countries display fertility levels that are quite similar to their predicted values; indeed, Nigeria, Zaire, and Tanzania show modest shortfalls of actual fertility relative to predicted. Botswana and Zimbabwe exhibit somewhat lower fertility levels than predicted, whereas the Kenyan TFR remains above that suggested by its socioeconomic standing.

In summary, we find strong evidence that African fertility levels are higher than those obtaining elsewhere in the developing world, even net of socioeconomic variables, but there is little in these cross-sectional data to support the proposition of greater resistance to change.

Household-Level Research

Household-level research can also be used to explore this proposition. Socioeconomic differentials in fertility at the household level in sub-Saharan Africa have been reviewed by Cochrane and Farid (1990) for a sample of 10 countries based on World Fertility Survey (WFS) data. They give attention primarily to differences in total fertility rates according to urban-rural residence and women's education. The size of the differentials provides evidence regarding the hypothesis of resistance to change: The smaller a socioeconomic differential at a given time, the greater is the implied resistance of fertility to changes in socioeconomic factors over time. (See footnote 13 on the dangers of using cross-sectional comparisons to draw such conclusions.)

As is true elsewhere, urban residence in Africa is associated with lower total fertility rates. Comparing rural women to those in the major urban centers, Cochrane and Farid find a mean difference of 1.16 in the TFRs; the bulk of the difference is due to nuptiality (or timing of entry into childbearing) rather than marital fertility. Similar gaps in total fertility rates appear in the WFS data for Asia, but the differential by residence in Latin America is much larger, amounting to 2.6 children.

In regard to women's education, Cochrane and Farid find a mean differential in TFRs amounting to two children between women without education and those with seven or more years of schooling. Like the rural-urban differential, that for education in sub-Saharan Africa is similar to the gap in Asia but less pronounced than in Latin America, North Africa, or the Middle East. The differential in sub-Saharan Africa is again in large part the product of nuptiality.

One interesting aspect of the educational differentials in fertility in Africa is an apparent nonlinearity in the effect of women's schooling. In the majority of the countries examined by Cochrane and Farid, women with one to three years of schooling, and in some cases those with four to six years, display higher fertility rates than do women without schooling. The relationship takes the form of an inverted U, with women in the middle schooling group having the highest fertility. These nonlinearities are thought to derive from the reductions in postpartum abstinence and breastfeeding that accompany higher levels of education. They may also have to do with the unmeasured effects of income or wealth on fertility that come to be correlated with women's schooling via marriage.

Tambashe and Shapiro (1991) present additional evidence on educational nonlinearities in a multivariate analysis for Kinshasa. In their sample, the difference in lifetime fertility between women with primary schooling (the highest-fertility group) and those with secondary schooling is on the order of one child. Women with no schooling generally have lower fertility than women with primary schooling and higher fertility than women with more than primary schooling. They show that education is positively associated with contraceptive use. There is little difference in length of breastfeeding for women with no schooling compared to women with primary schooling, however, for women with at least primary schooling, education is associated with shorter periods of breastfeeding.

Two general conclusions can be drawn from this research. First, one should expect continuing advances in female schooling, particularly in later primary and secondary schooling, to exert an important antinatalist influence. The effect of continued urbanization appears less powerful, but in the same direction. Second, the changes in fertility associated with these socioeconomic differentials are not always large, especially in comparison to those of Latin America,[14] and in this sense the proposition of greater African resistance to fertility decline could be said to receive support. But the socioeconomic differentials evident in Africa are nevertheless important and suggest a range of receptivity to further family limitation.

The WFS-based research is somewhat compromised by a lack of information on income, which has the potential to distort findings regarding schooling. We know of only one study of African fertility with proper controls for income, that of Ainsworth (1990) for Côte d'Ivoire. Ainsworth finds that lifetime fertility significantly decreases with female education, holding income levels constant. There is no evidence of nonlinearity in the education effects, although this result may be due to the very low levels of female educational attainment in the sample. The income coefficients reveal that cumulative fertility increases with household income. Ainsworth concludes that if income growth goes unaccompanied by increases in female educational attainment, fertility will very likely rise in Côte d'Ivoire.

These studies leave unclear precisely what behavioral mechanisms are at work in the link between female schooling and lower fertility. Certainly one aspect has to do with the nuptiality effects of education, but the nature of the education effect within African reproductive unions has yet to be elucidated. The connection usually emphasized in developed-country studies, which has to do with the greater opportunity cost of time in child care for better-educated women, is of doubtful relevance to sub-Saharan Africa. Another possibility, perhaps more plausible in the African setting, is that better-educated women place greater emphasis on child quality, as opposed to child quantity. This is the view stated, albeit in different terms, by Caldwell (1982) in his discussion of schooling and the adoption of Western conceptions of the child-centered family.

We now turn to a more detailed exploration of three areas that appear to be critical for future trends in fertility: progress in lowering child mortal-

---

[14]It should be recognized that Latin America is highly socially stratified. Therefore, one might expect larger socioeconomic differentials than those found in Africa. Comparisons between Asia and Africa might be more appropriate, and the evidence from Cochrane and Farid (1990) suggests similar differentials.

ity, changes in the costs and benefits of child schooling, and the notion of a crisis-led transition.

EVIDENCE ON CHANGES IN CHILD MORTALITY

Hill's (1990, 1991a,b, 1993) findings regarding child mortality trends document an impressive decline in African mortality over the period from World War II to the mid-1980s. As Hill (1991b) observes, in the 1950s most African countries displayed child mortality rates in the range of 160-400 deaths per 1,000 live births, and in only a few countries was the rate lower than 220. By the mid-1980s the range of child mortality had shifted to 60-270 per 1,000, most countries then being found in the 120-220 range. This progress is remarkable by any standard; yet in all but a few African countries, child mortality remains very high.

Although the gap is closing, a mortality differential between eastern and southern Africa, and western and middle Africa, is still in evidence. Child mortality has long been highest in the western and Sahelian regions, next highest in middle Africa, somewhat lower in eastern Africa, and lower still in southern Africa. However, recent data indicate continued blurring of these regional distinctions, particularly among midlevel-mortality countries (Hill, 1993). These regional differentials in survivorship are not easily explainable in terms of standard development indicators, such as education levels or incomes per capita; they may have to do with climate, long-standing patterns of population settlement, or various epidemiological peculiarities (Hill, 1991b).

The empirical record for the 1980s is not yet complete, but it seems that despite the economic reversals of the period, most countries managed to sustain at least modest improvements in survivorship. Experiences have been enormously varied across the continent. The situation in what are now the lowest-mortality countries in Africa—Botswana, Zimbabwe, and Kenya—presents a marked contrast to that prevailing in the largest countries of the region—Nigeria, Ethiopia, Zaire, Sudan, and Tanzania. In the former, child mortality rates have achieved the 50-100 per 1,000 range, a level comparable to much of Latin America and Southeast Asia. The improvements recorded by Kenya are especially noteworthy, given its still-modest level of income per capita. In the largest countries, by contrast, mortality remains high, and it seems that rather little progress has been made over the last two decades.

Among the largest countries, uncertainty attaches to the mortality record of Nigeria, owing to doubts regarding the reliability of data collected in the World Fertility Survey of 1981-1982. Using the Demographic and Health Survey (DHS) results, which she believes to be of higher quality than the WFS, Hill (1993) tentatively concludes that child mortality has been relatively stable since the mid-1970s, with a probability of dying before age 5, $_5q_0$, ranging from 190 to 200.[15] No recent data are available for Ethiopia, but it is doubtful that any substantial improvement could have been recorded over the past decade and a half. Hill's estimate for Zaire, placing $_5q_0$ equal to 210-220 per 1,000, is based on a 1984 census; no figures are available covering the post-1984 years of deepening economic crisis (Hill, 1993). Child mortality in the Sudan (northern) apparently leveled off at a $_5q_0$ of 150 per 1,000 in the mid-1980s with possibly some decline in the late 1980s (Hill, 1991b and 1993). Little is known about recent trends in survivorship in Tanzania. In short, the degree of progress sustained by Africa's largest countries over the past decade is much in doubt; the fragments of data available suggest only modest improvements, if any.

Elsewhere in Africa, child mortality rates continued to decline through the mid-1980s even in the face of difficult economic circumstances and cutbacks in government spending. Even the Sahelian countries (including Senegal, Mali, Burkina Faso, and The Gambia), beset by drought and economic stagnation, show appreciable and sometimes substantial improvements. The experience of Ghana, in which mortality either leveled off or increased from the late 1970s to the early 1980s in the face of difficult economic circumstances (Pinstrup-Andersen et al., 1987; Working Group on Demographic Effects of Economic and Social Reversals, 1993), and Uganda with its political turmoil appear to be exceptions.

Taken together, Hill's findings can be summarized as follows: There is nothing automatic or self-sustaining about improvements in African survivorship (although recent data indicate continued mortality decline for many countries during the last 20 years). Mortality improvement is likely in part the result of economic development and service delivery. Change can be slowed or suspended by periods of sociopolitical instability (Hill, 1991a) and accelerated by continued investments in the social sector. In Hill's (1991b) view, investments in the health sector provided something of a short-term demographic cushion for a number of countries (notably in the Sahel, but also in Togo and Côte d'Ivoire) through the 1980s. For a time the accumulated investments in health services may continue to sustain improvements in survivorship, even in the face of spending retrenchments and macroeconomic adversity. Eventually, however, as in the case of Ghana, such protection must erode in the absence of any new investments in health.

---

[15]Both the DHS first country report for Nigeria (Nigeria, 1992) and Hill (1991a and 1993) caution that mortality estimates based on the 1981-1982 World Fertility Survey for Nigeria are likely to be biased downward. A conclusion of increase in Nigerian mortality, seemingly implied by the difference between Hill's best guess for 1978 and the DHS 1990 figures, is probably unwarranted.

Links to Fertility

Although positive correlations between child mortality and fertility do not prove a causal relationship, because of the possibility of a common cause, we think the uncertain survival of children in Africa remains one of the strongest motivations for high fertility. Hill's research shows that at least among the largest countries of the region, mortality improvements would appear to have been slight. If even now, one in five births in Zaire or Nigeria fails to survive childhood, how persuasive could the logic of lower fertility be? The experiences of Kenya, Botswana, and Zimbabwe, by contrast, are as distinctive in respect to mortality levels and trend as they are in contraceptive use and fertility. It is difficult to escape the view that there must be a close connection.

In judging the prospects for fertility decline elsewhere, as these prospects may be linked to mortality, one issue surfaces that has curiously received rather little study. It concerns the perceptions of mortality decline as viewed by different socioeconomic strata. Given the progress that has been made over time against child mortality, have the views of African parents indeed kept pace with the empirical realities? Is there an appreciation of the extent of improvement in child survivorship? Or, perhaps, do perceptions and therefore fertility decisions respond only with a long lag? One study for Lagos (Adegbola et al., 1991) found that perceptions of mortality change varied considerably across socioeconomic groups. Respondents with completed primary schooling agreed that mortality had been reduced in the present generation compared to the past, whereas those with less schooling denied that any such change had taken place. Indeed, in the latter group, perceptions of long-term mortality increase were found to be as common as perceptions of decline. One wonders whether such perceptions mirror the actual experience of mortality among socioeconomic subgroups, or whether the educated are simply in possession of better information concerning the facts.

EVIDENCE ON CHANGES IN THE
QUANTITY-QUALITY TRADE-OFF

There have been surprisingly few studies of the relationship between fertility and child schooling at the household level in Africa. DeLancey (1990) reviews the evidence from a handful of investigations based on data for the late 1960s to mid-1970s for Kenya, Botswana, and Sierra Leone. This early research suggests that the relationship between child schooling and fertility has been weak in Africa, and that where a significant association is uncovered, it tends to be positive rather than negative as is the case elsewhere. This positive relationship appears to have been due to income effects, such that households with higher income can afford both to have more children and to provide each child with more education.

Although recent quantitative studies are lacking, there is reason to believe that changes in policy and economic conditions in the past decade have rewritten the terms of the quantity-quality trade-off in Africa. As discussed below, policy shifts in some countries have caused dramatic increases in the direct costs of schooling, particularly in the past decade. Focus group results from Nigeria and Niger (Wawer, 1990; Adegbola et al., 1991; Makinwa-Adebusoye, 1991; Okojie, 1991) suggest that parents are becoming increasingly conscious of the costs of schooling and cite these costs as being among the principal disadvantages faced by large families.

Opportunity Costs of Schooling

The opportunity cost of a year of schooling has to do with the value of the child's forgone labor.[16] These costs will vary with the age of the child in question, with urban or rural residence, and with the economic circumstances in which the household finds itself. For a child of primary school age, who resides in an urban environment and is a member of a comparatively high-income household, the opportunity costs of schooling may well be trivial. But if the child is older or resides in a rural setting where his contribution to the family economy can be considerable, or if the household as a whole is in strained economic circumstances, the opportunity costs of school attendance can be considerable.[17]

To the extent that economic conditions continue to favor the urban sector in sub-Saharan Africa, where child labor may not have the significance that it does in the rural sector, and to the extent that income growth returns to the region, we would expect the opportunity costs of schooling to continue to decline in importance.

---

[16]Because the opportunity costs of schooling measure the value of child labor, they measure one aspect of the benefits of high fertility. A decline in the opportunity costs of schooling thus has two effects: a direct effect that presumably reduces the net benefits of high fertility, and a presumably positive influence, akin to a price reduction, on the demand for schooling. In other words, as the value of child labor decreases, the incentives for parents to have large families to provide labor also decline. In addition, schooling for children becomes a more attractive option, because the child's contribution at home is less valuable.

[17]There is another dimension of opportunity cost to consider. Okojie (1991) records a consistent complaint among Nigerian parents that schooling leaves their children harder to handle and more resistant to discipline. These findings echo the views of Caldwell (1982) on the extent to which child schooling may disturb the distribution of authority within the household.

Direct Costs

Although the experiences of the past decade are varied and difficult to quantify with any precision, the trend in the direct private costs of schooling in the region appears to have been upward. The World Bank (1988) estimates that as of 1975-1980, private expenditures accounted for some 14 percent of total national spending on education in the Sudan, 23 percent in Tanzania, 31 percent in Zimbabwe, 48 percent in Sierra Leone, and 53 percent in Ghana.[18] The private share of total spending has increased over time as governments place greater emphasis on the collection of fees and other charges for educational materials, and increasingly transfer responsibility for capital expenditures to local communities, which in turn pass them on to parents.

For Nigeria, Makinwa-Adebusoye (1991) draws a sharp contrast between present-day private costs of schooling and those of an earlier era when education (and health) services were highly subsidized. She presents examples drawn from focus group studies confirming that the perceived costs of education are high in both Lagos and Calabar. Okojie's (1991) results for Bendel and Kwara State also show that parents are conscious of a dramatically changed situation with respect to educational costs.

For Kenya, Kelley and Nobbe (1990) and Robinson (1992) see increases in the costs of schooling as being associated in part with the educational reform of 1985 (which added an additional year to the primary curriculum) and with the introduction of new financing mechanisms that required parents to pay in direct proportion to the number of children enrolled. (Kenyan parents do not pay tuition fees; rather, they are responsible for school supplies, books, uniforms, and a share of capital costs.) Most of the capital costs for primary schools have been transferred from the national to the local level. Taken together, the private costs borne by Kenyan parents are said to be high, perhaps amounting to as much as 10 to 15 percent of household cash income per child.

In Zimbabwe, Lucas (1991; citing Davies and Sanders) notes that primary school fees were abolished in the early 1980s and then, in the face of a very rapid rise in enrollments, were replaced by various levies and capital charges (also see World Bank, 1988). In Botswana, by contrast, public sector primary school fees were reduced through the 1970s and finally eliminated altogether in 1980. Secondary school fees (at state-supported schools, which enroll roughly two of every three secondary students) were eliminated in

---

[18]The World Bank (1988) does not provide a source for these figures, but they appear to include outlays on private educational institutions as well as the fees and capital levies borne by families with children in public sector institutions.

1988. Evidently the elimination of fees in Botswana was not counterbalanced by increases in other charges.

In summary, the general trend is that of an increase in the direct costs of schooling, although Botswana may provide an exception to the trend and the net change in Zimbabwe is unclear. Very little information is available regarding fees and other costs in the private educational sector, which is a significant presence at the secondary school level in a number of African countries (see World Bank, 1988).

Perceived Benefits of Schooling

If the direct costs of schooling are indeed on the rise, will the perceived benefits of schooling in Africa be substantial enough to sustain a quantity-quality transition? The evidence on this critical issue is conflicting. By all accounts, African parents express a continued commitment to schooling and display a willingness to make sacrifices in other areas so that their children can be educated (see, among others, World Bank, 1988; Adegbola et al., 1991; Okojie, 1991; Makinwa-Adebusoye, 1991). But there is great uncertainty regarding the economic benefits of schooling in African economies and therefore in the extent to which educational aspirations, however deeply felt, will be reflected in educational investments.

The benefits are expressed principally in the gradient of earnings with respect to education; earnings, in turn, depend on the relative supplies of and demands for labor by educational level. The demand for educated labor depends in part on the growth of modern sector employment, which continues to be slow in sub-Saharan Africa (Hansen, 1990; Vandemoortele, 1991). The public sector component of employment will continue to be affected by cutbacks in government budgets. Vandemoortele (1991) finds a compression of wage scales in the public sector and general declines over the past decade in the real earnings of civil servants. To the extent that educational investments in children are made in the expectation that they will eventually secure employment in the public sector, these changes may reduce the private returns of schooling. However, as Vandemoortele points out, countries in which public sector pay is deteriorating often show counterbalancing increases in private sector earnings. The net effect on the anticipated payoff to schooling remains unclear.

There is clear evidence of an erosion in the quality of schooling in sub-Saharan Africa, such that the economic gains gleaned from schooling by older cohorts may no longer be available to younger cohorts. The evidence regarding quality decline is drawn from a mix of statistical and impressionistic accounts. In a careful study of the Ghanaian wage sector, Glewwe (1991) finds that the returns to schooling evident in wage differentials have declined for more recent cohorts; indeed, the cognitive achievements of recent cohorts per year of schooling are lower than those achieved by older cohorts.[19]   Glewwe attributes this change to difficulties in sustaining school quality over the postindependence period of rapid expansion in primary and secondary enrollments (also see Schultz, 1987).

Among other factors influencing school quality, the World Bank (1988) draws attention to the very low level of public spending per pupil in Africa at the primary and secondary grades (if not at the tertiary).   There is evidence that spending per pupil may have even declined in the 1980s (see below).   In the important category of educational materials, sub-Saharan governments make very small contributions.   Public expenditures for educational materials (World Bank, 1988) amount annually to less than 60 cents per pupil.   The share of the primary education budget going to instructional materials is only 1.1 percent, compared to a 4.0 percent share among developed countries.   (Recall that the responsibility for these expenditures is increasingly being shifted to parents.)   All these factors are consistent with the relatively poor performance of African students on standardized tests of achievement in math, reading, and the sciences, even by comparison to their counterparts in other low- or middle-income countries (World Bank, 1988).   Moreover, the impression of decline in school quality in Africa is not confined to statistical accounts.   It is also a widely shared perception among African parents and a common theme in conversation.

To sum up, we regard the prospects for a quantity-quality demographic transition in the region as being decidedly mixed.[20]   Recent accounts taken from focus group studies (e.g., Adegbola et al., 1991; Okojie, 1991) suggest that changes in the costs of schooling are perceived to add significantly to the financial burdens of large families.   In time, these relative price effects

---

[19]Recent studies show that with native ability held constant, cognitive achievement explains a large part of educational differentials in earnings.   That is, an extra year of schooling is rewarded in the labor market primarily because it produces a change in the cognitive skills that are valued in the market.   Among wage earners in Nairobi and Dar es Salaam, Boissiere et al. (1985) find strong evidence that cognitive achievement is a more powerful determinant of earnings than years of schooling per se; achievement is itself affected by years of schooling as well as by innate ability.   Glewwe's (1991) findings for Ghana are similar.   In summarizing the results for Kenya and Tanzania, the World Bank (1988) suggests that an earnings differential of 25 percent for secondary relative to primary schooling is attributable to the improvement in cognitive skills produced by secondary school.

The above is not to deny the importance of credentialism and other factors in determining the private returns to education in Africa.   But tests for "diploma effects" (Boissiere et al., 1985; Glewwe, 1991) show that the effects are weaker than the influence of cognitive achievement, save perhaps in the public sector.   Credentialism may have its largest effect on earnings at the outset of the work career.

[20]The picture is further muddied when child fostering and spouse decision making are considered in relation to the quantity-quality transition (see Chapter 4).

may help to bring about a fertility transition. But we cannot assume that African parents will continue to make sacrifices to invest in human capital if the payoff to that investment is in doubt. Indeed, in some countries, primary school enrollment rates fell in the 1980s, as discussed below. Policy-driven changes in the direct costs of education can have little long-run effect on fertility if the economic benefits of schooling cannot be sustained and improved.

ECONOMIC STAGNATION AND ADJUSTMENT: EFFECTS ON FERTILITY

The 1980s and early 1990s witnessed a contraction of incomes across sub-Saharan Africa, such that many countries were left only slightly better-off in terms of average incomes than they had been in the early 1960s (Vandemoortele, 1991). During the decade a number of countries responded to economic stagnation and crisis with structural adjustment programs. These programs sought to redirect government spending and to reduce the size of the government sector; in addition, they were often designed explicitly to influence the relative prices of food, education, and health care. Thus, the past decade has been one of profound change not only in income levels, but also in relative prices and policies determining access to social services. In an influential paper, Lesthaeghe (1989a) speculated that the economic reversals and turmoil of the 1980s in sub-Saharan Africa might hold the seeds of what he termed a "crisis-led" demographic transition.

In one sense, the idea of "crisis" breaks no new ground, in that it simply revisits many of the socioeconomic factors that have already been discussed above. The difference is that these factors are brought together in a particular configuration, and in addition, the concept introduces a distinction between short-term demographic effects at work in the crisis period itself and the potential longer-term consequences. Thus, comparatively temporary income contractions may have effects on fertility decisions that depend on expectations regarding longer-run income growth. Government retrenchments, intended to ameliorate short-term problems in the balance of payments, may have a long-run effect on access to education and health services. And a temporary receptivity to family limitation on the part of households under economic pressure may translate, over time, into a greater acceptability of family planning in more normal circumstances.

There is little doubt about the depth of economic crisis in many African countries, although experiences are perhaps more varied than might have been thought. In some countries the term "stagnation" better describes the situation during the past decade than does "crisis." Figure 3-8 depicts the changes in income per capita between 1975 and 1987 in the five largest countries of the sub-Saharan region. Population-weighted averages for sub-

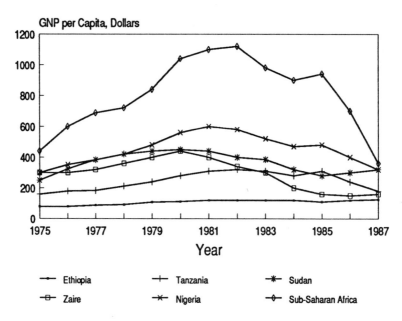

FIGURE 3-8 Per capita GNP, 1975 to 1987 (1980 dollars). SOURCE: World Bank (1990a).

Saharan Africa. A steady deterioration in income levels can be observed in the region from the high point in 1981. Among the larger countries, the collapse of incomes in Nigeria is particularly marked, but Zaire has also experienced a long decline. By contrast, among the three countries with higher prevalence, Botswana has exhibited a reasonably steady advance in income over the decade, and Kenya and Zimbabwe have displayed fluctuating incomes with little apparent deterioration (see Figure 3-9).

In considering the longer-run prospects for demographic transition, it is important to separate the effects of income on fertility from the effects of changes in relative prices. As long as fertility remains a normal good (one whose consumption increases with income) in the economic sense of the term, one would expect income contraction to be accompanied by a fertility decline, or at least by a pause in family building. One would equally well expect a return to high fertility as income levels improve. Thus, if current economic circumstances are to set off a demographic transition in sub-Saharan Africa, the origins of the transition must lie in a transformation of both incomes and relative prices, which is precisely the argument employed above in reference to the quantity-quality transition.

The implications of relative price changes induced by structural adjust-

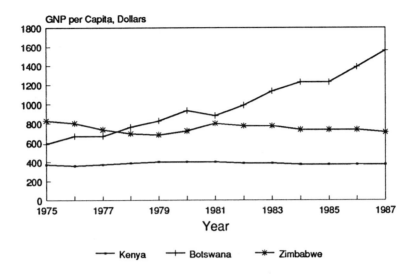

FIGURE 3-9 Per capita GNP in Botswana, Kenya, and Zimbabwe (1980 dollars).
SOURCE: World Bank (1990a).

ment for fertility are less than clear-cut (World Bank, 1990c). Food price
increases, which drive down the standard of living for urban consumers,
may well improve living standards among rural producers (indeed, this is
the prime motivation for adjustment policies that remove artificial food
price ceilings). If conditions in agriculture improve, might that not increase
the derived demand for child labor and exert a pronatalist influence on rural
fertility? Would improvements in agricultural earnings reduce the disper-
sion in earnings levels according to schooling, further dampening the prospects for a quantity-quality transition? Do cutbacks in public sector salaries
and employment, however well justified with respect to longer-term economic efficiency, further depress the private returns to schooling and thereby
delay the quantity-quality transition?

The task of documenting the distribution of benefits and costs associated with economic reversals and adjustment policies is just under way in
sub-Saharan Africa (World Bank, 1990c; Working Group on the Demographic Effects of Economic and Social Reversals, 1993). Nothing definitive can be said about these complex matters, and given the many interlock-
ing markets that are involved, economic theory alone can provide no clear
guidance. However, the current economic situation, which combines income contraction and various increases in childrearing costs, may well have
rendered acceptable, for the first time, the notion of family limitation. Such

a development is certainly consistent with the views expressed in the results of qualitative studies in Nigeria (Caldwell and Caldwell, 1987; Adegbola et al., 1991; Makinwa-Adebusoye, 1991; Okojie, 1991), in which Nigerian parents seem to comprehend rather fully the negative consequences of high fertility in the new regime of income and prices. The negative aspect, however, is that macroeconomic austerity may reduce the capacities of governments to improve access to education, family planning, and health services. It is therefore important to assess what has happened to public investments and access to services over the past decade.

Access to Education and Health

How have the social sectors, including education and health, fared in an era of general retrenchment in government spending? Hicks (1991; also see Hicks and Kubisch, 1984) finds that in periods of overall reduction in government expenditures in developing countries, recurrent expenditures on the combined social sectors (including all spending on health, education, housing, and other social services) tend to be well protected in comparison to the productive, infrastructural, and general public sectors.[21] That is, the social sectors tend to experience less-than-proportionate cuts in budget as total government budgets decline. Capital expenditures tend to be cut much more severely than do recurrent expenditures, and these cuts tend to be in roughly the same proportion across all sectors. Thus, perhaps contrary to expectation, the policy response to economic crisis and adjustment has typically been to compromise in the dimension of physical capital investments.

However, even if the education and health sectors have been able to protect their shares of government budgets, they have not been able to escape cutbacks on a per capita basis.[22] Figure 3-10 shows the trends in per capita central government spending on education, both for the largest countries in the region and for sub-Saharan Africa as a whole (for the latter, results are weighted by population). There is an unmistakable downward

---

[21]The sample used by Hicks (1991) includes, but is not limited to, countries from sub-Saharan Africa. The productive sector includes expenditures for industrial and agricultural development; infrastructure includes power, transportation, and communications; and general public services encompass administration, police, and the judicial system.

[22]In their analysis of the 1979-1983 period in sub-Saharan Africa, Pinstrup-Andersen et al. (1987) note a stagnation or decline in per capita expenditures on health and education, with the decline being more apparent in respect to health expenditures. They note considerable diversity among countries in the extent to which the health and education sectors maintained their budget shares. Like Hicks (1991) and Hicks and Kubisch (1984), they find that capital expenditures tended to be cut more than recurrent expenses, particularly in the economic services sector.

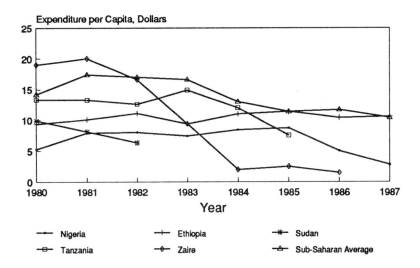

FIGURE 3-10 Central government educational expenditure per capita. SOURCE: World Bank (1990a).

trend in per capita education spending for the region; among the large countries this trend is mirrored in the experiences of Zaire, Tanzania, and Nigeria. Figure 3-11 considers health expenditures per capita; here, there is less evidence of a systematic downward trend. However, the very low levels of per capita expenditure on health in sub-Saharan Africa certainly did not improve.

Consequences for Human Capital Investment

With regard to primary enrollments, the 1980s appear to have marked the end of an era of expansion in sub-Saharan Africa. Primary enrollment ratios, which reached their high point of 74 percent in 1981 (population weighted), gradually slipped back to less than 70 percent by the end of the decade (United Nations Educational, Scientific and Cultural Organization, 1990). Among the largest countries, Nigeria, Zaire, and Tanzania experienced sharp declines in enrollments from about 90 percent in the early 1980s to 65-75 percent in the latter part of the decade. These declines are no doubt due in part to income effects and in part to policy-driven increases in the private costs of schooling described above. Let us emphasize again that the more responsive the demand is for education with respect to price, the less likely are the prospects for a quantity-quality transition in fertility. Moreover, the primary-age cohorts of the mid-1980s are now entering their

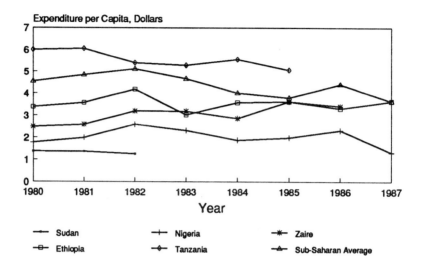

FIGURE 3-11 Central government health expenditures per capita. SOURCE: World Bank (1990a).

childbearing years. They will be without the benefits of the schooling levels that they might otherwise have enjoyed in the absence of an economic crisis.

The situation with respect to secondary schooling is very different. Enrollment ratios at this level continued to advance through the decade, although Zaire again and Tanzania present an exception to the general trend, with Zaire showing a dramatic decline and Tanzania showing little change. The advance in secondary schooling by Nigeria, from less than 20 percent in 1980 to about 24 percent in 1987, is especially noteworthy, given the decline in its primary enrollments over the period (United Nations Educational, Scientific and Cultural Organization, 1990).

Also of interest is the continuing increase in the enrollment ratios of women relative to men. Although males continue to outnumber females at both the primary and the secondary levels, the enrollment gap between them is being reduced progressively (United Nations Educational, Scientific and Cultural Organization, 1990).

Summary

The diverse experiences among countries show that there is no necessary connection between macroeconomic stagnation and crisis, and cutbacks in access to services (Pinstrup-Andersen et al., 1987). In Kenya, for example, the period from 1979 to 1982 saw an annual decline in per capita gross domestic product on the order of 1 percent per year, yet government expenditures on health and education continued to increase. Cornia and Stewart (1987) cite the cases of Botswana and Zimbabwe, which met their episodes of severe drought in the early 1980s with well-designed drought relief programs that targeted health care and children's supplementary feeding programs. Health expenditures increased, in general, even as economic conditions deteriorated; primary school enrollments also continued to rise. Moreover, the recent study by another working group of the Panel on the Population Dynamics of Sub-Saharan Africa, the Working Group on Demographic Effects of Economic and Social Reversals (1993), indicates that the effects of economic reversals have varied considerably from country to country.

CONCLUSION

The socioeconomic record offers few general lessons regarding fertility transition that can be applied across the whole of sub-Saharan Africa. Certainly the steady increase in female educational attainment, albeit from very low levels in some regions, may remove one of the props supporting high fertility. But in other respects the likelihood of fertility decline is very much a country-specific matter. Although mortality has fallen substantially in many sub-Saharan countries, the decline is not universal. Most of the largest countries still exhibit relatively high levels of child mortality. In Nigeria, the largest country, little progress, if any, has been made in the last decade and a half. Changes in the costs of living, and specifically the costs of education, may well hold the key to fertility trends in some countries, but as we have argued, the responses to higher education costs depend on the nature of the benefits to schooling. The economic crises of the 1980s may have opened the door to the acceptability of family limitation, but if income growth resumes without structural change, fertility decline need not follow.

The experiences of sub-Saharan countries have been so varied in respect to socioeconomic development, and governments so heterogeneous in their social sector policies, that no general forecast regarding fertility and contraceptive use should be made. Enough has been said to indicate that the three countries that may be the forerunners of fertility change, Kenya, Botswana, and Zimbabwe, are distinctive with respect to policy and socioeconomic setting. Among the larger countries, Nigeria shows some indications of sensitivity to the costs of schooling, but its decline in primary enrollments is worrisome. Ethiopia and Sudan remain in sociopolitical turmoil, which will necessarily limit the reach of policy; Zaire gives evidence of severe deterioration over the past decade with worsening conditions since 1990. None of these large countries displays the steady advances against mortality characteristic of the higher use countries, and it is doubtful that major fertility declines at a national level can be initiated without such improvement.

Yet even in the larger countries, economic stagnation, and structural adjustment may have brought into relief previously latent demands for family limitation among important subgroups of the population. In an atmosphere of austerity, policies addressed to these subgroups may find a newly receptive audience.

4

The Household, Kinship, and Community Context

This chapter considers whether long-standing forms of African social organization will continue to inhibit contraceptive adoption and support high fertility. There can be little doubt as to the pronatalist past: Evidence from a wide range of African countries suggests that social institutions and shared values have supported high fertility well into the postcolonial era. What is under debate is the prospect for change. Are the past structures so deeply embedded and immutable that high fertility will persist? Is Africa indeed so unique with respect to social organization, and so different from the remainder of the developing world where fertility decline is in progress? Or might pronatalist values and constraints give way in the face of new socioeconomic pressures, as they have elsewhere?

Much of the demographic literature, as exemplified by the writings of Caldwell (1991; Caldwell and Caldwell, 1987, 1988, 1990; Caldwell et al., 1989, 1991), Goody (1990), Frank (1987, 1988; Frank and McNicoll, 1987), Lesthaeghe (1989b), and Page (1989), has emphasized the probable continuity of pronatalist forms of social organization. African productive and reproductive systems are described in terms of functional coherence and internal logic; high fertility is seen as an essential building block in this larger edifice. Implicit in such a perspective is the view that, absent some sweeping system-wide transformation, one should not expect modern sub-Saharan Africa to join in the fertility declines in progress elsewhere in the developing world.

The very persistence of high fertility in the region is cited as testimony to the perseverance of pronatalist values. Yet as Chapter 3 has indicated, this aspect of the empirical record can be given a rather different interpretation. Persistent high fertility in Africa may well reflect the persistent high mortality characteristic of the region, its low levels of industrialization, the comparatively weak economic returns to schooling, the belated evolution of population policy, and the still-sporadic coverage of family planning programs. In this alternative view, the absence of fertility decline across the continent is evidence not so much of deep-seated cultural resistance, as of the continued unevenness and superficiality of economic and political development. The recent surges in contraceptive adoption in Botswana, Kenya, and Zimbabwe testify to the profound influence of new socioeconomic forces associated with modernization; where similar forces prevail elsewhere in Africa, it is argued (see Chapter 3), fertility decline will follow.

What is really at issue in these competing perspectives, therefore, is the degree of adaptability to be expected of African social organizations and cultures. There is a growing recognition in the literature that the African demographic situation is now in flux. As many of the authors cited above acknowledge, the changing economic circumstances of the 1980s and the gradual westernization of certain aspects of family life may have unsettled the past high-fertility regime (e.g., Caldwell and Caldwell, 1987; Lesthaeghe, 1989a; Caldwell et al., 1992). Some observers detect a growing detachment of these older values from day-to-day behavior and note the potential for rapid change. For example, with reference to Kenya, Robinson (1992:454) asserts that cultural beliefs often "persist as ideals or values which become more and more divorced from practice until they end up being dropped or becoming meaningless rules like 'love thy neighbor'." He cautions,

> Establishing that traditional Kenyan culture and custom was supportive of high fertility in no way establishes how strongly held are these practices today or how quickly they may change as the socio-economic basis of the real day-to-day society changes. Culture and values are adaptive . . . .

The task in what follows is to weigh the evidence regarding continuity and change. We view three broad areas of family and kinship organization as essential to an understanding of fertility decision making in Africa:

- lineages and systems of descent;
- kinship networks and child fostering; and
- the nature of conjugal bonds.

In each of these areas, African social organization has been uniquely pronatalist or, at the least, strikingly different in degree from that prevailing elsewhere. No doubt in the past these forms of social organization provided a powerful rationale for high fertility, but as our examination shows, that rationale is no longer wholly intact.

Much of the evidence brought to bear on these matters is ethnographic in nature, and the record is regrettably thin for the 1980s—a decade of social and economic turmoil in many African countries, which saw the beginnings of fertility decline in Botswana, Kenya, and Zimbabwe. Although the empirical base cannot support strong conclusions, we find numerous indications of a desire for moderate levels of fertility among certain socioeconomic groups and hints of a broader receptivity to change. We conclude that the long-standing supports for high fertility, although still strong across much of the continent, may no longer prevent fertility decline.

We then ask whether existing forms of social organization at the level of the local community might facilitate fertility decline. That is, in what way might African local voluntary associations, on the one hand, and local government organizations, on the other, serve as conduits for information about modern contraceptive methods or even as providers of such methods? To put it differently, what aspects of local social organization might assist in the diffusion of family planning information and services? Such questions, first advanced for Africa by Lesthaeghe (1989a) and recently taken up by Watkins (1991) and Hammerslough (1991a), are of special relevance for policy in an era of macroeconomic austerity, when African central governments may have little alternative but to rely on a network of nongovernmental organizations and the private sector to extend family planning service delivery.

THE HIGH-FERTILITY RATIONALE: AN OVERVIEW

The case for the uniqueness of African high-fertility regimes is based on several interrelated points. Each point is said to be more characteristic of historical than modern African social systems, but each, nonetheless, is viewed as being persistent in influence and still potent in affecting reproductive decisions. The relevant factors include

- the importance accorded to descent and perpetuation of the lineage;
- the economic value inherent in children, not only as sources of labor, but also as a means of securing access to land and other resources;
- the implications of a lineage orientation for the bond between wives and husbands, and the degree to which the boundaries of the conjugal household are penetrated by other kin;
- the availability of mechanisms for sharing child costs and benefits among kin, principally through child fostering; and
- the special interests of women in the maintenance of high fertility.

For example, a 1987 article by Caldwell and Caldwell argued that African societies have historically given great emphasis to perpetuation of the lineage. High fertility is the logical consequence if a family line is to be maintained in the face of high mortality risks. In this perspective, reproduction becomes a matter of concern not only for the individual couple involved, but also for a wider network of kin, and the duty to ensure lineage survival assumes something of the character of a religious obligation.

Labor, rather than physical or human capital, was the principal economic resource in historical African settings[1] and the economic benefits of high fertility remain significant in what are still predominantly agricultural economies with few sources of savings, insurance, and economic security other than those derived from kin. Moreover, it was through control of labor that individuals laid claim to the other important agricultural resource, land. Land was itself held by corporate groups such as lineages, rather than being privately owned, and was allocated by the lineage to households who possess the requisite labor to establish and maintain use rights.

Where descent is patrilineal, as it is in much of sub-Saharan Africa, the husband's lineage secures rights to the reproduction of the wife through the device of bride-price. The bonds linking husband and wife in marriage are weak in relation to the claims on spouses asserted by their respective lineages; the marriage bond is further undermined by the presence of co-wives and by high rates of widowhood and divorce. Within marriage the wife and husband shoulder different economic responsibilities for childrearing and may therefore assess the overall level of child costs rather differently. And the costs of high fertility need not be borne by the conjugal household alone but can be shared, through child fostering, among kin and even nonkin.

In such settings, women may find benefits in high fertility that are distinct from the benefits enjoyed by men. In particular, high fertility may help women secure for themselves continued access to economic resources. Childbearing provides women with one avenue to the resources held by their husbands or other men; it may help to fend off the competing claims of actual or potential co-wives; and following marriage dissolution, children may constitute a woman's only means of access to the household resources jointly produced by her husband and herself within the marriage (Bledsoe, 1990b). A widow's claims on household resources via inheritance are severely circumscribed throughout sub-Saharan Africa, and often her only path to such resources runs indirectly through her children (see, among

---

[1]Henn (1984:5) writes that "the key measure of a man's wealth was the number of dependents in his household. The association of wealth with persons rather than with material goods is explained by the conditions of production. Unlike many other world areas, labor—not land—was the scarce factor of production in Africa. A man's ability to expand his control over land and his production of food and livestock depended crucially on the number of dependent men in his household and on the number of women farmers whose agricultural and domestic labor he could mobilize."

others, Ladipo, 1987). Because both widowhood and divorce are common (the former being due to the wide age gap between spouses characteristic of polygynous societies), women must anticipate an extended period of economic reliance on their children.

If one takes a long historical perspective (Goody, 1976, 1990), these factors might be traced back in time to a few fundamental and enduring material elements characteristic of the sub-Saharan region: historically high mortality; a general lack of good soil that repays intensive cultivation; a general abundance of (adequate) land in relation to labor, so that in a sense labor becomes the more valued resource; and a great instability in income, giving rise to a need for kin and other social contacts to serve as networks of mutual insurance.[2]

This depiction is an essentially functionalist view of African social organization. The critical examination to follow uncovers in this view numerous elements of caricature and instances of overgeneralization (Messina, 1992). Nevertheless, the perspective outlined above has much to recommend about it.

It is especially important to appreciate the nature of its challenge to the usual conceptual models of fertility decision making employed in demography, wherein the conjugal couple is viewed as the primary locus of reproductive decisions. The demographer's notion of the conjugal household, with its pooled resources and shared responsibilities, is very much at odds with the portrait of the African household sketched above. This theoretical emphasis on the conjugal household, which has shaped demographic data gathering and interpretation, is wholly inappropriate to sub-Saharan Africa. A review of the ethnographic record confirms that African households are internally divided (along cleavages of age as well as gender) and participate in a network of economic relations with kin that put into doubt the economic demographer's notion of a simple household budget constraint.

To anticipate much of the argument to follow, we can state more precisely here the limitations of the conventional economic model as regards African family structure and decision making. To describe adequately the African situation, the conventional microeconomic household budget constraint would have to be amended in several fundamental ways.

1. The possibilities of transferring resources from one life-cycle period to another are severely constrained by the absence or limited penetra-

---

[2]On the issue of insurance networks, Guyer (1981) cites Lewis (1978) to the effect that in Mali, families incorporated in large patrilineal groups can exhibit greater variability in food production per capita, by comparison with more isolated families who must more closely match their production to subsistence needs.

tion of formal financial institutions. Thus, liquidity constraints are an essential feature of the intertemporal budget constraint.

2. One must recognize the possibility of transfers to and from other kin, both in the budget constraint and in the function describing intertemporal utility. Indeed, the notion of transfers among kin must include transfers between husband and wife; as noted later, sub-Saharan husbands and wives have distinct economic responsibilities and interests with regard to childrearing and resource allocation issues more generally. To suppose that the interests of husband and wife can be merged in a single utility function maximized subject to a common budget constraint, is to apprehend the situation badly.

The term "transfer" is itself inadequate, because it does not fully convey the sense of mutual and reciprocal obligation involved in resource flows among kin. One receives assistance but in so doing incurs an obligation to reciprocate in the future; thus a transfer can be viewed as akin to borrowing, with the terms of repayment left vague and perhaps dependent on future circumstances. The lender may in turn derive positive utility from the act of lending, since being able to lend enhances one's standing within the kin group. Not lending, when one is in fact able to lend, threatens the system of mutual obligations and may incur severe social sanctions.

The network of kin among whom transfers take place is a dynamic configuration. It changes with time, as the elders to whom one owes support die, and the children, in whom one has inculcated an obligation, come of age.

3. Another necessary amendment to the conceptualization of the budget constraint is that transfers and bargaining within marriage may take place in a polygynous setting, where norms of fairness and equality across wives place constraints on the manner in which a husband can allocate his resources among his wives and children (Fapohunda and Todaro, 1988; Bledsoe, in press).

4. It is necessary to incorporate the uncertainty in individual access to a given spouse's resources that arises from marital dissolution and remarriage. In particular, a wife's claims on her husband's resources may be only temporary and superficial unless she can lay down a basis for long-term claims by having children with him.

5. Owing to the material conditions surrounding agricultural production and the present weaknesses of industrial development, all incomes are subject to considerable uncertainty. Given the limited possibilities for individual savings, this uncertainty accentuates the need for a wide network of social contacts and contingent claims, many of which are established through children.

On the whole we would agree with Page (1989:402), who writes that "one can question the extent to which one can even speak of a husband-wife-child unit since neither economic nor kinship links are traditionally thus defined." African family structures, in which conjugal units are at once internally subdivided and permeable from the outside, may demand both a new conceptual model for demographers and new routes for effective policy intervention.

LINEAGE AND DESCENT

As outlined above, matters of descent and lineage are central both to African social organization and to the rationale for high fertility, and much of the ethnographic literature on sub-Saharan cultures has been in agreement. For instance, Bleek (1987:139) writes for the Akan of Ghana that "the lineage is the great, permanent and fundamental institution which permeates every aspect of life." Yet there is an important dissenting perspective, summarized by Kuper (1982a,b), in which the concept of lineage is seen not so much as a fundamental organizing principle, but rather as one among a great number of elements that make up social organization and shape individual identity. In this alternative view, the religious, social, and economic importance attached to the lineage is highly variable both across and within societies, and in terms of demographic behavior, the various descent ideologies of the region submit to no easy generalizations.

In what follows we shall first summarize the predominant view in the demographic literature regarding the role of African lineages and ideologies of descent, and then consider the demographic implications of the alternative perspective.

The Predominant View of African Lineages and Descent

An African lineage exhibits a depth of three to four generations among the living (Bleek, 1987, for the Akan of Ghana; Caldwell and Caldwell, 1987) and stretches infinitely back in time through ancestors. A larger grouping, the clan, is more difficult to define in any precise way, but it is generally regarded as being a set of lineages who view themselves as being related via a distant and perhaps mythical common ancestor.

The lineage is often envisioned as a finite collection of souls or spirits moving through time, such that each new birth to the lineage provides a vehicle for the return of an ancestor. In consequence, enormous spiritual weight may be invested in maintaining the continuity of the family line (Caldwell and Caldwell, 1987). In indigenous African religions the dead of recent generations were regarded as being "powerful shades," with an interest and a capacity to intervene in the affairs of the living. To restrain fertility is in effect to forbid the rebirth of such an ancestor and thereby condemn that ancestor to oblivion. To risk childlessness through low fertility is to threaten indirectly the survival of the lineage as a whole, and to be childless by choice is all but unthinkable. Caldwell and Caldwell (1987) find that attitudes such as these remain deep rooted even among modern African elites, many of whom would be outwardly dismissive of these religions.

Certain fundamental economic and social functions are vested in the lineage and the wider clan, among which allocation of land is of prime importance. In the past, land was rarely owned by individuals; rather, it was controlled by the lineage and allocated to its male members, who retained use rights in the land and could pass these rights under certain conditions to their male heirs (see Brain, 1976, for Tanzania). To these functions were added a host of social sanctions that derived from the authority of the descent group. It is the lineage that buries its members, and the refusal of the lineage to do so is said to be the greatest sanction that can be brought to bear upon any individual (Bleek, 1987, for the Akan of Ghana). Even if such a sanction is rarely applied, it serves to reinforce the power of the earthly old, who are themselves near to becoming powerful shades and who may exert their influence on younger members of the lineage by threatening to bring down an ancestral curse. Thus the emphasis given to descent and to ancestors in sub-Saharan societies bears a logical relationship to gerontocracy, filial piety, and age grades of authority among the living (Caldwell and Caldwell, 1987).[3]

Marriage is the means by which the lineage ensures its perpetuation, and in the vast majority of cases, marriage arrangements are accompanied by payments of bride-price (Lesthaeghe et al., 1989a).[4] In patrilineal societies, the payment of bride-price gives the husband's lineage claim to the children borne by the wife (Caldwell and Caldwell, 1987; Frank and McNicoll, 1987, for Kenya; Page, 1989). Frank and McNicoll (1987) note that for Kenya, there has been a practice of paying bride-price in installments, with a payment following successful births of the first, second, and third children. In matrilineal societies, by contrast, the children belong by right to their mother's lineage, and bride-price is much reduced in social importance.

A woman's fear in limiting her reproduction therefore lies not only in the breaking of an understanding or contract between families, but even more deeply in the possibility of angering the ancestors—her own, in the case of matrilineal societies, or her husband's ancestors in the patrilineal

---

[3]Sudarkasa (1981) describes such age grades of authority among the Yoruba of Western Africa.

[4]However, Guyer (1988b) has observed a recent decline in bride-price payments in Nigeria, which may reflect a broader decline in many types of tribute payments.

case. In addition, should fertility limitation threaten the bride-price agreement, the woman's relations might be required to forfeit valuable resources. Thus, an array of relatives on both sides may confront the contraceptive innovator. Caldwell and Caldwell (1987:414) argue that the influence of lineages in reproduction is such that "even educated women working in the modern sector regard their reproduction—as distinct from their sexuality—as being the decisionmaking province of their husbands and their husbands' families."

The pressures from the lineage that can be brought to bear upon individual couples can be daunting, as is illustrated in a study regarding attitudes toward voluntary sterilization in five regions of Zaire: Kinshasa, Bas Zaire, Sud Kivu, Haut Zaire, and Shaba (Chibalonza et al., 1989). Focus group results show that a husband's family could exert considerable leverage on the couple, even if the husband and wife had agreed between themselves as to the desirability of sterilization. The wife's not continuing her childbearing can be construed by the family as a failure to honor the agreement implicit in her bride-price. Even if the husband's family at first agrees to sterilization, it may eventually seek another wife for the husband so that he can continue to bring children into the lineage.[5]

In general, the ties between a husband and wife in marriage are regarded as being weak and subordinate to the interests of their respective lineages (Bleek, 1987, for the Akan of Ghana). A lineage needs marriage for procreation but sees to it by various means that the loyalty of the marriage partners remains with the lineage. With reference to the Akan of Ghana, Asante-Darko and van der Geest (1983:246) say that "relatives look askance at a marriage in which husband and wife develop a close relationship." A woman in no sense joins her husband's lineage upon marriage; rather, she remains part of her own (Caldwell and Caldwell, 1987). Moreover, it is not uncommon for women to return to live with their own lineages upon completion of childbearing (Sanjek, 1983, for Accra, Ghana). Indeed, if both wife and husband have relatives near at hand, they may maintain separate residences throughout the marriage, living with members of their own lineages (Robertson, 1976, for the Ga of Accra, Ghana; Abu, 1983, for Ashanti of Ghana; Hagan, 1983, for the Effutu of Ghana; Bleek, 1987).

---

[5]In Bas Zaire, by contrast, where the basis of descent is largely matrilineal, the husband's family was not viewed as so important in sterilization decisions (Chibalonza et al., 1989).

Distinction Between Patrilineal and Matrilineal Societies

Certain significant features differentiate patrilineal from matrilineal descent groups.[6] It is important to note first that the implications of matrilineality do not extend to patriarchal authority as such. Even in matrilineal societies, men still assume control over matters of inheritance, land, marriage, and politics (Henn, 1984). In a matrilineal society it is the maternal uncle who passes his property and social position to his sister's sons.[7] The key demographic differences between these descent systems have to do with the social importance accorded to marriage, and with certain mechanisms that in matrilineal groups are thought to enhance the social and economic security of women.

By comparison to patrilineal societies, matrilineal societies typically place much less emphasis on the marriage ceremony. For example, Bleek (1987) reports never having seen a marriage ceremony, so little import attaches to it, in his field work among the matrilineal Twi-speaking Akan of Ghana. It seems that the husband-wife bond may be even weaker among matrilineal groups than among patrilineal groups, although little direct evidence is available on this point.[8]

Several features of matrilineal societies contribute to the economic and social security of women (Henn, 1984). First, a woman in such a society is less likely to move away from her maternal village upon first marriage. If her husband has not yet inherited land from his maternal uncle at the time of marriage, he may establish a household and begin to farm in his wife's village.[9] Second, if the marriage dissolves, a divorced woman who has moved away can reactivate land rights in her maternal village much more easily than a divorced woman in patrilineal societies. Third, upon divorce, a woman's children remain with her because they belong by right to their maternal rather than to their paternal kin (Brain, 1976, for Tanzania; Bleek, 1987; Page, 1989). Thus, to the extent that economic insecurity per se

---

[6]In the Human Relations Area File data for Africa examined by Lesthaeghe et al. (1989a), 18 percent of ethnic groups are classified as matrilineal and 12 percent are both matrilineal and matrilocal.

[7]Yet the relationship between a man and his sister's son can be difficult, in part due to uncertainties surrounding inheritance. Sister's sons expect to inherit according to the seniority by age of their mothers, but their abilities to manage the inheritance also enter into the decision by the lineage head and elders.

[8]There does appear to be a well-documented and significant association between matrilineality and rates of divorce; see Lesthaeghe et al., (1989a). However, this association may reflect the greater ease with which women in matrilineal societies can obtain a divorce, instead of weaker bonds between husbands and wives.

[9]See Munachonga (1988) for a discussion of the implications of such arrangements for the authority of the husband vis-à-vis his father- and mother-in-law.

provides women with an incentive for high fertility, it would seem that pronatalist pressures might be somewhat reduced in matrilineal settings. Yet because there is also a greater assurance of economic returns to children over the long term, the value of children may be greater in matrilineal groups—that is, greater from the woman's perspective. These are complicated issues, to which we return below.

The contrasts between matrilineal and patrilineal groups should not be overdrawn. For western Africa, Sudarkasa (1981:54) writes, "It was common for women to have important roles within patrilineages as well as within matrilineages in West Africa, and in their roles as sisters and daughters of the lineage, they often exercised de facto authority and/or power within the 'public sphere'." For the patrilineal Zulu and Swazi of southeastern Africa, Ngubane (1987) describes a set of special provisions made in the bride-price agreement for the economic security of the bride.

An Alternative Perspective

The region's documented high fertility has been consistent with an emphasis on lineage orientation in sub-Saharan Africa, but the debate in the anthropological literature about the importance of lineage should not be overlooked. Kuper (1982a,b) has traced the course of the debate to nineteenth century theorists of British anthropology, who were concerned with whether the origins of statehood could be found along the lines of kinship or territory, or as Kuper puts it, in "blood" or in "soil." Those arguing in favor of territory viewed lineages as being "secondary and often unstable embroideries" on the more fundamental territorially based patterns of group residence and economic organization (Kuper, 1982a:78, citing Kroeber, 1938).

The work of Evans-Pritchard on the Nuer of Sudan, when coupled with that of Fortes (1945, 1949) on the Tallensi of northern Ghana, established the primacy of the lineage model in the British school of African anthropology, and it is of course this conceptual model of fully corporate lineages that dominates today's demographic literature. Yet even the fit of the lineage concept to the Nuer is in doubt. Evans-Pritchard (1940) himself (as quoted in Kuper 1982a:84) admitted that a Nuer rarely spoke of his lineage as being distinct from his community. As he wrote,

> I have watched a Nuer who knew precisely what I wanted, trying on my behalf to discover from a stranger the name of his lineage. He often found great initial difficulty in making the man understand the information required of him, for Nuer think generally in terms of local divisions and of the relationships between them, and an attempt to discover lineage affiliations apart from their community relations, and outside a ceremonial context, generally led to misunderstanding . . . .

The linkage between the conceptual model of the lineage and the empirical data was evidently never very clear; indeed, as Kuper (1982a:82) observes, Evans-Pritchard "increasingly came to glory in the lack of fit between the model and the empirical reports."

This is not to suggest that lineage concepts be dismissed as irrelevant to demographic concerns. Rather, the point to be extracted from the debate is that principles of descent do not necessarily exert any fundamental or dominant influence on African reproductive decision making. In some settings, lineage orientation is of so little importance that an individual's identity in respect to a lineage is itself adaptable: He may align himself with one or another lineage depending on the gains to be secured from such a manipulation of identities (see Guyer, 1981, and the discussion in Messina, 1992). Thus, lineages may be amplified in demographic significance in some circumstances, whereas in others they may be safely ignored. Even among the Yoruba of western Africa, whose ethnography has shaped so much of the demographic discourse for Africa, "corporate descent groups are contingent on other factors; they cannot be taken as the primary units of analysis" (Eades, 1980, quoted in Guyer, 1981:92). The centrality of lineage orientation is a matter to be explored on a society-by-society basis with due consideration for other aspects of social organization. We would agree with Guyer (1981:89), who writes,

> What has emerged over the last twenty years of scholarship on kinship is that the concept of the lineage and typologies of lineage systems disguise far too much of the variability in the way things get done: children brought up, livings made, authority achieved and assigned, land distributed . . . .

Certainly, the more sweeping generalizations about African descent systems, wherein the duty to perpetuate the lineage is invested with religious significance and the ancestors seem to figure in day-to-day reproductive decisions, are of very doubtful reliability if applied across the whole of sub-Saharan Africa.

Summary of the Implications of Lineage Orientation

To sum up, several implications for modern reproductive behavior follow from a consideration of lineage and descent in sub-Saharan Africa. The first implication derives from the weight attached to the continuity of the broader family line. To the extent that lineage orientation assumes social, religious, and cultural importance, we would expect the fertility response to mortality decline to be slower in African settings, in comparison to that elsewhere in the developing world.

As just noted, the emphasis on lineage continuity must be set in perspective and judged in relation to other elements of local social and economic structure. Furthermore, although it may run deep in certain African cultures if not in all, a lineage orientation is hardly peculiar to sub-Saharan Africa. Such an orientation is found among any number of cultures, including several in Asia that have gone on to record very rapid fertility declines. Perhaps the key difference between the African and Asian experiences is that despite some downward change, mortality levels have remained relatively high in sub-Saharan Africa. Moreover, as noted in Chapter 3, not all African groups in fact perceive child survival to be more likely now than it was a generation ago. Thus, parents and the elders of the lineage may not appreciate that where continuity is concerned, the need for high fertility is not as compelling as it was in the past.

Second, the emphasis on lineage and ancestors is logically connected to age gradings of authority. This connection may matter in an era of rapid social and economic change, since the lineage surrenders decision-making powers to those individuals who are perhaps least well equipped to understand the nature of contemporary society and the direction of change.

Third, a lineage orientation involves in reproductive matters a whole set of relevant decision makers beyond the wife and husband. For instance, in a matrilineal group a wife's brother may take an interest in the reproduction of his sister. This multiplicity of interests is associated with weakness in the conjugal bond: As Bleek (1987:139,142) writes for the matrilineal Akan, "The lasting association of women with their lineage provides them with a strong 'solidarity group' which cuts right through their conjugal bond . . . On the whole . . . the lineage has the better cards."

Fourth, lineage organization has a bearing on the distribution of economic returns to childbearing, and in particular on the support children are expected to provide to their mothers and fathers. From the woman's point of view the longer-term prospect of returns from children may well be less in patrilineal societies than in matrilineal. If a woman's marriage ends in divorce, her children remain with her husband's lineage in patrilineal societies, although she may be allowed to retain an unweaned or very young child (Schildkrout, 1983, for the Hausa of Kano, Nigeria). If she is widowed, the children can remain with her if she marries the husband's brother (the levirate); otherwise, she can only hope that the children will transfer to her some portion of their own inheritance (Henn, 1984, on widowhood; Frank and McNicoll, 1987, for Kenya; Ladipo, 1987, for the Yoruba of Ife). In matrilineal settings, by contrast, a woman has greater assurance of continued support from her children irrespective of the course of her marriage. This arrangement would seem to enhance the returns from children and the motivation for high fertility among women in matrilineal societies.

Yet in the short term, a woman in a patrilineal society may have a greater need for children to help secure her access to land held by her husband's lineage, and children constitute her only possible claim on the wealth produced in the marriage but held by the husband for his heirs.

Conversely, in matrilineal societies it is the husband's motivations for high fertility that are at issue. Once again a distinction must be drawn between the long-run prospects of returns from children, which would not appear to favor husbands in matrilineal settings, and the advantages for men that can be wrested from fertility in the shorter term. These are complex matters, and the literature does not provide any consensus on the net consequences for fertility that follow from the matrilineal-patrilineal distinction.

Finally, we should take note of one general area of agreement in the literature: The demographic significance of the lineage has been progressively undermined by economic development and modernization. Caldwell et al. (1991) describe lineage authority as being under attack from a variety of directions even in the colonial era. Lesthaeghe et al. (1989a) suggest that the integration of rural and urban economies, and the emergence of human capital as a movable economic asset, have combined to weaken the control of lineages over economic resources and decision making. Thus, the view that lineages and long-standing systems of descent must continue to inhibit fertility decline in modern Africa is in doubt.

KIN NETWORKS AND CHILD FOSTERING

With regard to day-to-day economic assistance and support, the conjugal family tends to rely not so much on the lineage as a whole as on its closest relations within the lineage.[10] Lloyd and Brandon (1991) show that the great bulk of remittances and income transfers in Ghana travels within a tight circle: spouses, children, parents, and siblings. The economic assistance provided by close kin is also evident in studies of migrant remittance flows in Kenya (Knowles and Anker, 1981); the vast majority of documented transfers are those between children and parents, and among siblings. Urban-to-rural transfers are used to help sustain consumption in rural areas and are said to be important in financing the schooling of rural children (Rempel and Lobdell, 1978; Stark and Lucas, 1988).

Among the Ga of Accra (Robertson, 1976:128), mothers and daughters are said to share "one money-bag." A substantial number of transfers take place as well between women and certain mother substitutes: the mother's sisters, father's sisters, and so on. For the matrilineal Akan, Okali (1983:176) reports that "a good mother's brother is expected to help his sister's sons, thereby obliging the latter to reciprocate in the next generation either through their own sisters' sons or through other matrilineal dependents." Educated

---

[10]As Bleek (1987) notes for the Akan of Ghana, the wider lineage tends to provide services of a social or ritual character rather more often than it does economic assistance.

children are thought to owe special obligations to those who gave them support.

Child Fostering

Demographers have only recently begun to explore the implications of child fostering for fertility in sub-Saharan Africa, and with one significant exception (Ainsworth, 1991), economic demographers have yet to address the issue with data adequate to the task. Yet as Page (1989:401) has argued, the institution of child fostering presents a fundamental challenge to the dominant conceptual model of the household: "We find analyses of fertility in terms of the costs and benefits of children, or in terms of the demand for children, all cast in a model in which the childbearer (or begetter) is assumed to be the person responsible for bringing the child to full adult status . . . . quite inappropriate for most of sub-Saharan Africa."

The prevalence of child fostering in sub-Saharan Africa is impressive indeed. An analysis of World Fertility Survey (WFS) data by Page (1989) shows that among children aged 0-4, perhaps 6 to 8 percent live with someone other than their mother; the figure increases to 18 to 20 percent among children aged 5-9, and 22 to 25 percent among those aged 10-14.[11] Considering various ethnic groups in Ghana, Blanc and Lloyd (1990) find that the proportion of households with a fostered-out child ranges from 20 to 48 percent. Lloyd and Brandon (1991), also with reference to Ghana, show that the percentage of households with fostered-in children ranges from 17 for households headed by a male of working age, to as high as 74 percent if the head is a woman of age 60 or older. Evidently the practice of fostering occurs on a very considerable scale.[12]

Most children are fostered to kin, although a significant proportion

---

[11]The figures cited are median values for WFS data classified by some 56 subregions in Cameroon, Ghana, Côte d'Ivoire, Kenya, Lesotho, Nigeria, and the Sudan, taken from Page (1989:Figure 9.3). There is considerable variation in these data: The upper quartiles are 10 to 12 percent for children aged 0-4; 20 to 23 percent for children aged 5-9; and 28 to 30 percent for children aged 10-14. Note that children may live with their father (especially in patrilineal societies after the divorce of the biological parents), so the percentages of children who do not live with their mother may overstate, to a degree, the prevalence of child fostering. However, closer examination of the situations among the Mende (Isaac and Conrad, 1982) and in Côte d'Ivoire (Ainsworth, 1991) suggests that the figures are not much overstated and provide a generally reliable guide to the prevalence of fostering.

[12]Lloyd and Desai (1991) have also examined this issue from the child's point of view. They find that in Kenya and Burundi, where fostering is generally less prevalent, children spend less than 10 percent of their childhood years living away from their natural mothers. In Botswana and Liberia, by contrast, 30 percent of the childhood years are lived away from the mother.

reside with nonkin.[13] As Ainsworth (1991) notes, the prevalence of fostering to relatives can be explained in terms of minimizing transaction costs
for both the sending and the receiving households, and reducing the burdens
of monitoring and supervision. A kin relationship may also be put to advantage by the host household, to help ensure flows of resources from the
natural parents.

The institution of fostering performs a number of important economic
and social functions. It is useful to distinguish among these according to
the motivations for fostering-out and fostering-in, and by the age of the
child. From the fostering-out point of view, the institution (1) provides a
mechanism for reducing the costs of rearing young children, especially if
the child is fostered to a rural area (for the Avatime of Togo, see Brydon,
1983; for the Mende of Sierra Leone, Bledsoe and Isiugo-Abanihe, 1989).
(Rural areas are commonly viewed as safer and more tranquil environments
for the rearing of young children; Page, 1989.) Fostering-out gives the
natal family a means of managing the consequences of its high fertility and
closely spaced births. It may also help a natal family living elsewhere to
strengthen its ties with a home village (Page, 1989; Bledsoe and Isiugo-
Abanihe, 1989, for the Mende). (2) For older children, fostering may position the child with a relative who is selected on the basis of ability to supply
some educational advantage, whether in terms of formal schooling (Isaac
and Conrad, 1982, for the Mende; Okojie, 1991, for Bendel and Kwara
states in Nigeria) or apprenticeship (Schildkrout, 1983, for the Hausa of
Kano, Nigeria). Fostering also widens the contacts of the child within the
urban social and employment network. Children may be deliberately placed
with potentially powerful patrons who can assist the child in later life (Goody,
1982, for the Gonja of Ghana). There is also the widely held view that
older children receive better discipline when they are raised by nonparental
caretakers (although this is not always the case as described in the next
section) (Bledsoe and Isiugo-Abanihe, 1989, on the Mende; Goody, 1982,
on the Gonja of northern Ghana, as cited in Page, 1989).

Regarding fostering-in, there are several potential motivations. (1) In
rural areas there is the value of child farm labor to consider (for the Avatime
of Togo, see Brydon, 1983; for the Mende, Isaac and Conrad, 1982), although this motivation was perhaps more important in the past than it is
today; for urban areas (Ainsworth, 1991, on Côte d'Ivoire), fostered-in children may provide significant assistance in domestic tasks and family businesses. (2) Fostered-in children supply additional dependents for the host
household, which in some settings may assist the household heads in their

---

[13]For the Mende of Sierra Leone, Isaac and Conrad (1982) find that 17 percent of fostered
children under age 15 are sent to nonkin.

own strategies for economic and social advancement.[14] (3) Fostering-in also provides a means of strengthening the obligations of the natal parents to the foster parent (Bledsoe and Isiugo-Abanihe, 1989, for the Mende).

Fostering of Young Children

Bledsoe and Isiugo-Abanihe (1989) consider the instructive case of granny fostering among the Mende of Sierra Leone. The grannies in question are usually based in rural villages. They are often, but need not be, the child's actual maternal or paternal grandmother; in some cases the granny is simply another relative of that generation.

Young Mende children are fostered-out simply to "raise them up" to learning age; until they reach the "age of sense," children are considered to be incapable of learning very much, and there is little harm in placing them with relations who have low status or little access to schools. When the fostered child reaches the age of sense, however, he or she is usually removed from the granny's care, perhaps to be fostered-out elsewhere.

In raising the children, Mende grannies are notorious for spoiling them, "petting" them, and being lax about discipline. In part, this treatment yields emotional rewards for the grannies, but it is also intended to inculcate a sense of obligation in the child, which will in time be expressed in support from the child himself and, in the nearer future, in flows of resources from the child's parents. Fostering gives the granny a means of acquiring resources from the modern world, to which a rural-based older woman might not otherwise have access. Thus, children serve to forge an economic link between adults, thereby providing an example of the "lateral strategy" of network building through children that has been explored in the work of Guyer (1988b), discussed below.

The grannies are said to levy great pressure even on young, educated urban women to maintain high fertility rates and to begin bearing children early. They can request that a child be brought to them, invoking as necessary the persuasive devices of pity, guilt, and the respect due a family elder. As Bledsoe and Isiugo-Abanihe (1989:466) write,

> This pressure does not stem simply from a desire to increase the size of the kin group. Rather, it stems largely from grannies' desires for modern goods and services from parents of the children they mind. As one young woman complained: "Whenever I come [to the rural area from Freetown], they [my elderly kinswomen] keep talking about getting married and hav-

---

[14]Among the Baule of Côte d'Ivoire (Etienne, 1983), fostering and adoption were key mechanisms for providing married women with additional dependents, who then could assist in the woman's own economic and social advancement.

ing kids. When I say I'm not interested in that now, they say 'Alright, just have the children and then send them to us to train.' As long as you can send them support, they will be happy. Then you can have your child when you are ready."

Fostering of Older Children

Whereas younger children are typically fostered to rural areas (Isaac and Conrad, 1982), fostering to urban households is much more common for children older than 5 years, who by virtue of their age "have sense" and are ready to begin intensive training and education in preparation for adult work roles (Isaac and Conrad, 1982). It is still predominantly kin who foster-in, but in contrast to the grannies, these are kin selected on the basis of urban position, ability to provide apprenticeships or schooling, and the like. Older children are sometimes sent out in response to economic hardship in the family, but it seems that parents usually foster-out in the hope of securing advantages for their children (Bledsoe and Isiugo-Abanihe, 1989).

Although in the past, older children were valuable as inputs into farm production, this motivation has receded in importance among the Mende. Children require some measure of supervision on the farm, and in consequence, adult and child farm labor are complementary to a degree. Many young adults have out-migrated from the Mende rural areas, and lacking supervision, children have become an economic burden in some rural settings.[15] Ainsworth (1991) also finds evidence against a demand for child farm labor as an explanation for fostering-in in Côte d'Ivoire: Rural households are more likely to foster-out children whereas urban households are more likely to foster them in.[16]

The role of schooling and apprenticeships, which is cited as the predominant motivation for fostering-out in a number of ethnographic studies, evidently merits closer attention. Ainsworth (1991), working with a large sample of observations from Côte d'Ivoire, finds that only trivial proportions of fostered-in children work as apprentices. The situation with regard to schooling is also more complex than might have been imagined. There are considerable within-household differences in enrollment rates, such that fostered-in children have much lower enrollment rates than do own children, especially in the case of girls. Moreover, Ainsworth's comparisons

---

[15]Isaac and Conrad for the Mende (1982:255): "Farming households were, thus, unburdening themselves of many children and making a conscious effort to seek educational advantage, whether through formal schooling or apprenticeship, for them."

[16]Ainsworth's sample is comprised of children ages 7-14, who are generally too old to be granny-fostered.

show that fostered-out girls have lower enrollment rates than do their nonfostered sisters in the households of origin, whereas fostered-out boys have roughly the same enrollment rates as their nonfostered brothers. Children fostered from rural areas have lower enrollment rates than do their own nonfostered siblings.

Yet Ainsworth also finds that the host households spend considerable amounts on the schooling of fostered-in children, if perhaps not as much as is spent on their own children. Thus, the picture regarding education is rather mixed. Perhaps a consideration of secondary schooling would have produced more evidence in favor of the schooling investments hypothesis.

It seems that host households do derive certain benefits from the labor of their fostered-in children. In rural areas of Côte d'Ivoire, fostered-in children are more likely to work on the farm than are own children of the household; in urban areas, fostered-in children are more likely to do housework than are own children. Thus, the dominant picture for Côte d'Ivoire is one in which fostered-in children provide substitutes for the labor that otherwise would have been supplied by own children, had those own children not themselves gone to school.

Regarding fostering-out as a means of managing the economic consequences of high fertility, Ainsworth (1991) finds there to be little influence of household permanent income on fostering-out of children (aged 7-14) in Côte d'Ivoire. This lack of influence is consistent with the reports of Isaac and Conrad for the Mende, and suggests that the managing effect is expressed, if it exists at all, in the fostering of younger children. By contrast, Blanc and Lloyd (1990) find for Ghana that the greater the number of living children in any age category, the greater is the likelihood that a child in that age range will be fostered-out.[17]

Summary of the Implications of Child Fostering

In summary, the institution of child fostering is of considerable demographic significance in sub-Saharan Africa. It is one aspect of social organization that is wholly distinctive to the region, certainly so in terms of scale. Fostering-out provides a way to spread the costs of childrearing by enlisting one's kin in the process, and thereby reduces the net expected costs of one's own high fertility. In addition, where fostering-in represents an obligation on the part of the receiving household, it may defeat the intent

---

[17]Other demographic behaviors are also related to fostering. Blanc and Lloyd (1990) note that fostering-out is more prevalent among recent migrants in Ghana. Page (1989) shows convincingly that fostering is related to the incidence of marriage dissolution; she terms this "crisis fostering."

of family limitation. As one man in Burkina Faso said, "If you limit your children to be able to take good care of them, and then they send you children for schooling because you don't have enough, there's no more family planning" (McGinn et al., 1989a:86).

THE CONJUGAL BOND

As has been indicated above, the conjugal bond is thought to be relatively weak in sub-Saharan Africa, that is, frail by comparison to the ties of lineage and the demands that other kin outside the marriage can place on the husband and wife. This weakness is important for three reasons: (1) a frail conjugal bond may prevent one or both members of a married couple from confronting the full costs of childrearing, thereby leading to a bargaining situation within the household in which the interests of the member with the lower perceived costs (presumably the husband) may prevail; (2) the uncertainties and conflicts in such settings may themselves provide an incentive for high fertility, as childbearing becomes both a strategy for capturing the continuing interest of the other party, and a means of ensuring economic security should the relationship dissolve; and (3) weakness in the conjugal bond may leave the couple vulnerable to the demands of other kin-group members (the Mende grannies being one such example) who have something to gain from the couple's high fertility and very little to lose in the way of childrearing costs. The implications for fertility are summed up by Caldwell and Caldwell (1987:421) as follows:

> The African family structure typically places reproductive decisionmaking in the hands of the husband and the economic burden mainly on the shoulders of the wife. Nothing could be more conducive to maintaining high fertility.

Lesthaeghe (1989a:485-486) also takes note of the contrast, admittedly something of a caricature, between African and Asian conjugal bonds. The Asian husband-wife dyad is often pictured as being much more unified and cohesive, such that Asian husbands are "directly and fully responsible for their offspring on the basis of a pooled family budget stemming from relatively fixed familial land resources . . . ." To the extent that this portrait is accurate, one would not be surprised to find less sensitivity to child costs and greater resistance to fertility decline in the African case.

The literature for West Africa, in particular, is emphatic regarding the relative weakness of the marriage bond. Caldwell et al. (1989:202) quote Omari on Ghana, "Throughout her married life a wife never identifies herself with her husband in his aspirations and interests." Men and women are often described as being members of two different societies with few points of intersection or common interest. Paulme (1963:13) observes that "the men put up with the presence of their wives but continue to regard them as strangers . . . ."

This division between wife and husband can be traced to the remarkable complexity of family and kin relations in sub-Saharan Africa. Sudarkasa (1981:56-59) writes,

> For the most part women in West Africa still function within the context of families that transcend the conjugally-based nuclear family. Women are born into lineages and most of them still grow up in compounds. When they marry, they move into compounds or otherwise join families that include many significant actors other than their husbands . . . . The West African wife is actively involved in a number of decision making domestic and kinship networks, only one of which is the immediate conjugal unit comprised of herself, her husband, and in some instances, her co-wives.

The cleavage in interests between husband and wife is further widened by the instability of African marriage, as evidenced in high rates of divorce and widowhood. Lesthaeghe et al. (1989a) have calculated the prevalence of divorce and widowhood for a variety of sub-Saharan countries primarily for the 1970s. They find that some 20 percent of women are either divorced or widowed at age 50 in Senegal, which is the country in their sample with the lowest levels of marital dissolution, and the prevalence of widowhood and divorce is in the neighborhood of 40 percent in western Cameroon, Lesotho, Zambia, Tanzania, and Malawi. These prevalence figures are instructive as to the likely incidence of divorce and widowhood.[18] Studies of incidence rates themselves are not common, but Lesthaeghe et al. (1989a) suggest that divorce is somewhat more frequent in eastern than in western Africa. Incidence rates have been calculated for four African countries that conducted a WFS: Kenya, Lesotho, Senegal, and northern Sudan (Smith et al., 1984). The probability of dissolution of first union by separation or divorce within five years of marriage was highest for Senegal (14 percent), followed by Kenya and Sudan (with 8 and 7 percent respectively). For Lesotho, there was a five percent probability of divorce or separation. As Pittin (1987:29) remarks for the Hausa of Katsina, "Given a high divorce rate, differential longevity of women and men, and the fact that women in their forties rarely remarry, and even women in their thirties may not remarry, it is clear that a woman works for her own and her children's security, and does not tie her fortunes to those of her husband."

---

[18]The data indicate very different age patterns of marital status in western and eastern Africa, probably as a result of including both widowhood and divorce in the numerators of the prevalence measures. Prevalence calculations have the disadvantage of confounding rates of marriage dissolution with rates of remarriage. Their advantage lies in indicating how much of the life cycle a typical woman or man might spend outside of marriage.

The husband and wife are further divided by the institution of polygyny, which may place women in a bargaining position vis-à-vis each other and the husband, and which is associated with large age gaps between husband and wife, hence with a greater likelihood of widowhood. A mapping of African zones of polygyny testifies to the enduring prominence of this institution (Lesthaeghe et al., 1989a). There is a long arc along the Atlantic coast where at least 40 percent of married women participate in polygynous unions, the only exceptions are among the matrilineal Akan groups of southeast Côte d'Ivoire and southwest Ghana, and the border areas of southeast Nigeria and southwest Cameroon. The incidence of polygyny is somewhat lower elsewhere on the continent, although there exist levels as high as 30 percent in an East African zone stretching southward from Kisumu in Kenya to Mozambique. Further inspection shows that matrilineal societies are less likely to practice polygyny, especially if they are also matrilocal (Lesthaeghe et al., 1989a).[19]

Lesthaeghe et al. (1989a) review the argument of Goody (1976), Boserup (1970), and others that links the economic value of female labor to incentives for men to establish polygynous households.[20] Traditional polygyny can be viewed as a response to the high productive value of women in hoe-based agriculture, and for western Africa one would also want to consider the economic surplus that can be derived from a woman's involvement in trade. In general, where these economic contributions are high, one expects higher levels of polygyny and relatively quick remarriage of widows. But where cattle raising, animal husbandry, and plow agriculture are more important, and trading is less common (as in eastern Africa), the value of women's labor may be relatively less, and from this perspective there is less incentive on the male side to enter into polygynous unions. As to the possible incentives for women that are inherent in the institution, Steady (1987) notes the economic benefits that can be derived when polygyny permits wives to specialize among themselves and coordinate their tasks under the supervision of the senior wife, whom Steady likens to the "foreman" of the family labor force.[21]

---

[19]In a matrilineal society a husband would be obliged to marry sisters if the household is to avoid a mix of children who belong to different lineages.

[20]The analysis is somewhat broader than indicated here, because male incentives to gather together a group of wives and offspring may also have to do with the economic surplus that can be gleaned from the labor of children and other dependents.

[21]In the fishing villages of Sierra Leone studied by Steady (1987), the processing, handling, and marketing of fish are entirely in the hands of women. Women buy fish directly from their husbands' boats, and transactions with the husband and other middlemen over the course of the season are managed much as a small business might handle its accounts payable and receivable. Specialization within a polygynous household might go so far as the delegation of one wife to the provinces, so that she can manage the profitable sale of fish away from home.

Yet these arguments regarding the functionality of polygyny should not obscure its elements of conflict.[22] Hagan (1983) remarks on the economic implications of a second wife for the first wife among the Effutu of Ghana, where wives handle, process, and market the fish caught by their husbands. When a second wife enters the marriage, the first wife thereafter receives only half of her husband's catch to sell; in effect she "splits her basket into two." Women often express anxiety regarding the character of the other wives entering the marriage and also worry about the potential for jealousy among wives and the possibilities of the evil eye. (The quotations below are taken from focus group sessions conducted in Lagos; see Adegbola et al., 1991.)

> If you say you will mind your own business and face your trade . . . you will struggle on your own. The other woman he will bring up [may have] a bad character, she is lazy, a pokenoser; the children you gave birth to will not have rest of mind because they would start using diabolical means on them and the children with brighter future will not be able to make it. [Yoruban woman, age 50+]

But there is also the clear-eyed view among women that polygyny simply underlines the need for a woman to be economically self-reliant:

> Some women do fear, that their husband would someday take a second wife. But if she has her job, she has no problem. If he likes let him marry, if he likes let him not, my own is my job. Once I sell my goods, I won't bother even if he marries ten. [Yoruban woman, aged 20-49]

These characteristics of marriage reinforce for women the necessity of achieving economic autonomy and independence, an achievement in which high fertility may play a strategic part. Guyer (1988b; also see Bledsoe, 1990b) has observed in contemporary Nigeria an increase in what she terms "lateral strategies" of network building for women. The notion is that women, lacking economic assets commensurate with those of men, must pursue various avenues of access to the economic resources held by men. A woman can make no claims of a lasting nature by virtue of a sexual relationship alone, nor are her possibilities much improved by marriage. Rather, it is the act of having a child with a man that advances a longer-term claim to his resources. In a sense, the rewards of childbearing, for the woman, are immediately at hand. Such immediate rewards associated with fertility may be more tangible than the distant and uncertain prospect of resource flows from the child itself. As Guyer (1988b:7) writes, "The fact of the child growing to adulthood and supporting [the parents] in older age can almost

---

[22]Bledsoe (in press) considers the conflicts among wives in respect to investments in the education of their children.

be seen as an unintended consequence, a bonus which may or may not materialise."

Moreover, marriage to any given man may be regarded as restrictive, in the sense that a woman might improve her prospects for economic security by creating links to several men (Bledsoe, 1990a,b). Within marriage, multiple links can be made via relationships with patrons or lovers, but over time they can be achieved by divorce and remarriage, as long as childbearing accompanies marriage. In each marriage a child stakes out the claim to resources, and as Guyer (1988b) notes, marriage itself becomes almost incidental to a woman's reproductive and economic career.

Separate Residence

In addition to the separation of spouses that arises from long-distance labor migration, as in southern Africa, the demands of seasonal agriculture also produce regular separations between the spouses in a variety of sub-Saharan settings.[23] Even among settled urban populations, however, it is not at all unusual for a husband and wife to live apart, especially if both spouses have members of their lineage living nearby.[24] Furthermore, continuous coresidence is really feasible only in a monogamous marriage; a polygynous husband usually lives with none of his wives or rotates his living arrangements among them (Abu, 1983, for the Ashanti).

There are life-cycle aspects to coresidence as well. As noted by Abu (1983) and Sanjek (1983) for Ghana, the probability of living with a conjugal partner tends to decrease for women after age 35. Most women from age 40 on live in households that they head or share with other adult women, and from this age many women embark on economic enterprises of their own.

Interestingly, among the Ashanti in Ghana described by Abu (1983), where perhaps half of spouses maintain separate residences, coresidence is said by women to be a desirable thing, because it brings all the household expenses to the attention of the husband and assists in matters of child discipline. Yet a significant minority of Abu's sample judged the practical difficulties attendant on coresidence to be simply insurmountable. As ex-

---

[23]See Hagan (1983) for an account of seasonal separations among the Effutu of coastal Ghana, a fishing group in which men leave to fish elsewhere in the off-season, often taking on other women to process and market their fish and look after their well-being.

[24]For the matrilineal Akan, see Bleek (1987); for the Ga of Accra, Robertson (1976); for the Ashanti, Abu (1983); and for Ghana, Lloyd and Brandon (1991:21). Vercruijsse (1983) finds that fewer than 40 percent of married women reside with their husbands among the Fanti of Ghana.

amples of such difficulties, both men and women mentioned quarreling among spouses, the fact that men will be too closely observed by their wives, the general lack of privacy when being visited by friends or relatives, and for women, the worry about what property belonging to the marriage would be taken away by the husband's relatives upon his death.

Separate Economic Responsibilities and Resources

Embedded in both ideology and centuries of practice is the expectation that an African woman must play the major role in feeding her family, either by growing the food herself or, through trade or other means, by earning the money necessary to buy the food (Henn, 1984). This expectation is implicit in the importance placed by African women on their work, which permits them to fulfill a fundamental responsibility and is therefore seen as being integral to a woman's identity. In Kenya, for instance, women take primary responsibility for the farming that feeds the family. Men have an obligation to clear and plow the land, or to make arrangements for doing so. Men also ensure that the bride-price payments continue to be met and cover any major family expenses beyond food and clothing, including school fees and perhaps the costs arising from health care (Frank and McNicoll, 1987).

Elsewhere the husband may have more extensive obligations in matters of childrearing expenses. Among the Ga of Accra, Ghana, the husband is expected to pay for the food and clothing of his conjugal family. His obligations extend to the children's education, although in many cases a woman will pay the school fees when her husband is unable to do so (Robertson, 1976). Adegbola et al. (1991) find a similar division of responsibilities in Lagos, Nigeria, where if the wife does pay the school fees, her husband is obliged to pay her back. Some variance of views is expressed in the Lagos study regarding the wife's responsibilities for school expenses other than fees. A number of respondents view school uniforms and materials as falling under the wife's set of obligations.[25] Regarding health care, however, Adegbola et al. (1991) found broad agreement that expenses are to be met primarily by the husband, with support from his wife should he be caught short.

In sum, there is general agreement that major items of childrearing expense, including food and clothing in some instances and by all accounts

---

[25]Kritz and Gurak (1991) report that Yoruba husbands have responsibilities for school fees and children's clothes. Okojie (1991) also reports that husbands in Bendel and Kwara states have an obligation to meet school fees as well as health-related expenses. Guyer (1988a) finds that in Cameroon, Beti men are responsible for school fees.

the major expenditures related to education, are the primary responsibility of the husband. Thus, to say that the burdens of childrearing fall almost entirely on the shoulders of the wife, which is the view advanced by Caldwell and Caldwell (1987) among many others, is to overstate the case considerably. In many sub-Saharan countries, the husband has his own large and regular commitments to the children that must be met as a part of his conjugal family obligations, although certainly many of the day-to-day expenses will remain the responsibility of the wife.

Beyond these central obligations to their children and to each other, however, the interests of the wife and husband may diverge sharply. Ashanti men (Abu, 1983) provide their wives and children with the basic necessities—such as chop (meal) money and school fees—but where capital investments such as houses and cocoa farms are concerned, the matrilineage takes precedence. Among the Ga of Accra, men are also said to give higher priority to financial obligations to their lineages than to those due their wives (Robertson, 1976).

Di Domenico et al. (1987:121), writing on the Ibadan and Abeokuta Yoruba of Nigeria, find that ". . . both wives and husbands had responsibilities in relation to their kin, and some were putting young relatives through secondary school. Few of the husbands gave their wives money to meet their obligations to kin, so wives needed to have their own source of income."

The literature is all but unanimous that resources of husband and wife are not pooled, even among the elites.[26] Separate budgets are a response to a situation in which conjugal family members have independent obligations to kin outside the conjugal family (Sudarkasa, 1981). A Ghanaian study (Gugler, 1981:174, citing Vellenga, 1971) found that some women

> attributed the continued viability of their marriages to the fact that the partners had not pooled their resources. With the wife's and the husband's relatives making different demands regarding school fees, funeral contributions, and the like, common property would create considerable difficulty. There were further problems in relation to inheritance, children outside the marriage, and other wives.

For the same reason, joint ownership of assets is unusual. The Ashanti firmly reject the notion that a wife and husband should join together in

---

[26]For western Africa as a whole, see Sudarkasa (1981) and Guyer (1988a). See Gugler (1981) and Fapohunda (1987, 1988) on Lagos, Nigeria; di Domenico et al. (1987) for the Ibadan and Abeokuta Yoruba; Mott and Mott (1985) for the Yoruba near Ondo, Nigeria; Pittin (1987) for the Hausa in Katsina, Nigeria; Abu (1983), as well as Bleek (1987) for the Ashanti; Robertson, 1976, for the Ga of Accra, Ghana; Okali (1983) for Akan cocoa farmers; and Gugler (1981) citing Grandmaison for Dakar, Senegal.

business, citing the ever-present possibility of divorce and the siphoning of profits to other wives or to the husband's outside liaisons (Abu, 1983). Fapohunda (1987) finds that few women in Lagos own farmland or houses with their husbands, but significant percentages own these assets jointly with their kin.

To be sure, it is a common practice for husbands to provide start-up capital for the businesses of their wives, but the capital is viewed by wives as a business loan and is treated in that spirit (Robertson, 1976, on the Ga of Accra). In particular, the loan does not give the husband access to his wife's profits, or even to knowledge of their amount. Okali (1983:170) reports that among the Akan cocoa farmers, even when wives worked the farms with their husbands, they were "always aware that they were not working on joint economic enterprises. They expected eventually to establish their own separate economic concerns . . . ."

Although husbands and wives each have well-defined responsibilities regarding the maintenance of the conjugal household, neither spouse expects to know the other's true income.[27] As Robertson (1976) observes, an illiterate woman is often wholly ignorant of the market value of her husband's labor and has no way of estimating his income. Yet as long as the amount of support given by the husband is up to expectations, a woman does not express much concern regarding his total earnings.

Abu (1983:166) says that among the Ashanti, "collaboration over domestic budgeting is clearly considered to be innovative and to be dependent on the understanding nature of the wife." Wives fear that the more they voluntarily contribute to household expenses, the greater is the risk that the husband may shirk his own responsibilities.[28] Men are more likely to think well of the notion of cooperative budgeting, doubtless for this very reason.

Obbo (1987:264), citing the views of low-income women in Kampala, reports that women believe pooling incomes to be foolish and regard it as something that only the naive or the elite would consider. These low-income women point out, with derision, that the husbands of their elite

---

[27]For the Hausa of Kano, Nigeria, see Schildkrout (1983); and for the Yoruba of Lagos, see Fapohunda (1988). We should note here the implications for collecting survey data on incomes in sub-Saharan Africa. It seems abundantly clear that the usual practice, whereby a single respondent (generally a male household head) is selected to report on the income of the household as a whole, is highly inappropriate in this setting.

[28]Robertson (1976:120) notes for the Ga of Accra, "Women did not like to let their husbands know the intimate details of their businesses. Only women who got along extremely well with their husbands trusted them with knowledge of their profits. One woman, who by all accounts had a good husband, explained her cautious attitude in this way. 'Once a husband gets to know about the finances of his wife, the man begins to be tight with money toward the wife. . . . A safe attitude is to keep him in the dark.' "

counterparts are often found in their own poor neighborhoods, seeing their "outside" wives and providing material support to their outside children.

Evidence for Emotional Nucleation

In the past, even among the elites (Gugler, 1981, citing Lloyd, 1971, for Ibadan in the 1960s), a husband and wife would tend to spend little of their leisure time together. Spouses shared few close friendships, and each spouse would occupy leisure time in visiting his or her own friends in exclusively male or female gatherings. Yet scattered and anecdotal evidence does suggest that change is under way in the direction of growing conjugal closeness.

Caldwell and Caldwell (1987) see evidence among the modern and educated elites of a gradual strengthening of the conjugal bond, which is linked to a decline in the period of postpartum sexual abstinence.[29] Oppong (1987a,b) also finds norms of shared conjugal residence and shared parental responsibilities among married male school teachers in Ghana, a group that would not be classed with the elites on the basis of economic status. She notes (1987b:173) that among school teachers, the men who have smaller families "expected more joint and equal conjugal relationships and less close kin ties. They were also more likely to think they personally [as opposed to the wife alone] should bear the costs of child-care . . . ."

Fapohunda and Todaro (1988) see the trend toward shared decision making as being, in part, an outgrowth of changes in childrearing costs and educational aspirations. Considering the Yoruba, they suggest that increases in school fees and other childrearing expenses have outstripped the financial capacities of women. If such large expenditures are to be made at all,

---

[29]The Caldwells argue that the decline in abstinence is in part due to a desire for greater conjugal closeness (also see Kritz and Gurak, 1991, and Fapohunda and Todaro, 1988, on the connection among education, income, and conjugality) and in part due to a greater fear among wives that continued abstinence will bring an outside wife to disturb the marital relationship.

In Burkina Faso (McGinn et al., 1989b), focus group research among women in Ouagadougou showed that they viewed abstinence as onerous for social, economic, and emotional reasons. In particular, it forces their husbands to go outside the marriage for sex, a practice that is both costly to the household, because husbands must buy presents for their girlfriends, and risky, because of the possibility of transmission of disease. Moreover, sex between husband and wife is regarded as an aid to marital harmony. Abstinence durations are shorter among younger women, the better educated, and those raised in urban areas.

For Zaire, Bertrand et al. (1985) report that urban living conditions discourage abstinence; their results are consistent with the view that modern contraception is substituting for postpartum practices as the duration of these practices is reduced.

they require the cooperation of the husband and therefore necessitate a degree of joint decision making.[30]

The roots of these changes are identified by Lesthaeghe et al. (1989a) in improvements in literacy, westernization, and the gradual erosion of the powers of the lineage. They note that in many parts of Africa literacy is itself a by-product of Christian missions and is therefore linked to an ideology that favors conjugal closeness. Gugler (1981:170) adds that "most Christian missions propounded a doctrine of the equality of marriage partners; schools taught boys and girls; print, radio, and screen extolled the overriding importance of love . . . ." Lesthaeghe et al. also emphasize the gradual evolution of free partner choice in the marriage search, which is associated with the erosion of lineage controls.

Yet it is difficult to say, for the present, just how deep a transformation of marriage is under way. Abu (1983:165) notes among the Ashanti "much talk by men and women of the need for trust between spouses, alongside evidence of a pervasive atmosphere of mistrust." Karanja (1987) contends that whereas elite Nigerian women reject polygyny, this attitude is not shared by their husbands. The conflicts between elite husbands and their wives may lead to surreptitious polygyny in the form of the "outside wife." Dinan (1983:351), reporting the views on marriage of white-collar single women in Accra, notes that women "accepted that it was hopeless to expect husbands to be faithful; at the same time they were highly critical and resentful of this adulterous behavior . . . ."

Implications of the Weak Conjugal Bond

We can draw together the various threads of this discussion in terms of the consequences of a weak conjugal bond for fertility. Much of the discussion has suggested that women may have separate and distinct motivations for high fertility that are independent of their husbands' motivations. Guyer's (1988b) concept of "lateral strategies" for economic advancement on the part of women is relevant here, in that children provide the leverage with which women gain access to a share of the resources of men. Given the separation of spouse incomes and responsibilities, marriage without continued childbearing will not provide a woman with sufficient support.

---

[30]The consequences, however, need not be antinatalist. As Fapohunda and Todaro (1988) go on to argue, the involvement of the husband in such expenditures may give him an even greater degree of leverage in reproductive decisions. And because co-wives would drain away resources that could otherwise be used in financing the education of her own children, a monogamous wife with educational aspirations for her children will perceive polygyny to be a greater threat. The net consequence may be that she has more children than she desires, so as to satisfy her husband's reproductive goals and fend off the threat of polygyny.

Yet if the benefits of high fertility differ for men and women, so do the costs. It is often said for sub-Saharan Africa (e.g., Frank and McNicoll, 1987) that men do not fully perceive the subsistence costs involved in rearing children, the bulk of which are shouldered by the wife, and the wife also bears the opportunity cost of lost child labor if her children are sent to school. As noted above, this view is something of a caricature and is less generally valid than one might have supposed. We present additional evidence below that suggests the salience of child costs to male attitudes on family limitation. Nevertheless, it is clear that many items of expense are not borne by men and the financial burden of childrearing relative to resources is doubtless far greater for women.[31]

The implications of polygyny for fertility also deserve further comment. Statistical analyses show that the fertility of women in polygynous unions is often little different from, and sometimes lower than, the fertility of women in monogamous unions (e.g., Goldman and Montgomery, 1990). Indeed, Adegbola et al. (1991) report for Lagos that a wife in a polygynous relationship possesses a certain amount of leverage in relation to a husband's demands for more children, in that she can ask him to seek out his other wives. Evidently the importance of polygyny does not consist solely in statistical differentials in fertility.

One area deserving of exploration concerns the implications of polygyny for the fertility of monogamous marriages. A consistent theme in qualitative research on Nigeria (Guyer, 1988b; Adegbola et al., 1991) is that continued childbearing demonstrates a woman's continued commitment to the marriage and ensures a continued flow of resources from her husband. A woman who contemplates family limitation must face the possibility that any interruption in childbearing may signal, both to the husband and to his lineage, that she has effectively abandoned the marriage. The family may begin to look for another wife for the husband, and the situation may end in divorce or polygyny. To forestall this possibility, a woman in a monogamous marriage may persuade herself to continue childbearing. The next child becomes, as it were, one more move in the strategic game for resources played out between husband and wife.

---

[31]Guyer (1988a) finds that among the Beti of Cameroon, women retain only one-fourth of their cash incomes for personal use, the remainder going primarily to purchase food for the family. Men, by contrast, retain nearly three-quarters of their cash incomes, after expenditures on housing, school fees, and bride-price. Despite their lower incomes, women contribute two-thirds of the total household cash expenditures for food and routine supplies.

Fapohunda and Todaro (1988) argue that as a rule, men take responsibility for household "overhead expenses," of which rent would be an example, that do not appreciably vary with family size. (School fees present an exception.) By contrast, women have obligations that expose them more directly to the full marginal costs of childrearing.

PROSPECTS FOR CHANGE

The aim of the discussion to this point has been to illuminate the features of African fertility regimes that support high fertility. What has this sifting of the literature revealed as the principal factors?

No simple answer presents itself, but we would argue that important clues are to be found in the multiplicity of roles and decision units in which a wife and husband participate in sub-Saharan Africa, and in the relative transience and impermanence of marital relations with any given spouse. Bleek (1987:148-149) describes the dilemma of family limitation exceedingly well:

> Why do rural Akan women rarely plan the number of their children? . . . For a woman, it is extremely hard to estimate the pros and cons of having a few or many children. It depends on how long her marriage will last; how many times she will marry; the financial position of her husband(s); what conjugal responsibilities her husband(s) or lover(s) will accept; how many of her children will be staying with her; how many children of others will be put in her care; how much help her lineage will give; how successful she will be in earning her own income; how much help her children will offer; how successful her children will be at school and in achieving a good economic position; how healthy her children will be, and how many of them will survive to adulthood . . . . The aggregate "decision" in such a complex and contradictory situation is most likely inertia.

Thus the eventual benefits inherent in family limitation are enveloped in a cloud of uncertainty, which itself arises from the very complexity and multiplicity of roles in African social organization. The greater this element of uncertainty is, the greater is the importance of risk aversion and adherence to norms in decisions about fertility.

Various other aspects of social organization also weigh against family planning. Family planning has the potential to upset the customary balance of social control between men and women. A worry often expressed by men is that access to family planning will give women freedom to act with greater autonomy and possibly behave promiscuously. (See, for instance, McGinn et al. 1989a, on Burkina Faso.) The weakness of the conjugal bond inhibits discussion about fertility in general, raises mutual suspicion, and renders less likely any mutual agreement between the spouses about family planning.[32]

---

[32]Mott and Mott (1985) find that for the Yoruba of Ondo State, three-quarters of women and men (separately interviewed) reported never having discussed how many children to have and who should make the decision with their spouse. Our analysis of 12 Demographic and Health Surveys found that the percentage of married women who had discussed family planning with their partners over the previous year ranged from 18 to 36 in western Africa (Mali, Senegal,

The duty to perpetuate the lineage and the fear of barrenness may generate a deep ambivalence regarding modern reversible methods of family planning. In many African settings the notion of reversibility does not seem to have been well understood. The pill and the intrauterine device are commonly believed to pose a permanent threat to the woman's physical capacity to reproduce (Caldwell and Caldwell, 1987). Men in Burkina Faso believe that if a woman uses contraceptives, she will not be able to have children again; the idea that modern methods could be employed for spacing purposes is largely absent (McGinn et al., 1989a). These fears could be viewed as a simple problem of misinformation regarding modern methods, or they could be seen as surface expressions of deeper fears.[33]

Voluntary sterilization, in such an atmosphere, would appear to have very limited potential. A study by Chibalonza et al. (1989:276) for Zaire indicated that even women who were currently using reversible contraceptive methods, cited pressures from the husband's family as weighing against sterilization: "The members of the husband's family will come to complain that you aren't having any children and to influence him toward a divorce . . . . They will oblige him to take a second wife, even though the two of you were in agreement about the operation before it was done." For the woman, sterilization not only puts her present marriage under risk, but also closes off one possibility for forging economic links with other men in the future.

Given these concerns, what forces could be expected to disturb the high-fertility regime? What features of economic and social organization might bring the benefits of family limitation into sharper relief and thereby prompt a transition to lower fertility?

From the evidence we present below—admittedly qualitative and only suggestive in nature—we nevertheless draw one clear theme: The supports for high fertility are not as strong as they might seem, given rapid change and even crisis in contemporary economic circumstances. Indeed, the evidence goes so far as to suggest an important role for female sterilization in Africa, unlikely as that may seem under the traditional calculus. We consider several factors in turn.

Liberia, Ghana, Togo, and Ondo State) and from 37 to 65 percent in eastern Africa (Sudan, Kenya, Uganda, and Burundi), and reached a high of 70 percent in Botswana and Zimbabwe. A multivariate analysis showed that discussion is more likely in urban than in rural areas, and increases with the education of the woman and the education of her partner.

[33]In the study by McGinn et al. (1989a), men expressed generally positive attitudes to family planning in focus group discussions, which would support the misinformation interpretation.

Land

In many regions of sub-Saharan Africa, increases in population density, and consequent reductions in the viability of agricultural holdings, may have reduced the value of farm labor. Land density was among the most powerful motivations for the rapid fertility decline in Thailand (Knodel et al., 1987). Its scarcity motivated Thai parents to invest in child schooling, substituting a new form of economic asset for the land they had previously passed down to their children. Although land scarcity is not an issue across the whole of the sub-Saharan region, there are pockets of high density in which a lack of land may emerge as a motivating factor in fertility control (e.g., in Rwanda or Burundi).

Kenya provides a case in point. Bertrand et al. (1989) found lack of land cited as a prominent motive for family limitation among their Kenyan respondents. Hammerslough's (1991b) focus group studies and analysis of Kenyan Demographic and Health Survey (DHS) data support this view. A consistent theme in focus group discussions was that "the land is getting smaller" as rural population density rises.

Interestingly, land scarcity in parts of Kenya has been accompanied more broadly by a change in the nature of land ownership. The traditional system, wherein land was controlled by communities and lineages, has today been largely replaced by a system of individual land ownership due to government resettlement and title registration schemes. The greater part of agricultural land and a significant fraction of pastoral land are now registered as private freehold (Frank and McNicoll, 1987). As Robinson (1992:456) notes, this change to private freeholdings of land "internalizes the economic costs and benefits of many activities and also the decisions including family size within the conjugal co-resident family unit." However, as Frank and McNicoll (1987) point out, the land titles have been granted almost universally to men. This policy may have removed one traditional source of economic security for women, perhaps increasing the need for women to rely on their children. Hence, the net fertility effect due to the transformation of land ownership in Kenya remains uncertain.

Schooling and Child Costs

Perhaps the fundamental threat to the sub-Saharan high-fertility rationale has to do with changes in the perceived costs of rearing children and, in particular, with the view that schooling is an increasingly necessary aspect of childrearing, yet so costly that it renders large family sizes impractical. Caldwell and Caldwell (1987:422) have expressed skepticism that the quantity-quality trade-off can be the decisive factor in a sub-Saharan fertility transition:

So weak [is the link between a man's reproductive decisions and his expenses], that there is little parallel to the situation in some other parts of the Third World where educated children will ultimately benefit parents but where there is such a financial crunch during the process of education that numbers must be restricted to ensure that any are sufficiently educated and adequately employed.

Yet in the same article, Caldwell and Caldwell (1987:431) acknowledge that relative prices underwent dramatic change in the 1980s; for Nigeria, they note that

the 1980s have witnessed growing unemployment, a decline in real wages, the imposition of school fees in all southern states, and most recently an exchange rate adjustment that has trebled the price of imported goods. Throughout the country there is an emphasis in conversation and in the media on the cost of children that encompasses all social classes and that would have been unthinkable only a few years ago.

Interestingly, changes in child costs seem to have seized the attention of men as well as women, a phenomenon that could not have occurred if men, as is so often alleged, do little to share in the costs of childrearing. Robinson (1992:450), writing on Kenya, notes that men express a "keen awareness of the rising cost of children, especially education costs. They also indicated acute awareness of the growing difficulties in providing for large families and agreed that times were changing." Economic pressures were also the most-discussed issue in focus group discussions among men in Burkina Faso (McGinn et al., 1989a). The much-repeated refrain in these discussions was that couples should have children only according to their means, a view that was also emphasized in the Lagos focus groups of Adegbola et al. (1991).

It is very likely that such economic concerns have affected male attitudes across the sub-Saharan region. As Robinson (1992:450) observes for Kenyan men, the picture at present is one of

inconsistency and contradiction among various male attitudes. They express "macho" values, but are worried about economic considerations. In short, the study shows traditional values under attack by modern economic considerations.

Economic Crises and Their Aftermath

If births are indeed analogous to the normal goods of economists, it should not be surprising that over the short term in Africa, income contractions associated with the turmoil of the 1980s might exert an antinatalist effect.[34]   As two Nigerian focus group participants reflected on the structural adjustment program (SAP) in place since the mid-1980s (Adegbola et al., 1991):

> Without any problem of childbearing I don't see the reason why you should do family planning. [But] when there is not enough food one would be compelled to stop. So if you say you will not plan your children, your pocket will plan it now [laughter] . . . . There is SAP in Nigeria and this makes us to plan our families. [Yoruba woman, aged 50+]

This antinatalist pressure is perhaps keenest in urban areas, where changes in the costs of food and other necessities have often been dramatic over the past decade.[35]

If fertility is "normal" in respect to income, however, one would expect a resumption of economic growth to be accompanied by a resumption in family building.   As Chapter 3 has argued, the basis for a longer-term fertility decline would then be found only in fundamental changes in relative prices, aspirations, and forms of social organization.

One possible change concerns the extent to which the costs of childrearing and schooling can continue to be shared by kin networks.   Lesthaeghe (1989a) speculates that in times of general economic crisis the conjugal family is left more isolated and dependent on its own resources than before, and that where assistance from relatives is given there will be harder bargaining over the terms of assistance.   This view is echoed in the comments of focus group participants in Lagos (Adegbola et al., 1991):

> I can't render help to anybody now not to talk of someone else doing same to me. Because I have not eaten, talk less of rendering any help. If anybody eats and has a left-over, that is when he eats and remembers his relatives. My own idea is that everybody, presently with the Nigerian situation, everybody takes care of their responsibilities and mind their own business because in case where my own child and that of his brother falls sick, he'll mind his own business and take care of his own child before taking care of another person's. [Yoruba woman, aged 20-49]

Okojie's (1991) findings for Kwara and Bendel states of Nigeria are similar.   Her respondents maintained that in the current economic crisis, one

---

[34]For views similar to those expressed below, see Ladipo (1987) on economic circumstances and motivations for family planning in Ife, and Okojie (1991) for Kwara and Bendel states in Nigeria.

[35]As Chapter 3 notes, little is known about the effects of structural adjustment in rural areas. To the extent that the increased prices farmers receive for their crops increase the value of child farm labor, one might expect structural adjustment to exert a pronatalist effect in rural areas; but high prices might exert an antinatalist effect in urban areas. See Working Group on Demographic Effects of Economic and Social Reversals (1993) for more discussion.

should not add any additional burdens to one's relatives through child fostering.

There are also indications that the perceived need for joint conjugal decision making is greater[36] in difficult economic times (Adegbola et al., 1991):

> You see nowadays, you cannot leave everything for the man. The two should join hands because things are very difficult now. I mean the (economic) situation of the country is very hard. So, you can't say the husband should or the woman should take full responsibility. So two of them should join hands and do everything accordingly because it is their child. [Igbo man, aged 20-49]

These changes in kin relations and conjugal decision making may well persist into the postcrisis era.[37]

Contraceptive Innovators

Yet how are couples to effect the change to family limitation in the face of opposition from lineage members and elders who may not fully comprehend the new economic environment? Here a study of female sterilization in Kenya (Bertrand et al., 1989) is instructive.[38] In some contrast to the earlier discussion of sterilization in Zaire, Kenyan women and men regard the economic burdens of large families as an important consideration, and the motivations of acceptors of tubal ligation were frankly economic in nature: Respondents mentioned a lack of land, financial constraints, and the expenditures required for children's schooling and daily necessities as being among their major motivations. Regarding the influence of the ex-

---

[36]It is interesting to note that the Ghanaian male school teachers studied by Oppong (1987b:174) were situated in difficult economic circumstances relative to their expectations: Within this group, contraceptive users "differed from non-users in several aspects of their familial roles and relationships. Greater equality and flexibility in conjugal roles, more marked tendencies towards closure of the conjugal family or a cutting-down of obligations and exchanges associated with kin ties, and more individual assumption of parental tasks and responsibilities, were characteristic features." Perhaps it is this coincidence of stressful economic circumstances and western-influenced views on conjugal obligations that facilitates family limitation.

[37]Other changes in kin relations may also occur. For instance, Lesthaeghe (1989a) speculates that the educational function of child fostering may be hit hard by rising costs and diminishing prospective returns to education, not only for the biological parents but also for the kin network. The implications for fertility, however, are unclear.

[38]Sterilization is being used here as an extreme example that may shed light on more moderate decisions regarding contraception. However, it may be mentioned in passing that the implications of voluntary sterilization for fertility levels in Kenya are considerable, even if sterilization takes place only at the high parities. Frank (1987), relying on 1984 data, estimates that a stop-at-six policy would reduce Kenyan fertility by some 34 percent.

tended family, which was a decisive factor weighing against sterilization in Zaire, the Kenyan response was rather different. There was a widespread perception among both men and women that the husband's family would be opposed to tubal ligation, "but the solution to this was simply not to inform them. There was strong consensus that this was a private matter between husband and wife" (Bertrand et al., 1989:286).

The results of Adegbola et al. (1991) for Lagos are similar. When asked about the role of the extended family in matters of family size and contraceptive use, a young Yoruba woman replied:

> What I know is that the husband's relatives must not have a knowledge of this issue. We young ones of nowadays that have just gotten married do family planning and if the husband's relatives know about it, it is the husband's mother who will look for another wife for her son. She will call her son and say "This your wife does not want to give birth again when I am still alive. I should look for someone else for you." They will cause confusion between the husband and wife. It is not a proper thing to let the husband's relatives know about it, neither is it a proper thing to let the wife's relatives know about. Both relatives must not intervene.

Thus, contraceptive innovators are more than aware of the pressures from the extended family that can be brought to bear upon them, but can themselves devise ways of evading such pressures.

Summary

We must emphasize in closing this section that many of the arguments just made, which suggest the possibility of fertility decline and increases in contraceptive method use, remain speculative and are grounded not in large and statistically representative samples but in small qualitative or anecdotal studies. Moreover, the factors that we have emphasized do not operate with equal force across Africa.[39] They are surely more important in urban areas and among the educated, and doubtless vary considerably by social and economic circumstances.

Furthermore, some observers make very different predictions regarding the effects of economic crisis and modernization on fertility. For instance, Frank and McNicoll (1987) argue that far from reinforcing joint conjugal decision making and helping to internalize costs and benefits, economic

---

[39]In addition, we do not expect these factors to have much effect on groups affected by involuntary sterility, because they may not have been able to meet their past fertility goals. As a result, these groups will likely be less receptive to family planning. Evidence from Zaire, for example, suggests that communities with historically high rates of primary sterility have experienced smaller fertility declines than communities in which fertility has been very high (Sala-Diakanda, 1980).

modernization in Kenya will more likely serve to further disassociate husbands and wives. Frank and McNicoll speculate that family systems may increasingly depart from a lineage basis without ever becoming more nuclear and conjugal in orientation.[40] They envision a future for Kenya in which family structure comes to resemble the Caribbean mode of visiting unions and spousal autonomy.

Boserup (1985) has also questioned the logic by which reductions in kin solidarity (as evidenced in child fostering, for instance) are expressed in lower fertility. She notes that in Bangladesh, a lack of wider kin support mechanisms and a greater dependence of parents on their children are advanced as explanations for continuing high fertility.

The principal theme that emerges from the discussion above is the great variation across sub-Saharan Africa in receptivity to fertility limitation and family planning. In some groups the high-fertility rationale remains largely intact. For others, however, the current economic situation has uncovered a demand for postponement or delay in family building, if not for lower lifetime fertility. And in certain selected subpopulations, principally in urban areas and among those better educated or with higher educational aspirations for their children, the profound changes of the past decade in incomes, relative prices, and social organization have produced a desire for lower lifetime fertility.

LOCAL SOCIAL ORGANIZATION AND
THE DIFFUSION OF FAMILY PLANNING

We have argued that among other factors, the economic crisis of the 1980s in parts of Africa has presented programs to increase contraceptive use with a window of opportunity. Yet as noted in Chapter 3, the irony of the situation is that the same economic forces that have opened the window on family planning have also reduced the governmental resources available to exploit the opening in settings where fertility decline is a policy goal.

The challenge for policy in such settings, then, is how to seize on the themes and motivations brought out by economic stagnation and crisis in a cost-efficient way, recognizing that initially the appeal of family limitation will not be in evidence across the full socioeconomic spectrum, and even the appeal of birth spacing via modern contraception may be resisted in some traditional quarters. One proposal, advanced by Lesthaeghe (1989a),

---

[40]Lesthaeghe (1989c) notes that in Lesotho and Botswana, weakening of traditional marriage patterns led not to increasing conjugality, but rather to a greater reliance by women on their own kinship groups and less reliance on husbands.

is to exploit the concept of diffusion and the potential presented by sub-Saharan forms of local social organization.

It is clear that the provision of information and the social legitimation of modern contraception will be crucial to the prospects for service delivery. Given the budgetary constraints and limitations of personnel with which sub-Saharan governments must cope, national delivery strategies must tap a variety of local social networks, including the private for-profit sector and nongovernmental organizations. What can the existing forms of social organization contribute?

A great variety of local groups and networks exist. Some of these grass-roots networks have their own roots in precolonial dual-sex systems;[41] others derive from the colonial era or have a more recent vintage. The following types of groups are of interest: (1) traditional birth attendants; (2) modern-day counterparts of the female secret societies in West Africa;[42] (3) producer cooperatives and other modern-day descendants of traditional local work parties;[43] (4) occupational groups, the most important of these

---

[41]The dual-sex systems described by Lesthaeghe (1989a) are cases in which female social-political organizations are a mirror image of male organizations. There were female counterparts to the male paramount chief or regional chiefs, and female counterparts descending to the level of local work parties. Such groups would have a "queen," for instance, at the top of market women's associations. In middle, eastern, and southern Africa, both male and female branches of the dual-sex system are thought to have been much less developed. Thus, in these areas, greater relative importance was accorded to associations introduced during the colonial period: churches and government-sponsored associations.

See Arhin (1983:93) on the traditional dual-sex system among the Akan of Ghana, where "female stools complemented the hierarchy of male stools." As in Nigeria (Okonjo, 1983), the British disrupted this system, failing to recognize women on their chief lists or as members of the native authority councils and courts. Such also appears to have been the case in Côte d'Ivoire for the Baule (Etienne, 1983).

[42]For example, in Liberia, Sierra Leone, Guinea, and Côte d'Ivoire, these societies were powerful in matters of procreation, infant and maternal health, education, local politics, and religion, and have been enlisted in formal health projects (Lesthaeghe, 1989a). Wipper (1984:74) notes that older women from the powerful land-owning lineages in Sande tended to be the most important midwives, and there was an important element of patronage: "Women prefer to patronize midwives of powerful lineages and those who occupy important leadership positions in the Sande society because they believe these women possess the most powerful medicine which will protect their own life and their baby's life. Women are highly dependent on the midwives' knowledge of obstetrics and gynecology and this knowledge is jealously guarded." Steady (1981:33), considering the Bondo or Sande secret societies in Sierra Leone and Liberia, says that "even in areas such as Freetown where, on account of urbanization much of the sacred aspect of Bondo societies is diluted rendering them more like voluntary associations and social agencies, they still serve to regulate relationships between the sexes through the maintenance of sororal bonds."

[43]Ladipo (1987) discusses family planning as a component of a women's cooperative in Nigeria.

being the western African market women's associations;[44] (5) mutual aid societies and rotating credit networks;[45] (6) a plethora of colonial-era associations including Christian missions, youth associations (Girl Guides and Boy Scouts, YMCA and YWCA), and church women's groups, the latter being particularly vigorous in eastern and southern Africa;[46] and (7) local associations with roots in government initiatives.[47]

Lesthaeghe (1989a:498) argues that with regard to family planning, the "main function of grass-roots networks is to discuss the subject and to legitimize contraception in the process, thereby eventually developing their own referral system, more than in their direct financial sponsoring of family planning clinics."

National Female Political Associations

Lesthaeghe (1989a) is skeptical about the family planning potential of national-level female political associations. He notes that these are often dominated by elites, who are widely divorced in interests and social status from the grass-roots associations that operate at the local level.[48] Furthermore, local associations may strive to maintain a respectful distance from national organizations. The local associations have "an interest in coming to terms with current regimes (especially if some of their activities are sponsored by governments), but also an interest in never becoming too closely identified with the political powers of the moment" (Lesthaeghe, 1989a:497).

---

[44]Lesthaeghe (1989a) notes that in eastern and middle Africa, by contrast to western Africa, trading is done primarily by men, and such powerful female groups are lacking.

[45]These include the esusu savings and credit groups of the Yoruba; their counterparts among the Ga (Robertson, 1976); rotating marriage and childbirth associations or associations that fund pilgrimages to Mecca, as among the Dioula of northern Côte d'Ivoire (Lewis, 1976). Wipper (1984) also mentions prostitutes' associations as mutual aid associations in Zaire, Ghana, and Nigeria, and beer-brewers' associations in Nairobi.

[46]Wipper (1984) discusses Protestant church associations in Sierra Leone (also see Steady, 1976); there are counterpart Muslim associations in Freetown, with interests in mutual aid. Muslim women's associations of Mombasa (descendants of the dance associations of the late nineteenth century and the colonial era) fall in this category, since they have taken interest in child welfare, adult literacy, and so on. See Strobel (1976) for a historical account.

[47]For instance, the so-called corn mill societies of Cameroon were government initiated in the 1950s; these first began around corn mills rented to the village by government and later expanded their functions (Wipper, 1984).

[48]Lesthaeghe's point is illustrated by the history of the largest women's association in Kenya, Maendeleo ya Wanawake (Progress for Women), as recounted in Wipper (1984). An initial militancy and close attention to the needs of its rural clubs degenerated as positions in the association began to be taken up by elite wives. A similar fate has met Muslim women's groups in Mombasa (Strobel, 1976).

Market Associations

Certain creative efforts have been made to tap the potential of local-level market women's associations in Ibadan, Ilorin, Lagos, and Accra (Center for Population and Family Health, 1989, 1990a-c; Webb et al., 1991). These market-based distribution projects employed market traders, with requisite training in family planning service delivery, to retail contraceptives in the market, usually (although not always) in combination with other health treatments such as oral rehydration therapy and treatment for malaria. The projects were all of a pilot nature, but displayed considerable potential (see Chapter 5).

In the case of Ibadan, market associations are a relatively new phenomenon; they may have arisen in response to growing local government intervention in market affairs and a need for an organization to represent traders' interests vis-à-vis external bodies. The market associations in Accra were predominantly women's associations, headed by a market "queen," whereas in Ibadan men tended to dominate the upper reaches of the organization.

It proved important that vendors of contraceptives be seen as legitimate agents of a major health institution (in the Ibadan case, it was the University College Hospital), no doubt because of the prevalence in western Africa of fake drugs and quackery. The research on contraceptive sales showed that the greatest proportion of clients were fellow traders rather than customers of the market, and many sales were made outside the market to neighbors of traders. Thus, the Ibadan project generated considerable diffusion of information and delivery of services, often through routes that were not at all anticipated by the researchers. In the Lagos project, the scheme was conceived as a two-way referral system, whereby private and government clinics would inform their clients about the marketing program, and at the market, those clients with problems, contraindications, or in search of other methods were told of the clinic system.

Local Women's Groups

Watkins (1991) and Hammerslough (1991a) have begun to explore whether local women's groups in Africa can provide a vehicle for the diffusion of family planning information. Hammerslough's analyses of the Kenyan DHS show that women who are members of such groups are more likely to know about modern methods of family planning and are also more likely to have used such methods. But the policy content of Hammerslough's analysis goes deeper. It appears that women who are not themselves group members, but who reside in communities in which such groups are important, also are more likely to know and to use contraception. This pattern is precisely what one expects to see in a setting where the diffusion of information is taking place.

As any one socioeconomic group comes to adopt innovative family planning behavior, knowledge of the new behavior begins to spread via what are termed "weak ties" to other socioeconomic strata. To the extent that the initial adopters serve as reference groups for those contemplating innovative behavior, a diffusion process is set in motion that may promise a broader adoption of contraception. The key point is that a diffusion process may very well begin with a few selected socioeconomic subgroups, but the process of social interchange extends the knowledge of innovative behavior along the links or weak ties among socioeconomic groups. Individuals must still evaluate, with reference to their own individual socioeconomic situations, the advisability of family limitation. That is, enhanced awareness does not translate automatically into contraceptive adoption. But to the extent that contraceptive adopters reduce the uncertainty surrounding this new behavior, and provide a concrete demonstration as to its benefits and costs, the broad base of attitudes and preferences concerning contraceptive use may begin to shift.

As far as we are aware, no one has yet investigated the role of men's groups in regard to diffusion. Yet study after study has emphasized the need to enlist African men in family limitation, and there is ample evidence of male receptivity to the economic rationale for limitation that the current economic situation has brought to prominence. Hence, this would appear to be a promising avenue for research and program development.

Local Government

Some observers remain doubtful about the likely role that African governments can play in the delivery of contraceptive services. Part of the issue is that state formation is so recent in much of sub-Saharan Africa, even by comparison to Asia; also, even within the complex and hierarchial African states that developed in precolonial times, there was little sustained bureaucratic penetration by the larger state to the local level (Hyden, 1990). Nor are African nations now in a position to use family planning as a part of the apparatus of nation building, in contrast to India, Indonesia, Korea, Singapore, and the Peoples's Republic of China as noted by Lesthaeghe (1989a).[49] Evidently, then, a key issue in the delivery of services will involve the decentralization of government authority and the devolution of

---

[49]Lesthaeghe (1989a:488) notes one interesting exception, in that "the present, allegedly strong program performance in Zimbabwe is a part of the ZANU government extending and consolidating its control over the country."

responsibilities to local levels, which may be more receptive and perhaps more flexible in responding to local concerns (Frank and McNicoll, 1987). The case of Nigeria will bear watching because there the national government has given great emphasis to the creation of local political and economic structures.

Summary

In short, it is possible that local organizations constituted for other purposes could be enlisted in the diffusion of family planning information and services in Africa. The process of involving such organizations in family planning efforts can only happen gradually, and no doubt will be met in many cases with political resistance or indifference. Yet as outlined in Chapter 5, the 1980s witnessed a striking change in the receptivity of certain African populations and governments to family planning, and the possibilities for tapping the energies of local organizations deserve continued exploration.

CONCLUSION

An analysis of African social organization clearly points to several factors supporting high fertility, namely, the high value attached to the perpetuation of the lineage; the importance of children as a means of gaining access to resources, particularly land; the use of kinship networks to share the costs and benefits of children, primarily through child fostering; and the weak nature of conjugal bonds. Changing economic circumstances, however, such as growing scarcity of land in areas with high population density, increased schooling and child costs, and perhaps deteriorating economies, are challenging this high-fertility rationale. These changing circumstances are resulting in lower fertility desires among certain populations, particularly those with high levels of education or with high educational aspirations for their children and those living in urban areas. The high-fertility rationale has not yet disappeared from the scene, to be sure, but it is certainly giving way. Thus, our summary judgment, hedged as it must be with qualifications and caveats, is that sub-Saharan Africa is entering a new era of fertility control.

5

Family Planning Programs and Policies

To concentrate primarily on cultural and socioeconomic barriers as a main reason for low contraceptive prevalence in the African region belies the fact that small, well-managed projects and programs throughout the subcontinent have been achieving prevalence rates of 20 percent or more in recent years.[1] These include projects in Muslim and Catholic francophone countries (e.g., projects in Matadi in Zaire, Ruhengeri in Rwanda, Niamey in Niger), Muslim Sudan, and a host of anglophone countries (Kenya, Ghana, and others). Although it may be argued that some of these projects achieved such prevalence levels in the more educated and urbanized sectors of society, this pattern of uptake was also common in Asia and Latin America in the earlier days of family planning. In any event, although none of the projects discussed in this chapter were located in the deepest rural reaches, some such as Ruhengeri were outside urban areas. It is instructive to examine those programs that are associated with increased contraceptive use in the last decade, as well as situations in which little program support and poor project effectiveness are associated with low prevalence rates.

A review of program directions and potentials is particularly called for in this period of economic retrenchment in Africa. As reviewed in Chapters 3 and 4, economic factors may have substantial effects on the acceptance of

---

[1]Programs influence prevalence in two ways: They meet existing demand and stimulate interest in the adoption of family planning among nonusers.

family planning. There is growing utilization of family planning services in Africa, and the first indications of fertility decline were observed in several African countries in the 1980s. The future role of programs in sustaining and increasing the rate of contraceptive utilization and the lessons learned regarding factors necessary to maintain viable programs are ripe for review. This chapter describes the historical development of population policies and contraceptive services in Africa, reviews the contributions of private versus public sector delivery, and discusses future prospects for family planning programs in the region.

THE AFRICAN CONTEXT FOR POPULATION AND FAMILY PLANNING PROGRAMS

The sub-Saharan context for family planning information and service delivery differs from that of Asia, Latin America, or North Africa. Important factors in sub-Saharan Africa, include weak policy support, relatively late program implementation, generally inadequate resources, weak absorptive capacity, and interregional disparities, each of which is discussed below.

Weak Policy Support

Of the first ten governments to promulgate policies supporting family planning and slower population growth, only one—Mauritius—was in the African region.[2] However, due to its unique cultural and geographic characteristics, Mauritius is not given emphasis in this volume. Until recently, political and policy support for family planning demonstrated by African governments was cautious at best. However, such support is increasing. In her analysis of policy support, Heckel (1986, 1990) indicated that by 1986, 13 sub-Saharan countries had established explicit population policies that encouraged slower population growth, 3 of them in separate policy documents and 10 as part of national economic or social development plans. Ten of these statements emphasized the need to reduce or stabilize rapid rates of population growth but did not set specific targets.

As of 1991, some 20 African governments had adopted population policies and established government agencies responsible for coordinating policies or programs (Roudi, 1991). Regardless of the status of their population policies (or lack thereof), almost all African countries now provide

---

[2]In 1951, India became the first country worldwide to have an official population policy; by 1965, five other Asian countries plus Fiji, Egypt, Turkey, and Mauritius had followed suit.

either direct or indirect support for family planning programs (United Nations, 1989b; Population Reference Bureau, 1990).

The rationale supporting policies has varied from country to country. In Kenya, the pressure on land resources has been highlighted (see Chapter 4 for discussion), whereas Botswana has noted unemployment and a high dependency ratio (Heckel, 1986).

Relatively Late Program Implementation

Although early family planning activities were initiated during the colonial period in much of Africa (particularly in English dependencies), post colonial implementation of programs in the 1960s was slow due primarily to low government recognition of the need for services and fluctuating government support, insufficient external assistance, opposition from the Roman Catholic Church in some regions, logistical problems, and lack of trained manpower (United Nations Population Fund, 1983). By 1969, only five continental African countries, Benin, The Gambia, Ghana, Kenya, and Zimbabwe (12 percent of the total countries discussed in this report, among them containing 10 percent of the African population), had officially committed themselves to the initiation of family planning programs (World Bank, 1985). As of 1991, only three had carried through on this commitment to any substantial degree. During the same period, 1969 to 1991, three of the five North African countries and all of the most populous, as well as many smaller, countries of Asia had established family planning programs. Moreover, although a few nongovernmental family planning organizations were active in Africa as early as the 1950s, most programs were not initiated until the end of the 1970s or later.

Not only did family planning programs generally start later in Africa, the strength of government commitment to existing programs has tended to lag behind that of other regions. Assessments of national family planning activities and family planning effort, based on contraceptive availability, policy statements, and program activity, indicate that in the early 1980s, only one sub-Saharan country, Mauritius, demonstrated strong program commitment; the other countries of the region were judged to have either weak programs or no programs at all. In contrast, more than half the countries of North Africa, Asia, and Latin America were deemed to have moderate or strong programs (Ross et al., 1988; United Nations, 1989a). A 1986 World Bank review noted that only Zimbabwe provided substantial access to family planning outside urban areas; although Botswana and Kenya had programs underway, the review indicated that "access by potential clients remained limited. Countries such as Ghana, Liberia, Malawi, Nigeria, Rwanda and Tanzania had all started programs but had made only limited progress to date." In the rest of Africa, "what services exist are provided in limited areas by small nongovernmental organizations that are often poorly funded" (World Bank, 1986:5).

Since then, family planning programs in Africa have been improving at a faster rate than those of other regions. In their assessment of policy and program strengths,[3] Mauldin and Ross (1991) indicated that between 1982 and 1989, the sub-Saharan countries showed the greatest improvement in program effort of all regions. However, the overall score for family planning programs in Africa still lagged well behind that in Latin America or Asia. Mauldin and Ross concluded that of 38 African countries, one (Botswana) had a strong program; five (Ghana, Kenya, Mauritius, Zambia, and Zimbabwe) had moderate programs; and the remaining countries had weak, very weak, or no programs. Of countries worldwide in the weak or no-program category, Africa accounted for 60 percent. Poor contraceptive availability continued to represent a substantial program weakness in the region (Mauldin and Ross, 1991).

Generally Inadequate Resources

Although it is difficult to obtain accurate information, available data suggest that per capita funding for family planning activities in the African region is less than half of that in Asia and Latin America. In most sub-Saharan countries, the annual per capita expenditure (government and donor sources combined) is less than $0.20 (Ross et al., 1988). Such disparities have long existed: In 1980, only four African countries provided more than $0.50 per capita in public expenditures for population programs; more than half the countries in North Africa and Asia provided this amount or more (World Bank, 1985). Resource disparities become even more important if we consider that per capita income, and thus personal resources available for the private purchase of health and family planning services, are substantially lower in Africa than in other regions.

Weak Absorptive Capacity

Merely increasing the funds for family planning services would not in itself address African resource problems. Absorptive capacity in the region is weak. To give but one example, the availability of health personnel, who may be expected to play a key role in contraceptive distribution, is much lower in sub-Saharan Africa than in other regions. World Bank data from

---

[3]The calculation of program effort is based on 30 items that fall into four broad categories: policy and stage setting activities, service and service-related activities, record keeping and evaluation, and availability and accessibility of family planning supplies and services (Mauldin and Ross, 1991).

the mid-1980s indicate that of the 33 sub-Saharan countries for which data were available, half had fewer than one physician per 15,000 population, and almost all had fewer than one per 5,000 population (World Bank, 1990b). In all other regions combined, only two countries (Nepal and Bhutan) had a physician/population ratio of 1/15,000 or less, and countries with fewer than one physician per 5,000 population were in the minority (World Bank, 1990b). Although less extreme, the same differential held for nursing personnel (World Bank, 1990b). Increasing resources for service delivery in Africa will require long-term emphasis on human capital and infrastructure development, as well as the development of strategies to increase available financing.

Interregional Disparities

Substantial interregional disparities in family planning program development exist within Africa. Historically, family planning programs have been more prevalent in anglophone than in francophone sub-Saharan countries. In their review of family planning programs in francophone countries up to 1974, Gauthier and Brown (1975a) indicated that none of them had a policy aimed at reducing the rate of population growth. By the mid-1970s, all the anglophone countries of the region, except for Somalia and Malawi, had private associations promoting family planning, whereas only four francophone countries had such associations (Gauthier and Brown, 1975a,b). Francophone African countries have generally been substantially more conservative in the promotion of contraception, whether their populations are predominantly Catholic or Muslim. Almost 10 years after the Gauthier and Brown analysis, Faruqee and Gulhati singled out six continental anglophone countries as making substantial progress in family planning program and policy development, but only one francophone country, Senegal; the latter was deemed to have the weakest policy and program support of the group (Faruqee and Gulhati, 1983).

In a number of francophone countries, a 1920 law based on the old French legal code (hereafter referred as the French law) still prohibits distribution of contraceptive supplies and information (United Nations, 1989b). Although the law is generally not strictly enforced, it exerts a negative influence on program development. Many francophone countries also have highly centralized, physician-based public sector service delivery, and regulations that specifically prohibit the provision of contraceptives by personnel other than doctors. Because the ratio of population to physicians is high in most sub-Saharan countries, as indicated above, such regulations severely restrict family planning availability. Moreover, as discussed below, community-based distribution, private sector delivery, and social marketing have all been introduced later in the francophone countries and continue to be less common.

Contraceptive prevalence rates in francophone countries are lower than those of their anglophone counterparts (see Chapter 2). That this difference is due primarily to programmatic rather than cultural factors is suggested by the fact that contraceptive prevalence in areas of Niger, Zaire, and Rwanda, where effective service delivery has been initiated, has risen to rates comparable to those of well-managed programs in anglophone countries (Direction de la Santé Familiale and Population Communication Services, 1989; McGinn, 1990; Wawer et al., 1990; Bertrand et al., 1993).

The weak policy support, relatively late program implementation, generally inadequate resources, weak absorptive capacity, and interregional disparities in Africa indicate the problematic milieu within which family planning projects and programs have operated, and suggest reasons for the pattern of success in family planning programs or relative lack thereof seen in different countries.

INTERNATIONAL AND REGIONAL INFLUENCES ON POPULATION POLICY DEVELOPMENT

A number of factors have influenced the gradual move toward government policies more favorable to family planning in Africa (Goliber, 1989). The rapidity of population growth has been documented authoritatively in a series of national censuses.[4] The degree to which rapid population growth is outstripping growth in social infrastructure (e.g., educational and health facilities) and job creation, has been brought home to governments through basic sociodemographic and economic analyses such as presentations by the Futures Group conducted to date in more than 20 African countries (Middleberg, personal communication, 1991).

The importance of external influences on policy development cannot be underestimated. In the early 1960s, the U.S. Congress passed legislation endorsing population research because of the perceived effect of population growth on economic development (Piotrow, 1973). U.S. foreign policy emphasized an economic interdependence between the United States and developing countries (Donaldson and Tsui, 1990). In 1967, Title X to the Foreign Assistance Act was passed, providing support to voluntary family planning programs overseas. The United States offered assistance to governments, U.S. agencies, and UN voluntary health or other qualified organi-

---

[4]Most censuses were conducted with the assistance of external donors, notably the United Nations Population Fund and the U.S. Agency for International Development, with technical assistance from the U.S. Bureau of the Census.

zations for program implementation (Piotrow, 1973), and $35 million was earmarked for population programs. Support for population activities had become part of U.S. national policy, rather than an occasional technical assistance foray supported by private citizens or organizations. The special role of the United States in international population programs is based not only on its early interest, but also on its continued financial support. In terms of total dollars, the United States was the dominant donor to international population activities between 1965 and 1980 (Donaldson and Tsui, 1990).

Another major international player in the population field is the United Nations. From 1962 to 1972, a series of resolutions were adopted in the governing bodies of the UN agencies advising governments to examine their demographic circumstances and take appropriate action (Finkle and Crane, 1975). The United Nations in 1969 designated a separate fund to respond to global population needs, the United Nations Population Fund (UNFPA), to be administered by the United Nations Development Fund (Futures Group, 1988b). The United Nations gave legitimacy to population programs because its endorsement meant approval of member states from developing countries. Population programs that might otherwise have been viewed with suspicion acquired credibility.

In 1972, a resolution of the UN Economic and Social Council called for a Draft World Population Plan of Action to be prepared for the 1974 Bucharest World Population Conference (Mauldin et al., 1974). This conference was the first major population meeting to invite political representatives from all over the world, rather than just international population specialists, to discuss population strategies (Mauldin et al., 1974). However, whereas developed nations regarded the Bucharest conference as a potential catalyst to increase the role of the United Nations and its member governments in limiting population growth, many developing countries viewed the same event as one that would strengthen the unity of the Third World in achieving a "new economic order" (Finkle and Crane, 1975). Amendments were introduced to the draft plan that shifted the focus away from demography to socioeconomic development. The final version of the World Population Plan of Action examined population variables within the context of social and economic development (Mauldin et al., 1974). At Bucharest, African countries did not indicate that rapid population growth was one of their major problems.

Ten years later, African views on the necessity of fertility reduction had changed. The Kilimanjaro Programme of Action for African Population and Self-Reliant Development was formulated at a regional conference for African governments, held in Tanzania in January 1984, to prepare for the second International Conference on Population, which took place in Mexico City later that year. The Kilimanjaro Programme declared that effective programs were needed in Africa to reduce the high levels of fertility and mortality (Finkle and Crane, 1975). It reaffirmed the rights of parents to decide the number and timing of their children, and called on all countries to ensure the availability of safe, effective, and affordable contraception (Futures Group, 1988b). At the Mexico City conference, Africa joined the other developing regions of the world in declaring that population problems must be addressed regardless of whether a "new economic order" was established (Finkle and Crane, 1975). This stance represented a major change in attitudes and priorities.

HISTORICAL EVOLUTION OF FAMILY PLANNING PROGRAMS

On a national level, to what degree does the presence or absence of a population policy affect family planning programs? As demonstrated in the discussion of selected countries below, many pilot projects have been implemented successfully in the absence of a supportive government policy. Indeed, the presence of the projects themselves may promote policy development by providing evidence for government leaders that family planning will be culturally acceptable. However, there is evidence that the policy milieu is important for large-scale program success. Two of the three countries (Kenya and Botswana) currently having the most successful national programs and the highest contraceptive prevalence rates (CPRs) were among the first group to adopt population policies in Africa—Zimbabwe being the one exception where strong government support of programs occurred without an explicit policy. In countries with centralized government control over service delivery, such as the francophone countries, the lack of such policies has contributed to reluctance to expand programs and may in part account for their having, as a group, the lowest CPRs in Africa.

The implementation of family planning programs in Africa has tended to follow four stages, which occur within different time frames depending on the country.[5] These stages are:

1. implementation of early pioneering projects, most conducted by nongovernmental organizations (NGOs) or only weakly linked to the public sector;

---

[5]The four stages of African program development to date that are discussed here are congruent with a program typology developed by the U.S. Agency for International Development (USAID) to guide its assistance efforts in the 1990s and beyond (Destler et al., 1990). According to the USAID model, most African countries are at the emergent (modern method prevalence of 0-7 percent) or launch stages (prevalence 8-15 percent). Only three (or four if Mauritius is included) are at the growth level or beyond (prevalence greater than 16 percent). The implications of the different stages of program development for international donor technical and funding assistance are discussed later in this chapter.

2. family planning service expansion, usually including both discrete projects and preliminary government involvement, setting in motion the initiation of a national program;

3. broad-based service expansion and consolidation, particularly in the national program, and relative policy stability that results in appreciable effects on the CPR;

4. substantial and sustainable increases in CPR resulting in a fertility decline. In most sub-Saharan countries in the fourth stage (principally Botswana, Kenya, and Zimbabwe), the public sector is the primary, although not the sole, service provider.

First Stage: Pioneers

Pioneer projects throughout Africa have introduced family planning and demonstrated its political and cultural acceptability. In most cases, such programs have been implemented in milieus having little or no experience in contraceptive delivery and weak or no policy support. The weak support resulted in part from the very dearth of experience: Lacking empirical evidence to the contrary, African leaders were concerned that contraception would not be perceived as a need by their populations. The role of the pioneer programs has been crucial in changing political attitudes.

The early program activities have most frequently been implemented by NGOs, missionary groups, or as joint endeavors between in-country and developed country universities and research groups. In almost all cases, such projects have received external funding and technical support. With few exceptions, public sector involvement has been relatively minimal. Even where some degree of government involvement has been inevitable, such as within the highly centralized service delivery systems of francophone Africa, the pioneers have generally been small operations research programs, or other discrete entities outside the main health service delivery system. As such, they can be deemed "experimental" and disavowed quickly if the government perceives political fallout (Wawer et al., 1991b). In francophone countries, the first stage has generally been limited, due to the relatively monopolistic and centralized role of government in service delivery. This limitation accounts for the slow development of family planning in these countries; francophone countries have had less exposure to the small, successful nongovernmental family planning projects that have influenced policy in anglophone countries.

Exceptions to the general rule of weak government support for or involvement in early projects can be found in a few African countries. Kenya and Ghana were the first to formulate population policies, in 1966 and 1969, respectively. In these countries, government support of program activities occurred relatively soon after or in parallel with many of the early

NGO activities (World Bank, 1980, 1986). In Zimbabwe, the preindependence government, although not declaring an official population policy, was concerned about rapid population growth and, since the mid-1960s, has strongly supported private family planning activities (World Bank, 1982).

The implementation of pioneer projects in Africa has occurred in two distinct waves. The earliest projects were implemented in a small group of countries (Kenya, Ghana, and Nigeria) between the mid-1950s and the 1970s, and demonstrated that family planning was acceptable to substantial portions of the target populations even in what were considered to be pronatalist settings. Examples of such projects include those of the Family Planning Associations of Nairobi and Mombasa, which began providing contraceptive information and services in 1955 (World Bank, 1980); the Gbaja Family Health Nurse Project in Nigeria (1967-1970) (Ross, 1986); the project in Danfa in Ghana (Reinke, 1985) begun in 1969; and collaboration with the International Postpartum Program of the Population Council, which also began in Ghana and Nigeria in 1969 (Castadot et al., 1975). For cultural and political reasons, many pioneer projects concentrated on family planning as a maternal and child health issue. A number of the early projects demonstrated that service delivery strategies that had been or were being tested in Asia, including community-based distribution (CBD) and variations on commercial sales of contraceptives, could be adapted to African settings (Black and Harvey, 1976; DeBoer and McNiel, 1989).

A second wave of "pioneer projects" was implemented or begun in the period from the mid-1970s to the present in countries that for political or cultural reasons were slower to promote family planning. (The early stages of family planning service delivery in Africa have thus occurred over a 30-year time span, depending on the country.) These projects have yielded lessons already learned elsewhere (i.e., family planning can be culturally acceptable; CBD can work in African settings; and contraceptive services can be successfully integrated into health care) (Senegal and U.S. Agency for International Development, 1982; Bertrand et al., 1984, 1993; Wawer et al., 1990), but served to demonstrate again the acceptability of family planning on a regional level.

In virtually all cases, the early pioneers helped to introduce family planning, but did not have a great effect on contraceptive prevalence rates, except in small, select populations. In the project populations themselves, ultimate contraceptive prevalence rates have varied substantially: from less than 5 percent in the Nigerian Oyo State CBD project, Sine Saloum in Senegal, Bouafle in Côte d'Ivoire (Ross, 1986; University College Hospital et al., 1986; Columbia University, 1990) to almost 20 percent or more in the populations served in Danfa, Ruhengeri in Rwanda, Matadi in Bas-Zaire, Niamey in Niger, and the Sudan (Ross, 1986; Farah and Lauro, 1988; McGinn, 1990; Wawer et al., 1990; Bertrand et al., 1993). The definitions of "success" for early programs are thus highly variable. In the case of the Oyo State or Côte d'Ivoire projects, success was not necessarily demonstrated in the effect on the CPR, but rather in the very fact that these projects were implemented, showed some influence on prevalence (albeit limited), and laid the groundwork for an expansion and replication of these models in other regions (Wawer et al., 1991b).

No attempt was made to assess the community CPR achieved as a result of the Market-Based Distribution Project in Ibadan, Nigeria (see Chapter 4), which focused on contraceptive sales by traders in an urban market. (The project did record the quantities of contraceptives sold.) However, this project has been replicated in two new settings in Nigeria and one in Ghana, at the behest of local governments (Wawer et al., 1991b), suggesting "success" in making innovative family planning delivery more acceptable to policymakers and political leaders.

With respect to the prevalence achieved, what may account for the great disparities among the various pilot projects? Given the great variations in project design and implementation, direct comparisons are not very instructive. However, it seems that projects that established a clear identity for the family planning component (whether integrated with other health services or not) performed better. In both Oyo State and Sine Saloum, for example, there are indications of shortcomings in the promotion of family planning services: greater emphasis on the curative program elements at the expense of preventive and contraceptive services, and perhaps reluctance by project management or workers to stress family planning (Ross, 1986; University College Hospital et al., 1986). The Ruhengeri project in Rwanda achieved more than 19 percent prevalence in one area, compared to 8 percent in the second project site. Although dissimilarities in the educational level of the target populations accounted somewhat for the results, project staff emphasized the differences in the level of local political support for the projects, which were said to affect the degree to which project workers carried out their promotional and distribution activities (McGinn, 1990).

Second Stage: Mixed Private and Public Activities and Service Expansion

In the wake of the pioneering projects, countries have tended to follow one of several directions. In one model, found in Nigeria, early projects have loosened political constraints on the development of other, larger, nongovernmental projects. Countries such as Kenya and Ghana have expanded both governmental and nongovernmental activities. In a third model, found particularly in the francophone countries, governments have been reassured and have expanded their own services, but they continue to be reluctant to promote private sector delivery and NGO involvement.

Third Stage: Increasing Consolidation of Service Delivery

In the third stage, service delivery is sufficiently well established, advertised, and accessible to result in substantial contraceptive prevalence rates at the national level. It is interesting to note that the three African countries that have progressed through this stage (Zimbabwe, Botswana, and Kenya) had one thing in common: strong government involvement in family planning. Although the private sector played and continues to play a role in each country, in none is it the primary source of supplies (Botswana, 1989; Kenya, 1989; Zimbabwe, 1989).

Experience from these three countries may have implications for several other African nations. For example, in Niger, a dramatic government reversal of its negative stance on family planning has resulted in strong government support for the public sector distribution of services. In Niamey, CPR has increased from less than 6 percent in 1984 to more than 25 percent in 1989 (Direction de la Santé Familiale and Population Communication Services, 1989; Wawer et al., 1990). Although services are not yet available on a national level (in part because of weaknesses in the coverage provided by the government infrastructure), the results in Niamey suggest that intrinsic cultural or religious barriers to acceptance may be limited and that distribution itself is a major determinant of CPRs in this setting. In Rwanda, as a result of the favorable experience of the Ruhengeri project, the government is embarking on a national program of family planning promotion by community agents and is strengthening service delivery in all public sector outlets (McNamara et al., 1990).

Based on the experience of the current African front-runners, it would appear that government involvement is an essential step in the attainment of substantial contraceptive use in Africa. Although the government infrastructure may be weak, it remains the only means of providing truly national coverage in most settings. The primary and valuable role of the nongovernmental sector at the third stage of program development appears to consist in the testing of innovative service delivery strategies that are then adopted by and adapted to the public sector.

Fourth Stage: Effects on Fertility

The three countries in the fourth stage, Botswana, Kenya, and Zimbabwe, demonstrate not only strong government involvement in family planning service delivery, but also significant associated increases in contraceptive use, as discussed in Chapter 2. These increases have been accompanied by decreases in fertility. In Chapter 7, we examine the contribution of contraceptive use, relative to postpartum infecundability, to these declines (see also Jolly and Gribble, 1993).

Although not yet a major factor in family planning delivery in the sub-Saharan region, it is conceivable that private sector contraceptive delivery may become more important over time. Such a shift could occur as the result of donor emphasis on social marketing and other commercial strategies (a current trend in support by the U.S. Agency for International Development (USAID), for instance), sufficient client motivation to use family planning even in the face of some extra costs, and financial pressures on the public sector resulting in service cutbacks. At present, however, it is not possible to predict the degree to which the private sector will become a more important factor in the coming decade.

PROGRAM DEVELOPMENT IN SELECTED COUNTRIES

This section reviews the development or lack thereof of family planning activities in a number of countries with different policy and program commitments.

Countries with Programs Demonstrating the Most Success to Date

Kenya

Among the earliest organized family planning services in Africa were those provided by the Family Planning Associations of Nairobi and Mombasa, starting in 1955. In 1961, the Nairobi and Mombasa associations joined as the Family Planning Association of Kenya (FPAK), and a year later became the first tropical African affiliate of the International Planned Parenthood Federation (IPPF) (World Bank, 1980). As indicated earlier, Kenyan government interest in population programs began earlier than in most other African countries: In 1966, several years after a demographic survey revealed an annual population growth rate of 3 percent, the government included family planning as part of its development policy (Krystall, 1975). Assigned to the Ministry of Health (MOH), the program was launched in 1967, with the goal of providing information and services in all government hospitals and health centers throughout the country (Krystall, 1975). In its early years, due to the lack of an effective health infrastructure and shortages of skilled personnel, the Ministry of Health (MOH) relied heavily on FPAK and expatriate staff for technical assistance (Kenya, 1989). Close cooperation ensued between the pioneering family planning providers and the government, as evidenced by the fact that by 1968, the FPAK operated 40 clinics, the majority of them in MOH facilities (World Bank, 1980). In addition, the MOH program was supplemented by services provided by the Nairobi City Council and other smaller organizations.

In the early stages, a number of nongovernmental programs in Kenya tested service delivery outside the clinic structure. The Kinga Experiment launched in 1972, and supported by Population Service, tested condom commercial social marketing techniques in one district. An aggressive advertising campaign used various media (radio, movies, and displays) and initiated subsidized condom sales through village stores. Current use of condoms among survey respondents increased from 4 percent before the program to 15 percent a year after project initiation; current use of any method increased from 21 to 35 percent. No such changes were discerned in the control population. It is reported that in its early stages, the project encountered opposition from community members, particularly a potential competitor (an influential physician). Local support from project shopkeepers quelled the issue. On its termination in 1974, the project was replicated by another condom social marketing program in the area (Black and Harvey, 1976; Ross, 1986).

The Health for the Family/Chogoria Hospital program has been in operation since 1974, with support and funding from a number of sources, including the Presbyterian Church of East Africa, Family Planning International Assistance, and the Ford Foundation. The program conducts both clinical and community-based distribution of integrated health and family planning services. By late 1983, survey data indicated that almost 30 percent of all eligible women in the area were active users of contraception (DeBoer and McNiel, 1989; Ross, 1986).

The data from these pilot projects suggest that family planning uptake can be rapid in well-conducted programs. Such information is instructive in an examination of progress within the Kenyan national program. Starting with the five-year plan of 1975-1979, the government launched its information and service delivery activities. One goal was to reduce the annual rate of natural increase from 3.3 percent in 1975 to 3.0 percent by 1979 (Kenya, 1989). A World Bank review concluded that in its first four years, the national maternal and child health/family planning program had made satisfactory progress in reaching operational targets, particularly in establishing about 300 service delivery points (World Bank, 1980). Initially, however, the family planning component met with limited success. Although by 1978, the national CPR (modern methods only) was 6 percent (Kenya, 1980), the program had succeeded in recruiting only 55 percent of the acceptors targeted for 1976 and 60 percent in 1977. In part, the shortfall was ascribed to the setting of unrealistically high targets (World Bank, 1980; Kenya, 1989). However, important problems were also noted in sustaining the rate of adoption, in client retention and continuation, and in ensuring access and quality of care. Distance, short hours of operation, insufficient outreach, personnel problems, and inadequate training were all said to contribute to the shortfall (World Bank, 1980). The lack of coordination between different providers exacerbated these difficulties.

In 1982, partly in response to such problems, the government of Kenya established the National Council for Population and Development to coordinate public and private sector activities (Kenya, 1989). Throughout the decade, the government has worked closely with a large number of multilateral and bilateral donors (the World Bank, UNFPA, USAID, other governments, and more than 25 international nongovernmental and private associations) to improve both public and private sector programs (United Nations Population Fund, 1991).

Between the mid-1970s and 1990, the use of modern methods throughout Kenya more than tripled (see Chapter 2). Services have been expanded such that even in rural areas, prevalence is now 16 percent compared to 26 percent in cities (see Chapter 2 and Kenya, 1989). The public sector continues to be the major provider of contraceptives (67 percent of all users of modern methods receive supplies from government facilities, 13 percent from the FPAK, and 16 percent from various private sources) (Kenya, 1989). Among women knowing at least one modern method, more than 90 percent cite a government clinic or pharmacy as a source for contraception (see Table 2-9). Although initial progress in increasing the CPR and reducing fertility was slow, the rate of change appears to be accelerating (Working Group on Kenya, 1993). Increased use in Kenya has been aided by the facts that government commitment has been reasonably consistent, both the public and the private sectors provide family planning, and the country has not undergone major political or economic disruptions, as occurred for example in Uganda and Ghana.

Botswana and Zimbabwe

Botswana and Zimbabwe, the other continental African countries that have achieved substantial rates of contraceptive use, have experienced long-term and strong government involvement in family planning service delivery. Botswana implemented a small maternal and child health and family planning project in 1967, in conjunction with the IPPF affiliate (Botswana, 1989). The government adopted a policy favorable to the development of family planning in 1970 (Gauthier and Brown, 1975b). From the beginning, family planning was integrated into the general context of MCH rather than being established as a separate program. In 1973, a national program was instituted under the aegis of the MOH. MCH and family planning services are available during operating hours in all government health facilities. According to the 1988 Botswana Demographic and Health Survey (DHS), the public sector supplies 96 percent of all current users (Botswana,

1989). Among women knowing at least one modern method, almost all cite a government clinic or pharmacy as a source for contraception (see Table 2-9).

Zimbabwe has achieved a CPR of 36 percent for modern methods (see Chapter 2). Prior to independence, the government had not established an official population policy, but encouraged the development of family planning services. From the 1970s onward, most government, private, and mission health facilities dispensed family planning information, and the government subsidized the private family planning association (Gauthier and Brown, 1975b). In 1981, after independence, MOH assumed responsibility for family planning activities as part of its child spacing program. The Zimbabwe Family Planning Association, the IPPF affiliate, became a corporate body under the wing of the ministry and later developed into the Zimbabwe National Family Planning Council (ZNFPC). Personnel from the disbanded private association became employees of the ministry. Contraceptive services were made available at a nominal charge (Nortman, 1981). At this time, service delivery continues to be coordinated by the ZNFPC, and three-quarters of acceptors receive their services from national or municipal branches of public programs, including the ZNFPC community-based distribution program (Zimbabwe, 1989). Most multilateral, bilateral, and NGO family planning assistance is channeled through ZNFPC programs (United Nations Population Fund, 1991).

Countries with Historical Variation
in Policy Development and Program Implementation

Ghana

Ghana was among those countries demonstrating early support for population activities and, starting in the late 1960s, served as the testing ground for a number of innovative delivery strategies. Unlike Kenya, Botswana, and Zimbabwe, however, Ghana has not lived up to the early promise of rapid progress in family planning program development.

Ghana promulgated its official population policy in 1969, and the National Family Planning Programme (GNFPP) was established a year later. Coordination of public and private sector activities was delegated to the Ministry of Finance and Economic Planning. Participating agencies included the Christian Council of Ghana and the IPPF-affiliated Planned Parenthood Association of Ghana (PPAG), private sector agencies that had been offering family planning services since the 1960s (McNamara et al., 1990). In 1972, the GNFPP was still small and expended an estimated $23 per acceptor at the time, compared to $3.60 for the postpartum program (Ross, 1986).

In part because of the positive policy milieu, Ghana was among those

African countries in which innovative service delivery strategies were first tested. Between 1969 and 1973, Ghana and Nigeria served as the only two African countries to participate in the International Postpartum Program, which was initiated in 1966 by the Population Council with USAID support.[6]   Ghana (and Nigeria) ranked near the bottom in terms of the acceptance ratio: There were 9,000 direct acceptors (persons initiating use of contraception within three months after delivery) in Ghana among 93,000 delivering women, with another 11,000 indirect acceptors.   It should be noted, however, that in Ghana the ratio of direct and indirect acceptors to deliveries/miscarriages rose more than fourfold during the life of the program (Ross, 1986). Although progress in the African centers lagged behind those in other countries, the program experience represented a new and substantial program direction.

Ghana was also the site of the Danfa Comprehensive Rural Health and Family Planning Project, which ran from 1969 to 1979 in Danfa district, about 25 miles outside of Accra. The project served a population of approximately 60,000, and was conducted by the University of Ghana Medical School, Department of Community Health and the University of California, Los Angeles, School of Public Health. Funding was made available by the government of Ghana and USAID. The project tested three different combinations of health and family planning service delivery, with a fourth site serving as a control. In 1975, the quasi-experimental design was eliminated to loosen constraints on service delivery and in response to a government policy decision that family planning would be integrated with basic health services. By 1977, contraceptive prevalence had risen to 18 percent in the most successful project area that received comprehensive health and family planning services. (Prevalence in the control area was 5 percent and only 2 percent in the area receiving family planning services without health services.) It has been noted that project proximity to Accra and inputs from the two collaborating universities may have resulted in better management and supervision than that found in less visible project sites, and thus affected the high prevalence achieved in at least one project area (Ross, 1986).

Ghana served as one of the first African regions to experiment with social marketing. In 1970-1971, the GNFPP sponsored the Ghana Social Marketing Experiment, with the parastatal Ghana National Trading Corpo-

---

[6]By 1974, the program had expanded to 138 hospitals in 21 countries (Castadot et al., 1975; Gauthier and Brown, 1975a,b; Ross, 1986). Three of the seven participating African hospitals were in Ghana. Worldwide, participating hospitals conducted 3.2 million deliveries and had more than 1.0 million family planning acceptors. More than 500,000 (or 16 percent) of all postpartum women were direct acceptors who initiated family planning use within three months of delivery (Ross, 1986).

ration. However, only two weeks into the promotional campaign, all press and radio advertising was stopped because of criticism by influential public officials, and the television and film components were never initiated. Between 1976 and 1980, the government of Ghana and Westinghouse Health Systems established a sales program for contraceptives through existing commercial networks. Sales in the 18-month period commencing January 1979 amounted to about 37,000 couple-years of protection. The peak months of sales coincided with the peak months of advertisement (Ross, 1986). Problems included large monthly swings due to supply disruption. Like its predecessor described above, this project experienced problems with administration and wavering political support, raising the question of whether such difficulties are inherent in mixed private-public sector approaches (Ross, 1986).

By 1974, the GNFPP had expanded considerably. Family planning was offered in 135 clinics throughout the country; more than half were MOH facilities. In that year, the GNFPP also extended its commercial distribution program by allowing nonprescription contraceptive sales through nongovernmental commercial outlets; prior to that, all social marketing had been conducted through the parastatal Ghana National Trading Company, which supplied more than 600 outlets (McNamara et al., 1990).

Between 1970 and 1974, the GNFPP enrolled 110,000 new acceptors (approximately 6 percent; Armar, 1975). Of these new users, 42 percent were recruited in MOH clinics and 39 percent in PPAG facilities, with the Christian Council and other private clinics recruiting the remaining 19 percent. However, by 1974, only some 47,000 women, or 3 percent, continued to use a method (Armar, 1975). The total number of users in 1974 was well below the GNFPP target of 10 percent. The target itself may have been unrealistically high. Also, the numbers may represent an underestimate because of irregular reporting from clinics associated with the national program; in addition, other private sources reached an unknown number of clients. However, problems with program coordination, quality control, and high contraceptive discontinuation rates were all cited as contributing to slow progress (Armar, 1975; McNamara et al., 1990). Political support for family planning was uneven, as illustrated by the problems experienced by the social marketing experiments described above.

As shown in Chapter 2, 5 percent used modern methods in 1988, close to the level of 3 percent in 1979. Persisting programmatic and economic difficulties help explain this lack of progress. Although population policy has been retained through successive administrations over the past 20 years, political commitment has been erratic (McNamara et al., 1990). Poor institutional coordination and support, interagency tensions, poor management accentuated by a lack of skilled personnel, and inadequate government funding also contributed (Nabila, 1986; Benneh et al., 1989). Economic deterioration, beginning in the early 1970s and reaching its lowest point in 1983, led to less investment in the country's health service infrastructure (see Chapter 3). Material shortages curtailed MCH and family planning services.

Since 1985, there have been signs of renewed public sector commitment to family planning programs. A short-term primary health care plan for 1986 gave priority to MCH and family planning, and signaled a turnaround made possible by improvements in the national economic situation. By 1986, 330 clinics offered family planning, up from 135 in 1974 (Nabila, 1986). A new contraceptive marketing program was launched in 1986. Important roles in the new initiatives were and continue to be played by governmental and nongovernmental donor agencies such as IPPF and Family Planning International Assistance. The Ghana Social Marketing Program (GSMP), funded by USAID, supports a network of approximately 3,000 pharmacists selling contraceptives, a national program to train traditional birth attendants in rural areas, and an expansion of the GSMP to encourage traders in the markets to sell contraceptives (Kenya, 1980; McNamara et al., 1990).[7]

The potential for rapid uptake of family planning in segments of the Ghanaian population is illustrated by an operations research project supported by USAID, the Ghana Registered Midwives Association Project. In this project, an 18-month follow-up conducted in December 1989 on a sample of 130 project midwives, indicated that this group had performed 18,884 deliveries and serviced 12,411 new family planning clients in the period under review, for a relatively high ratio of one family planning client to 1.5 deliveries.[8]

The 1988 Ghana DHS results indicate that the government supplied 35 percent of current users, compared to 23 percent who received services from pharmacies (representing in part the Social Marketing Program), and 18 percent who cited the PPAG (Ghana Statistical Service, 1989). Among women who know of at least one modern method and a source for the method, 88 percent cited the government as a source (Chapter 2).

Nigeria

In Nigeria, government interest in population issues has been slow to develop. Nigeria's Second National Development Plan, 1970-1974, con-

---

[7]The last two programs were initiated as operations research projects, assisted by Columbia University.

[8]Almost 40 percent of the midwives were in rural practice, and all reported that at least part of their clientele came from villages or urban slums (Ghana Registered Midwives Association and Columbia University Center for Population and Family Health, 1988; McNamara et al., 1990).

tained a chapter on population policy. The gist of the document was that the demographic situation did not call for emergency action. Subsequently, in 1975, following several delays in the development of its terms of reference, the National Population Council was created by the government to advise on population policies and activities. However, by the mid-1970s, none of the actions in the second plan's population policy had been carried out; voluntary family planning services had not been integrated into the overall health care delivery system, and there was no discernible federal support for contraceptive services (de Sweemer, 1975). As of 1974, whatever family planning services were available were provided commercially through pharmacies or private maternity homes, as part of university-operated studies, or through the clinics of the Family Planning Council of Nigeria, an IPPF affiliate (de Sweemer, 1975). As in many other places in Africa, the IPPF affiliate had initiated small-scale activities as early as 1969 in a number of states in Nigeria (Nigeria (Ondo State), 1989).

It is interesting to note that despite its lack of government commitment, Nigeria served as the site of several of the earliest innovative service delivery projects in Africa. As indicated above, Nigeria was one of only two African countries that participated in the International Postpartum Program of the Population Council. As in the case of Ghana, participating hospitals generally lagged behind those of other developing countries. Approximately 5 percent of all obstetric/abortion cases became direct acceptors, and another 8 percent were indirect acceptors. However, in the final analysis, the ratio of all acceptors to all obstetric/abortion cases rose from 4 percent in 1969 to 16 percent in 1972-1973 (Ross, 1986).

The Ishan Experiment (1969-1972) in Midwestern State, covered a population of roughly 300,000. The project consisted of hospital-based family planning service delivery and full-time community motivators. Within four years, contraceptive prevalence in the target population rose from 1 to 24 percent. During the three years of project operation, a sizable number of private and semiprivate maternal and child health clinics in Ishan began to offer family planning services; of the 24 percent of women using modern methods, 9 percent received supplies from the project hospital, and 15 percent cited other sources (Ross, 1986). It is likely that the family planning motivation provided by the project had a positive effect on acceptance from these other sources as well.

The Calabar Rural Maternal and Child Family Health Project was conducted between 1975 and 1980 in Cross River State, serving a population of approximately 200,000 in 280 villages. The project was initiated by the State Ministry of Health and the Population Council with UNFPA financial support. Calabar was part of an international program designed to test methods of delivering maternal care and family planning services to rural populations lacking health infrastructure (Taylor and Berelson, 1971; Ross,

1986). Four countries participated: Nigeria, Turkey, the Philippines, and Indonesia. The Nigerian version of the trial has been described as best reflecting the original intent in trying to determine what it would take to provide basic MCH and family planning services to all eligible rural women (Ross, 1986). Results were mixed. Although 63 percent of all women in the area remained uninformed about modern family planning as of a 1979 survey, those who had interacted with project workers had higher levels of knowledge and use. Ever use of family planning was 18 percent among those who had discussed contraception with project personnel, compared to 8 percent among all respondents. However, the discontinuation rate for all women was high, so that only 2 percent of the sample of all women aged 25-54 used a method at the time of the 1979 survey. Problems included the limited coverage provided by the clinic-based system, substantial population migration, and centralized supervision, which worked against the integration of family planning within the operation of the health centers. In addition, because the project was operated independently of the State Ministry of Health, it had little effect on local decision makers, who ultimately did not accept the concept of a low-cost, low-level personnel strategy for rural health care (Ross, 1986).

The subsequent Oyo State Community Based Delivery of Health and Family Planning Project (1981 onward), conducted as an operations research project by the Department of Community Medicine, Ibadan University, and Columbia University, also had relatively little effect on prevalence of use. The proportion of all women in the target population using modern methods did not exceed 5 percent (University College Hospital et al., 1986), a finding thought in part to reflect the greater emphasis placed on health service delivery to the detriment of the family planning component. However, the project met with political approval, illustrated the feasibility of integrating family planning with basic health care in a community-based distribution strategy in rural Nigeria, and showed that government personnel could sustain and expand the project after the involvement of the University College Hospital had ended. The successful transfer of the pilot project was the result of a carefully planned "apprenticeship." State personnel first observed the functioning of the pilot program, then participated in the training of trainers, observed and assisted university staff in the initial steps of the expanded project, and gradually took over the operations (Ross, 1986; University College Hospital et al., 1986).

A number of social marketing activities have at present been tested by university groups and local governments. The Ibadan Market Based Distribution Project, implemented as an operations research project by University College Hospital, Ibadan University, and Columbia University, has been replicated in Lagos and Ilorin with local government support.

On the national front, results from the 1973 census showed that the population had risen to more than 80 million and that the annual population growth rate was greater than 3.5 percent. The findings influenced national leaders to fear that population growth was outstripping food production (de Sweemer, 1975). However, it was not until 1988 that an official policy fostering the provision of family planning services was adopted (Nigeria (Ondo State), 1989). Although there is still no comprehensive national family planning program, a large number of NGOs conduct projects at the local and state levels, many with local and state government support (United Nations Population Fund, 1991). Among many other activities it supports, USAID is providing funding to expand private sector distribution through commercial and other channels (United Nations Population Fund, 1991).

Modern contraceptive prevalence in Nigeria in 1990 was 4 percent (see Chapter 2), reflecting the relative lack of federal government support. Nigeria represents one site where private sector delivery may provide a substantial alternative to the relatively slow government implementation of services. The relatively low prevalence achieved to date, however, suggests the difficulties inherent in trying to provide extensive coverage to a large population in the absence of a broad-based program.

Uganda

As in the case of Ghana, Uganda realized early the problems inherent in rapid population growth, but made little subsequent progress in program development largely because of severe economic and political problems. The government first discussed the high population growth rate in its Third Five-Year Development Plan, 1972-1977. The Ugandan government also assisted the Family Planning Association, an IPPF affiliate, in providing family planning information. In 1973, 20 out of 28 clinics offering contraceptive services in Uganda were run by association staff (Nortman, 1981). As of 1981, the government planned to integrate family planning services into all medical units (Nortman, 1981). Needless to say, subsequent political chaos precluded any effective implementation of these plans. In 1988-1989, contraceptive prevalence in Uganda was 3 percent, and half the current users received their supplies from the Family Planning Association of Uganda and from private sources (Chapter 2 and Uganda, 1989).

Countries with Consistently Weak Support
for National Family Planning Programs

Sudan

In the Sudan, lack of government interest in population issues is now coupled with civil and economic disturbance to create a situation in which little progress seems possible. Family planning for birth spacing is nominally a part of MCH services, although it is not a priority. The MCH infrastructure through which contraceptives are to be delivered is itself very limited in the coverage it provides (McNamara et al., 1990). A 1985 UNFPA needs assessment mission noted the lack of an institutional base for MCH, administrative difficulties, the absence of guidelines for service delivery, and economic hardship as reasons that family planning delivery has not progressed (United Nations Population Fund, 1991). Public health officials are cautious in view of social values supporting high fertility and the perception that Sudanese women hold negative views about birth control (McNamara et al., 1990)

However, even within this context, it has been possible to mount a successful family planning project. In 1980, the Department of Community Medicine, University of Khartoum, initiated the Community-Based Family Health Program (an operations research project conducted with technical assistance from Columbia University and USAID funding) to test the delivery of contraceptives and selected primary health care services by village midwives. The project site was a rural area north of Khartoum. A project extension was implemented in 1984 in 60 villages north of the original area. Both the original and the extension sites achieved 20 percent prevalence of current use of modern methods by 1987—the original area starting from a base of 8.5 percent in 1980 and the extension area from 6.8 percent in 1984. The extension area achieved the same level in approximately half the time of the original project (Farah and Lauro, 1988). One reason for the accelerated progress in the new villages was application of the lessons learned through operations research, which identified weaknesses in components such as supervision. It is interesting to note that religious beliefs did not appear to represent an insurmountable barrier to family planning acceptance in the villages.

Mali

Mali was the first francophone country to adopt a policy favorable to the development of family planning. To establish the policy, in 1972, Mali repealed the French law of 1920, and in 1980, the Family Health Division was created in the Ministry of Public Health and Social Affairs (Mali, 1989). As of the early 1980s, family planning services were available in government-operated maternal and child health centers. The private Association Malienne pour la Promotion et la Protection de la Famille (AMPPF) was given responsibility for providing family planning information and education (Gauthier and Brown, 1975a; Nortman, 1981). Although family planning is nominally available, it is not emphasized within the MCH system, which itself provides only limited population coverage (Mali, 1989). The AMPPF, an IPPF affiliate, which was created in 1971, is the only nongovernmental agency involved in family planning in the country. Given the lack of emphasis on family planning and the limited coverage, it is not surprising that in 1987 the use of modern contraceptives in Mali was only 1 percent (see Chapter 2).

Zaire

In 1972, in Zaire, President Mobutu declared the government's policy on family planning as being one of support for *naissances désirables* (desirable births). No demographic objective was attached to the policy, and in the 1970s, the government was generally favorable to rapid population growth. A clinic offering contraceptive services was established in 1973 at Mama Yemo hospital in Kinshasa, directly under the authority of the Office of the President. A few MCH/family planning clinics were established as offshoots of the hospital service. Religious or private groups operated a small additional number of clinics in Kinshasa and in the interior of the country (Gauthier and Brown, 1975a). In the early years, donor agencies supported a few service and research projects, including programs of the Association Zairoise pour le Bien-Etre Familiale, an IPPF affiliate (United Nations Population Fund, 1991). The Projet des Services des Naissances Désirables (National Family Planning Project) is nominally national in scope, but problems with communications and transport preclude true national coverage. Even in such a weak policy and program setting, however, a well-managed project did substantially increase prevalence rates in its target populations. Operations research projects in the cities of Matadi and Kananga reached prevalence levels (modern methods) of 23 and 17 percent, respectively, in the late 1980s (Bertrand and Brown, 1992). Yet even these geographically limited gains have been undermined by Zaire's current political turmoil. In view of political instability, major donor agencies have withdrawn their support from Zaire. Local organizations are attempting to maintain program activities, but these activities are threatened by the lack of donor support and general deterioration of living conditions in Zaire.

Countries Where Rapid Progress in Family Planning May Occur

Rwanda

Until fairly recently, Rwanda exemplified countries with slow development of family planning programs. However, increased political will to address population issues is resulting in progress. Rwanda's growing commitment to population programs is influenced by two demographic factors: a population density of about 270 persons per square kilometer and an annual rate of natural increase of 3.5 percent (World Bank, 1990b). The rate of population growth was already recognized as a problem in the colonial era prior to 1962. However, it was not until the five-year plan of 1977-1981 that research was proposed on issues such as desire for family planning.[9] The 1982-1986 plan was more specific: It proposed to maintain the population growth rate of 3.7 percent per year while the conditions for rapid decline after 1986 were set in place. The Office National de la Population (ONAPO) was established by decree in 1981, and the political will to support its efforts has since been strong and consistent. By the mid-1980s, with financial and technical assistance from USAID, UNFPA, and other donors, ONAPO and the Ministry of Health had instituted family planning services in about 65 percent of the government health clinics throughout the country (McNamara et al., 1990)

Problems remain. By late 1988, estimates from service statistics indicated a national prevalence of 4.2 percent, an increase from the 1.0 percent reported by the 1983 National Fertility Survey, but nonetheless representing a sizable gap between national policy and individual practice (McNamara et al., 1990). Existing outreach efforts are still underdeveloped; at many centers, family planning is offered during fixed days and hours separately from other services. The position of the Roman Catholic Church continues to present an obstacle of considerable magnitude. (Approximately 40 percent of the population is Catholic.) According to May et al. (1990), up to 60 percent of the Rwandans use health facilities operated by the Catholic Church, which offer only natural family planning methods.

Despite these cultural, religious, and programmatic constraints, Rwandan pilot projects have demonstrated that a sizable proportion of the population may be ready to accept family planning services. The Ruhengeri operations research project introduced community education and distribution of contraceptives by volunteers belonging to the network of the Centers for Development and Continuing Education of the Ministry of the Interior and Community Development. Three noncontiguous communes were selected for the project. In one, volunteers provided information and clinic referrals, and distributed contraceptives. In the second, information and referrals were the only interventions. A third, which originally had three service sites and twice the number of family planning clients as the experimental areas, served as the control. Between January 1988 and June 1989, prevalence rose from 2.3 to 6.4 percent in the distribution area, from 4.5 to 28.5 percent in the family planning referral area, and from 6.9 to 7.4 percent in the control area. Overall, 70 percent of women with one to three living children indicated that they wished to use family planning in the future. Project person-

---

[9]Prior plans had concerned themselves with population distribution issues (Emmanuel, 1988).

nel attributed the success in the second area to somewhat higher levels of education among women in this area, higher levels of activity among the volunteers at this site, and particularly strong support from local community leaders (McGinn, 1990; McNamara et al., 1990). In the distribution site, the first area, several changes in commune leadership over the 16 months weakened support for the volunteers (McNamara et al., 1990). Nonetheless, government officials were encouraged by the project findings and launched a new national effort. Based on preliminary project results, ONAPO set in motion a national information, education, and communication (IEC) program, and 17,000 volunteers have been trained as family planning promoters, though not as community distributors.

Niger

Although the government of Niger has allowed contraceptives to be sold in public and private pharmacies since the 1970s (Gauthier and Brown, 1975a), it did not abrogate the French law of 1920 until the late 1980s. As of 1983-1984, however, the government dramatically reversed its previously lukewarm stance regarding family planning. With UNFPA support, the Centre National de Santé Familiale was inaugurated in late 1984 to coordinate family planning research, training, and program planning. A 1988 national conference on family health served as an official takeoff point for the population program. The chief of state, President Kounche, made a surprise visit to the conference and stated that population planning and contraceptive services were necessities given population growth rates. Since then, partly through operations research and other pilot projects, contraceptive services have been made available through clinics to the population in the national capital of Niamey and in several smaller cities. Prevalence in Niamey has risen from less than 6 percent in 1984, to more than 25 percent by 1989 (Direction de la Santé Familiale and Population Communication Services, 1989; Wawer et al., 1990). The results suggest substantial latent demand for fertility regulation, and the potential for further progress in family planning in the strengthened policy milieu. The greatest current challenge may be ensuring adequate coverage in this Sahelian country facing economic hardships.

MAJOR DONORS FOR POPULATION ACTIVITIES

Estimates of the proportion of population related expenditures covered by developing country governments range from 60 to 75 percent, with donor agencies contributing between 15 and 20 percent, and the remainder of expenditures covered by individuals (Population Crisis Committee, 1990; United Nations Population Fund, 1991). More than three-quarters of foreign assistance for developing country population programs comes from the public sector, either directly from the governments of developed countries or through the United Nations' membership assessments. The remaining amount is derived from the private sector through voluntary organizations, foundations, and nongovernmental organizations (Nortman, 1981). Developed countries finance population programs in a variety of ways. Approximately 30 percent of such funding goes directly into bilateral programs; one-third is disbursed multilaterally through the UN agencies; and the remaining funds are distributed through organizations in the private sector (United Nations Population Fund, 1992).

In all, it is estimated that in 1988, $290 million was expended in the provision of family planning services in Africa (or approximately $0.60 per capita). However, a substantial proportion of these funds were used for expatriate administrative and technical assistance costs, reducing the amounts spent on direct services in Africa. This amount represents both African and international donor support for family planning activities; information, education, and communication (IEC) programs; and the provision of services. Expenditures for Africa by donor governments increased from $128 to $153 million from 1989 to 1990, the greatest proportional increase for any region (United Nations Population Fund, 1992).

The private sector made the first overtures of population assistance on the African continent. Private charities, foundations, and nongovernmental organizations did not encounter the bureaucratic and political obstacles in conducting fieldwork that foreign governments faced. The implementation of relatively small programs by private voluntary organizations did not require the innumerable authorizations and reviews that governmental agencies require. Private voluntary organization's missions were expressly humanitarian, raising fewer host country anxieties that assistance might be linked to complex political or economic agendas.

The International Planned Parenthood Federation (IPPF) was formed in 1952 and was the first agency of any magnitude to provide family planning in many African countries.[10] Africa became IPPF's sixth region of the world at a meeting in Ghana in June 1971 (Suitters, 1973). The geographical coverage of the IPPF Africa region includes the 42 independent mainland and island countries south of the Sahara (United Nations Population Fund, 1991). Twelve countries signed up to be members of the new IPPF region in the early 1970s (Suitters, 1973). Today that number has.doubled to 24. In addition there are several other countries in Africa, such as

---

[10]IPPF is the largest nongovernmental agency providing family planning services and educational programs to increase public and government awareness of population programs (Johns Hopkins University Population Information Program, 1983). The IPPF operates through its 134 member family planning associations throughout the world.

Zimbabwe, that have no independent family planning program but where IPPF is nevertheless helping to support family planning.

The African federation members are about evenly divided between francophone and anglophone countries (United Nations Population Fund, 1991). IPPF's strategy is to stimulate the formulation of national family planning associations to satisfy local demand for activities. IPPF provides cash grants, technical assistance, and commodities to its member associations. Outside funding from local supporters or other foreign donors supplements IPPF contributions. Africa has become IPPF's priority region and in 1990, Africa's 24 member associations received $13 million.[11] IPPF has played a major role in encouraging service delivery through its support of community-based distribution and other innovative service delivery strategies.

Like IPPF, the Population Council was founded in 1952 with a mission to promote knowledge and action leading to fertility reduction (Suitters, 1973). In its early years, the Population Council emphasized demographic studies and building research capacity at other institutions. The Population Council has received most of its funding from USAID and from the Ford and Rockefeller Foundations (Johns Hopkins University Population Information Program, 1983). The Population Council helped to launch worldwide pioneering programs for fertility reduction in the 1960s and 1970s, including the postpartum program discussed earlier. Over the years, the Population Council has also invested in biomedical research, technical assistance, and training and fellowships for professionals in the population field. A current regional project is assisting the development of country-specific population policy documents in 16 French- and Portuguese-speaking countries (Population Council, 1989). In 1990, total population funding of sub-Saharan African projects amounted to $5.9 million and was distributed among 23 countries.

In 1952, the Ford Foundation began supporting population activities.[12] The Ford Foundation played a leading role in drawing world attention to population questions, developing new contraceptives, and supporting academic research and training, and during the 1950s and early 1960s was the largest single source of funds for population activities (Warwick, 1982). By the 1980s, however, population assistance no longer received major funding from Ford. This situation recently changed; in fiscal 1990, a plan was approved to reorganize the population program to emphasize reproductive health, including social science research and the promotion of public

---

[11]The Western Hemisphere region also received $13 million, but this amount was divided among its 46 members (International Planned Parenthood Federation, 1990).

[12]It began with an annual commitment of $60,000. Its commitment rose to $26 million in 1966, then subsequently decreased to $14 million by the end of the 1970s (Warwick, 1982).

discussion surrounding legal and cultural issues in reproduction (Ford Foundation, 1990). During fiscal year 1990, a total of $1,492,700 was allocated to programs in Senegal, Nigeria, Zimbabwe, and Kenya (Ford Foundation, 1990).

In the late 1960s and 1970s UNFPA and USAID became major contributors to population assistance. The majority of funds committed to the United Nations by developed countries are given to UNFPA (Nortman, 1981).[13] UNFPA is active in 43 sub-Saharan African countries, of which 31 are UNFPA priority countries.[14] From 1983 to 1991, population program expenditures in Africa increased more than 300 percent, from approximately $16.9 to $55.0 million (or approximately 32 percent of total expenditures worldwide). In 1991, approximately one third of expenditures were spent on family planning, one fourth on IEC, one fifth on data collection and policy development, with the remainder spent on other population-related activities (Cornelius, 1992).

In addition to UNFPA, the World Bank has been a significant multilateral donor of population assistance to Africa.[15] The bank's first loan to the region was in 1974. In the 1980s, its efforts expanded to over 20 countries, and $68 million was loaned for population activities between 1982 and 1989 (World Bank, 1989). By the middle of 1992, almost $290 million in loans had been approved, representing 18.5 percent of total population lending (World Bank, 1993).[16] The majority of funds have been targeted to combined population, health, and nutrition projects with the view that family planning is best introduced through health efforts. Kenya is the only country that has received loans for free standing population projects. The

---

[13]As many as 130 governments have contributed to UNFPA, with the United States and Japan leading in cumulative contributions. In 1985 the United States withdrew its support of UNFPA, claiming that UNFPA was collaborating with a coercive family planning program in China. UNFPA spent more than $900 million on population funding from its creation in 1969 through 1982. Most of UNFPA's support goes toward family planning programs. The total allocation between 1969 and 1981 was about 45 percent, followed by basic data collection at 17 percent and IEC programs at 13 percent (Johns Hopkins University Population Information Program, 1983). UNFPA decides each year what portion of its funds to retain for direct execution of UNFPA activities. Remaining funds are distributed among developing country governments, private organizations, and other UN organizations for population projects (Nortman, 1981).

[14]UNFPA has a total of 55 priority countries.

[15]The World Bank, spent $366 million on population assistance worldwide during the 1970s (World Bank, 1992). World Bank loans tend to emphasize development of an infrastructure, as well as construction of facilities for integrated health and family planning programs (Johns Hopkins University Population Information Program, 1983).

[16]The dollar amounts cited here only include loans specifically for family planning activities and demographic survey work. Total project loan amounts are much higher.

World Bank has also promoted changes in population policy in Kenya, Nigeria, and Senegal and has aided in program development in Kenya and Rwanda (World Bank, 1989).

USAID has expended $3.9 billion on population activities over the past 25 years, of which $2.9 billion was provided in the last 10 years alone (Destler et al., 1990).[17] USAID provides the greatest amount of funds for population activities in Africa of all donor governments. By 1989, USAID had bilateral population programs in 37 countries, of which 16 were in Africa; another 20 countries received assistance through its central Office of Population (Destler et al., 1990). In fiscal year 1990, USAID spent almost $281 million on population and family planning assistance; $73 million, or 26 percent of these funds, was expended on support for African programs in 38 countries, having a total of 284 subprojects (U.S. Agency for International Development, 1991).

As in other regions, the greatest share of subproject funds in Africa was spent on service delivery activities (37 percent), followed by IEC (22 percent), and training activities (20 percent) (U.S. Agency for International Development, 1991). Policy development figured more prominently in the African portfolio than in other regions, because policy was less developed (U.S. Agency for International Development, 1990). More than one-third of the African subprojects were undertaken by government or parastatal organizations. Approximately 40 percent of the projects in fiscal year 1989 were undertaken by the private sector compared to 58 percent in Asia and the Near East (U.S. Agency for International Development, 1990).

In fiscal year 1990, contraceptive shipments to Africa totaled $10.9 million and represented 20 percent of USAID's contraceptive shipments worldwide. Kenya, Nigeria, Tanzania, Zaire, and Zimbabwe received three-fourths of the contraceptives. Condoms accounted for about two-thirds of the cost of the contraceptives sent to Africa, followed by oral contraceptives (17 percent), vaginal foaming tablets (12 percent), and intrauterine devices (IUDs; 5 percent) (U.S. Agency for International Development, 1991).

USAID has estimated that the total number of contraceptive users in the African region will have increased from 9 million in the mid-1980s to 32

---

[17]The objective of USAID's population assistance is twofold: to promote the ability of individuals to choose the number and timing of their births and to bring population growth in line with economic growth and production (U.S. Agency for International Development, 1991).

USAID seeks to assist developing countries that favor population reduction and have an existing infrastructure in which family planning programs can be developed. It provides funding directly to developing country institutions, as well as through numerous nongovernmental and private voluntary organizations. In the early 1970s, USAID contributed roughly half the budgets of the IPPF and the UNFPA, more than 90 percent of the funds for the Pathfinder Fund, and substantial amounts to the Population Council (Warwick, 1982).

million in the year 2000, and 66 million in 2020 (Destler et al, 1990).[18] Even if annual costs per user drop to $15 by 2010, the funding needed to supply users in the African region will have risen from approximately $180 million in the mid-1980s to almost $1 billion in 2010. It is estimated that approximately half of this amount will be financed by the African countries' private and public sectors, with the remaining balance financed by international donors (Futures Group, 1988a).

LESSONS LEARNED FROM PROGRAMS AND PROJECTS

A number of themes and findings emerge from the descriptions of programs and projects above and from program-related research.

Evidence of Demand for Fertility Regulation Services in Diverse Settings

Although strong pronatalist attitudes and tendencies can be identified in many African settings and have substantial cultural underpinnings, sizable proportions of many sub-Saharan populations are interested in child spacing or limiting family size and will consider using contraception. This interest is apparent from survey research (Chapter 2; Bongaarts, 1991; Wawer et al., 1991b), ethnographic studies (see Chapter 4), and the experiences of the many projects cited above. In recent DHS surveys, between one-quarter and one-half of the women in countries as diverse as Burundi, Ghana, Kenya, and Zimbabwe indicated they wanted no additional births (Bongaarts, 1991).

The need for high-quality contraception is also indicated by several studies that have reviewed the prevalence of legal and illegal abortion in African countries. Results of research conducted in the late 1970s and early 1980s generally suggest that there was a rise in hospital admissions for abortion complications throughout the region and that postabortion cases seen in hospitals represented only a small proportion of total procedures conducted by trained or untrained practitioners (Coeytaux, 1988). A study conducted in a Nigerian secondary school indicated that almost one-third of the female students had undergone an induced abortion (Nichols et al., 1986). Recently, a small case history study of abortion in Kenya noted that many of the urban abortion patients had previously used contraception and had discontinued use because of side effects or dissatisfaction, or were using a method at the time of the pregnancy and experienced a method failure (Baker and Khasiani, 1992). Such study results suggest that there are subgroups of women for whom the prevention of unwanted pregnancy is

---

[18]Estimates are based on current contraceptive prevalence and on country-specific projections of users corresponding to the United Nations high population growth scenario.

of crucial importance and that improved service provision will prevent abortion and unwanted births.

A Range of Service Delivery Strategies Have Been Successful

There appears to be no one "magic bullet" with respect to the type of delivery strategy that will be successful. In Ruhengeri, the most effective approach was intensive IEC and referral to clinics; in the Sudan and Bas-Zaire, door-to-door distribution proved feasible and effective; market-based distribution is showing itself to be a useful option in several sites in Nigeria. Both integrated and vertical service delivery programs have improved family planning utilization; equally, both strategies have at times had minimal effects (Taylor, 1979; United Nations Population Fund, 1979; Trias, 1980). Important components in achieving success are local support, good management, and a commitment to family planning by project directors, such that the service does not become lost among other interventions.

Pilot and Operations Research Projects Have Contributed Substantially

Pilot or operations research (OR) projects can be reassuring to local or national leaders who would like to see a test of family planning but are reluctant to undertake a potentially politically damaging activity. Under the guise of these projects, new approaches can be tested, carefully monitored, documented, and possibly, jettisoned as an experiment that failed should the need arise (an uncommon experience). In 1987, more than one-third of innovative service delivery approaches discussed at the Harare Conference on Community Based and Alternative Distribution Strategies in Africa had originated as operations research projects (Columbia University Center for Population and Family Health, 1987).

To some extent, the African situation with respect to pilot and OR projects mirrors the early days of family planning in Asia. Small demonstration and NGO projects preceded national involvement or continued to play a critical role even as government programs came into their own (Freedman, 1987).

Family Planning Effort Is Associated With Contraceptive Prevalence[19]

In 1985, Lapham and Mauldin developed an international family planning effort score based on policy milieu, stage-setting activities, service-

---

[19]The evidence in this section is based on data pooled from African and non-African countries. There is no evidence for Africa alone.

related activities, record keeping, evaluation, and availability and accessibility of fertility control supplies and services (Lapham and Mauldin, 1985). They then examined the interactions between national socioeconomic indicators (based on indices from 1970) and program effort variables as predictors of contraceptive prevalence in the period 1977-1983.[20] The key conclusions were

> . . . the two conditions—socioeconomic setting and program effort—work most effectively together. Countries that rank high on both socioeconomic setting and program effort generally have higher contraceptive prevalence than do countries that rank high on just one, and still more than countries that rank high on neither. Furthermore, the path analysis suggests that program effort components are strongly associated with the availability and accessibility of family planning . . . . Moreover, the chances of achieving increased contraceptive prevalence by means of an aggressive family planning program range from good to very good among all but the lowest socioeconomic setting countries (Lapham and Mauldin, 1985:132-133).

Bongaarts et al. (1990) have updated the Lapham and Mauldin analysis and reconfirmed the conclusions that both socioeconomic development and family planning program strength influence contraceptive use and fertility, and that they operate synergistically, with one reinforcing the other. Of the 29 African countries considered in their analysis, 16 countries were in the low-development category (1980 data), and 21 had very weak or no family planning programs (based on the program in place in 1982). Between 1965 and 1985, countries falling into the "low development index/very weak no program" category recorded on average no decline in fertility. The researchers concluded that "much can be done to improve service delivery, particularly in countries where programs are still weak. Although the development of effective programs is more challenging in settings where the demand for birth control is weak, well-designed programs can have a substantial impact on fertility and population growth" (Bongaarts et al., 1990:307).

In an examination of programs worldwide, Mauldin and Ross (1991) identified strong associations between family planning program vigor and contraceptive prevalence. The prevalence rate ranged from 6 percent in those countries with very weak or no programs, to 20 percent in those with weak programs, to 45 percent or more in those with moderate and strong programs. The correlation between program effort score and CPR was .70, and the correlation between the contraceptive availability score and prevalence was even stronger, .84 (Mauldin and Ross, 1991). Furthermore, they

---

[20]Of the 26 sub-Saharan countries included in the Lapham and Mauldin analysis, 14 were in the lowest socioeconomic grouping in 1970.

suggested that the association between program effort and prevalence would have been stronger were it not for the fact that positive population policies, which increased the overall score, were not necessarily related to strong program implementation. The relationship between contraceptive availability and decline in the total fertility rate was also noteworthy (Mauldin and Ross, 1991).

Access to Family Planning Is Associated With Contraceptive Prevalence

Modern contraceptive use cannot occur in situations where methods and information on correct use are unavailable. Lack of availability may be due to many factors, including distance to services, barriers intrinsic to delivery systems (such as limited hours of operation and low provider enthusiasm), and high cost. DHS has reported the effects of distance on service utilization for ten countries, of which three (Togo, Uganda, and Zimbabwe) are in sub-Saharan Africa. Despite some limitations inherent in the sampling methods used to collect much of the data (Wilkinson et al., 1991), the results are instructive. In Togo and Uganda, utilization rates of modern methods are highest among women living within 5 kilometers of a static family planning provider; in Zimbabwe, prevalence remained high even in women somewhat distant from stationary providers, in part due to adequate outreach and community-based approaches (Wilkinson et al., 1991). However, even in Zimbabwe, the use of contraception decreased for users living 5 kilometers or more from a provider, and the use of clinical methods (IUD, tubal ligation) increased. For all 10 countries examined, the effects of distance on use of modern methods were strongest in Togo and Uganda; in other countries, greater availability of clinical methods, alternative supply strategies, and better transportation ameliorated the effects of distance to some degree (Wilkinson et al., 1991).[21] Based on analysis of the 1988-1989 Kenyan DHS and Kenyan Community Survey, Hammerslough has suggested that the rise in service availability in Kenya accelerated but did not initiate the fertility transition; the acceleration was related in part to the increased likelihood that contraceptors used efficient contraceptives (Hammerslough, 1991b).

With respect to cost, as a rough rule of thumb, contraceptives are deemed to be "accessible" if their total cost does not exceed 1 to 2 percent of

---

[21]Care should be taken in interpreting results of the relationship of distance to contraceptive use because skepticism has been voiced about the validity of distance as a measure of accessibility. It has been suggested that a variety of data collection techniques are needed to measure accessibility (Commitee on Population, 1991).

household income per annum (Lewis, 1985). A recent set of studies conducted by the Population Council examined private sector costs of contraceptives in relation to per capita income in 94 countries (Population Crisis Committee, 1991). The annual cost of 100 condoms represented more than 2 percent of per capita income in 19 out of 23 sub-Saharan countries represented in the analysis. In Benin, Burundi, Central African Republic, Ethiopia, Madagascar, Mali, and Togo, it was estimated that the private sector price of 100 condoms represented more than 15 percent of annual per capita income. Similarly, for oral contraceptives, the annual cost of 13 cycles was estimated to represent more than 2 percent of per capita income in 20 sub-Saharan countries. The need for public sector or subsidized family planning delivery is thus evident in the African region; the Population Council study suggested that in many of the sub-Saharan countries in question, less than one-third of couples currently has access to such low-cost supplies.

Donor Support Is Essential

In 1986, a World Bank document noted that "the cost of providing family planning in Africa is not great in absolute terms, but it will not be easily met by domestic resources" (World Bank, 1986:6). The bank estimated that average costs per user fall to approximately $20 per year as contraceptive prevalence reaches 20 percent or more of couples of reproductive age. The document suggested that "an increase in external assistance not only for family planning but also for policy planning, data collection and analysis, and training will be necessary for several decades if family planning is to be a realistic option for Africans . . ." (World Bank, 1986:6). The authors urged that population assistance to Africa increase as rapidly as the absorptive capacity allows and pointed out that "even a tripling of the external assistance currently spent on population in Africa, from $53 million to $160 million, would imply an increase in assistance from $0.12 to just $0.36 per capita, half the $0.75 figure cited as a goal for overall spending" (World Bank, 1986:6).

The difficulty of developing strong family planning programs in poor socioeconomic settings has been noted (Mauldin and Ross, 1991). Most African countries fall into the lowest economic categories in rankings developed by the World Bank and USAID. Given the economic downturn in much of Africa in recent decades, coupled with the potential for major increases in contraceptive use, the critical role that donors can play in population programs in Africa cannot be overemphasized. To date, the history of population and family planning programs in Africa has been inextricably linked to donor support. Donor inputs into pilot and operations research projects, policy development, data collection, service delivery, information campaigns, and technical assistance at all phases have played a crucial role in achieving what success is now evident. The quality and effectiveness of many family planning projects have depended fundamentally on the interplay between donor organization budgets and technical assistance, and host country health care infrastructure, laws, and regulations. The importance of this assistance reflects economic constraints faced by African governments and NGOs, as well as the hesitancy of national leaders to undertake a controversial activity without some external assistance.

One important problem faced by donor agency grantees may be described as donor fatigue. Any one strategy for service delivery is likely to demonstrate its effects only slowly or may be applicable in only a limited segment of the population. Donors often feel the pressure from their own constituencies to show more dramatic results or at least demonstrate that they support dynamic innovation. Thus, over the years, programs in Africa have experienced sequential or short-lived donor enthusiasm for clinic-based approaches, community-based distribution, commercial retail sales, and variations on these themes. Donor support for innovation has many positive effects. However, it is detrimental if the emphasis on a new approach reduces support (financial, political, technical) for a tried-and-true strategy that can and will pay off over time.

As indicated earlier in this chapter, the USAID population program development typology was developed to guide funding and technical assistance efforts at different program stages (Destler et al., 1990). At the earliest emergent stage (prevalence less than 8 percent), it is argued that assistance needs are broad and substantial, and multidisciplinary technical assistance is required. At the launch stage (prevalence 8-15 percent), it is suggested that donor support may be directed to more specialized technical assistance and implementation agencies, in particular to meet training needs and promote programmatic and financial sustainability. From the launch stage onward, growing emphasis is placed on involving the commercial sector. The typology and the suggested directions for action provide a conceptual framework for donor strategies. The model recognizes that a mix of private and public sector involvement in family planning is desirable and that the move to sustainability is gradual. In the African setting, applications of the model would have to take into consideration the weak overall economic base and the potential for setbacks in population programs if national economies deteriorate further. True financial independence and autonomous sustainability will be harder to achieve in Africa than in settings having preexisting strong private sectors and more solid economic bases.

The current economic situation in Africa, the opportunity to expand family planning much more rapidly in the next decade, and a continuing need for technical input suggest that donor involvement will continue to be essential for the foreseeable future.

New Mechanisms Are Needed to Increase Resources

Governments, donor agencies, and programs need to address the problem of static resources at a time of growing family planning demand and costs. Strategies to improve the use of existing resources and to coopt new sources of manpower and funds include direct cost recovery (fees for service and supplies), social marketing, employer donations, leveraging of resources (matching requirements, collaborative service delivery arrangements, debt conversion), service coverage by third parties, expansion of private sector services, and increasing program efficiency (economies of scale, less costly service delivery models, introduction of more effective contraceptive technologies; Destler et al., 1990; Lande and Geller, 1991). USAID projections indicate that, over time, a greater proportion of service delivery costs will need to be met with local private resources (Destler et al., 1990).

There is evidence that some clients can and will pay for family planning services; indeed, acceptance of modestly priced contraceptives has at times been higher than that of free commodities in the same setting (Lewis, 1985). Within programs, the trend has been to provide services free of charge in the initial phases and to institute fees only after demand has been stimulated. The merits of such phasing in of payments remain controversial. In the Oyo State CBD project in Nigeria, contraceptive use fell in project areas where fees were introduced some time after project initiation; areas in which similar prices were charged from program inception achieved and maintained distribution levels equivalent to those in the initial free service areas (University College Hospital et al., 1986).

The more pressing question is not whether it is possible to charge for services, but rather the degree to which fee-for-service and other fundraising schemes can cover the true cost of family planning delivery. As indicated earlier, contraceptives may be considered accessible if their total cost does not exceed 1-2 percent of average annual income per capita. Lewis has concluded that most cost recovery efforts do not cover more than one-quarter of total costs, or half of noncommodity costs (Lewis, 1985). Commercial prices that reflect true costs are often too high for the average household, particularly in Africa where such prices relative to income are generally the highest in the world. Donor and government subsidization of services will likely remain important in Africa, whether contraceptives are distributed through the public or private sector. More small-scale research is needed to determine the extent of price elasticity and to improve market segmentation in order to set realistic fees for different population subgroups.

Worldwide, the proportion of the total population served by the private sector tends to increase as family planning services mature, with developed countries being much more dependent on private providers than developing countries (Destler et al., 1990; Lande and Geller, 1991). It is also noteworthy that a comparison of family planning costs in developing countries suggests that social marketing and clinics offering primarily voluntary sterilization were the most cost-effective family planning delivery modes (with respect to cost per couple-year of protection, CYP); community-based distribution services had the highest costs per CYP, but became somewhat more cost-effective if coupled with clinics offering long-term methods such as the IUD and tubal ligation (Huber and Harvey, 1989). The relative success of social marketing with respect to cost-effectiveness was attributed in part to such programs' ability to reach massive audiences quickly once they are introduced.

Project and Program Success Needs to Be Interpreted Broadly

Increase in contraceptive prevalence is not necessarily the only measure of success in many early family planning projects. The Oyo CBD project, for instance, may not have had a substantial effect on the use of modern methods but did result in greater acceptance of community-based distribution of family planning by the state government. Projects with limited size and scope have had important effects in reassuring policymakers of the acceptability and feasibility of family planning services and have resulted in policy changes and expansion of services (Destler et al., 1990; Wawer et al., 1991b). To ensure that the lessons learned have reached policymakers, the involvement of such leaders in the project from its early stages is frequently desirable, as in the cases of the Danfa project, the Oyo State CBD project, the Sudan CBD project, and Ruhengeri. All resulted in policy changes or were sustained and replicated by the public sector following their OR/pilot phase. Projects that provide less opportunity for policymakers to become aware of and comfortable with their approaches, as in the case of the Calabar project in Nigeria, may not stimulate future family planning efforts.

PRIVATE VERSUS PUBLIC SERVICE DELIVERY, INCLUDING SOCIAL MARKETING

The degree of coverage that may ultimately be provided by the private sector in Africa is still unknown. According to DHS data (Cross, 1990), there currently exist wide variations in the source of contraceptives by country. In Botswana, Kenya, and Zimbabwe, countries with the highest contraceptive prevalence in continental sub-Saharan Africa, government sources supply between 73 (Kenya) and 92 percent (Botswana) of all modern contraceptive methods. The public sector is also the major supplier in Burundi (87 percent of users) and Mali (76 percent of users); contraceptive prevalence in both these countries is less than 2 percent. In five other sub-Saharan countries (Ghana, Liberia, Senegal, Togo, and Uganda—all low-prevalence countries), the government sector supplies half or less of all users. Pharmacies supply between 11 and 23 percent of users in Ghana, Liberia, and Togo; other private sources (which may include private health providers or nongovernmental organizations) account for between one-quarter and one-half of users in Ghana, Kenya, Liberia, Senegal, and Uganda. Interestingly, government sources of contraception predominate in the three Asian countries with DHS data (Thailand, Sri Lanka, and Indonesia),[22] whereas pharmacies and other private sources service the majority of users in most Latin American countries. The patterns noted above persist when supply methods are considered separately from clinical methods.

Experience to date and the data above suggest that public sector involvement has been a critical element in national expansion of family planning services in Africa, and that those countries with relative success stories continue to rely in large part on government sources. The data also make clear, however, that in the majority of countries, the public sector, although it may be the predominant source of methods, is actually reaching only a portion of the population. Thus, there remains a need to expand the networks available for service provision, both in countries where progress is being made and in countries with little family planning delivery to date. Expansion of services into the private sector, including pharmacies, private practitioners, and nonmedical retailers and traders, has recently become an area of great interest. Social marketing, wherein contraceptive supplies are generally sold at subsidized prices, represents a model that may be used to involve private distributors.

As yet, social marketing remains a small component in family planning delivery in Africa. Statistics compiled by DK-Tyagi (DKT) International (a subsidiary of Population Services International) indicate that there were eight sub-Saharan countries where social marketing projects provided more than 10,000 CYPs in 1991 (DK-Tyagi International, 1992). The CYPs reported ranged from 18,000 in Côte d'Ivoire to 200,000 in Zaire. Condoms were the sole method delivered in five of the countries; the Zaire program also included foaming tablets; the Ghanaian, oral contraceptives; and in Zimbabwe, oral contraceptives and IUDs. In both Ethiopia and Zaire, the program was estimated to have provided coverage for 4 percent of the target market, the latter defined as being 80 percent of women in union, aged 15-44; in the other five countries, the coverage provided was 2 percent or less (DK-Tyagi International, 1992).

Social marketing programs, and indeed any attempts to reach the private sector (outside both governmental and NGO programs), are recent in origin

---

[22]In some Asian countries such as Taiwan, the private sector played a large role in service delivery in the early implementation of family planning programs.

and cannot be expected to have achieved their full potential. Unfortunately, there is a dearth of information from which to project what this potential may ultimately be. Data on the numbers and distribution of private sector providers not affiliated with public or nongovernmental programs are often unavailable for a given country. Country assessments carried out by the Social Marketing for Change (SOMARC) program of the Futures Group, point to potential obstacles to social marketing. The Togo assessment noted that the parastatal pharmaceutical company had a monopoly on pharmaceutical imports, which may reduce flexibility, efficiency, and resupply, and hinder plans for cost recovery and self-sustainability; the parastatal distribution network was limited, reaching only approximately 165 points of sale; and current regulations would permit the sale of oral contraceptives in fewer than 70 outlets nationwide (Baird et al., 1990). Commercial distributors lacked experience with the product line, and the report further noted that ". . . since the volume of product is limited and the profit margin very small compared to the rest of their product lines, there is the possibility of a lack of interest in the long term benefits of this program" (Baird et al., 1990). Based on these observations, SOMARC ultimately recommended that the social marketing program be housed within a nongovernmental organization, the IPPF-affiliated Association Togolaise pour le Bien-Etre Familial (Baird et al., 1990).

In Rwanda, it was noted that "the country's commercial infrastructure is rudimentary . . . . Distribution and marketing activities are passive in nature and advertising is not widely used. There are very few commercial entities which provide a significant coverage of the country in terms of distribution despite the fact that the network of pharmacies has increased from 28 in 1987 to 124 in 1989" (Karambizi and O'Sullivan, 1989). This report also noted that import duties on contraceptives, although lower due to their classification as essential drugs, were still "high enough to increase the retail price beyond the purchasing capacity of the majority of the people."

The concerns noted do not preclude the establishment of social marketing programs. However, they do suggest that commercial approaches are likely to become widespread much more gradually in the sub-Saharan region than, for example, in Latin America, and it is thus too early to dismiss the importance of CBD and other noncommercial approaches, despite their potentially higher cost. It should also be mentioned that the cost-effectiveness of social marketing mentioned above was based on assessment of programs in four Latin American, three Asian, one North African, and two sub-Saharan countries: the last two, Kenya and Nigeria, are not representative of the potential for social marketing in Africa as a whole. In neither case are programs overly constrained by restrictive policies, and both countries have better than average networks of commercial distributors who can be mobilized to provide services, thus achieving the broader distribution associated with lower unit cost. Thus, social marketing per se is unlikely to be a programmatic magic bullet for Africa, and diversified approaches will continue to be needed.[23]

THE IMPACT OF AIDS ON
FAMILY PLANNING PROGRAM ACTIVITY

No discussion on population activities in Africa is complete without some reference to the potential impact of acquired immune deficiency syndrome (AIDS) on family planning programs in the next decade. Unfortunately, little data is available and what can be said about the impact of AIDS is more speculation than fact. It is thought that AIDS may affect family planning services in two ways.

First, it may decrease the resources available for these services—both financial and human. Public health officials may target their limited resources to addressing the AIDS epidemic resulting in fewer resources available for other health services, such as the promotion and delivery of family planning. Health workers may be reluctant to promote family planning among populations severely affected by AIDS, for fear of going against the possible pronatalist response to AIDS or because they too believe it is important to promote childbearing to offset AIDS-related deaths. Furthermore, some health providers may be reluctant to insert IUDs because of the possible connection between the use of an IUD and increased spread of sexually transmitted diseases, including human immunodeficiency virus— which causes AIDS—and because IUDs may increase bleeding (Williamson, personal communication, 1993).

Second, AIDS may increase the demand for contraception, particularly condoms. Information, education, and communication (IEC) efforts regarding the use of condoms in preventing AIDS are already under way in Africa and the flow of condoms to Africa has increased dramatically (Williamson, personal communication, 1993). Although condoms are not as well accepted as other methods as a means of pregnancy prevention within marriage, such education efforts have at least made many Africans more aware of the potential usefulness of this method. In addition, it is generally believed that governments, in response to the spread of AIDS, have become more willing to broadcast information on condoms and AIDS via the mass

---

[23]It should also be noted that in a number of non-African countries there has been a decrease in the use of the private/commercial sector (particularly pharmacies) for family planning supply in the last decade. This decline has been attributed in part to an increase in the use of clinical methods (the IUD, sterilization) (Lande and Geller, 1991). In these cases, cost savings on a national level are more likely to result from the adoption of more effective methods than from commercial cost recovery per se.

media. In the wake of these efforts, messages in the media on other family planning methods may seem more acceptable in the future.

CONCLUSION

As noted by Freedman, ". . . in the rapidly changing world, the reports of traditional cultural constraints in developing countries may be more representative of the past than of the present. All developing countries increasingly are linked to the world communication and transportation network carrying ideas and messages that permeate cultural barriers to varying degrees . . ." (Freedman, 1987:58). Information regarding successful programs is being disseminated to other regions, through exchanges, conferences, and word of mouth, and is resulting in successful replication of service delivery strategies (Columbia University, Center for Population and Family Health, 1987, 1990; Wawer et al., 1991b).

The relative success or weakness of family planning implementation in each of the countries discussed above is largely predicated on very specific political and economic circumstances. Caution is therefore in order in drawing any conclusions as to the determinants of the different outcomes. However, in a general sense, programs have tended to encounter particular problems where original national commitment was weak, or where it faltered as a result of political instability or economic decline. To date, the contribution of nongovernmental sources to contraceptive use in African countries has been important in introducing the services, reaching specific target populations, and opening the door to innovations. However, private and voluntary services have had a modest effect at best on national contraceptive prevalence rates and coverage.

The qualitative evidence in this chapter suggests that limited access to contraceptives contributes to the relatively low use of family planning in sub-Saharan Africa. Government programs are beginning to have substantial effects on contraceptive use and to produce indications of an effect on fertility in a number of African countries (Botswana, Kenya, and Zimbabwe). The potential for major increases in contraceptive use in the next decade is great in a group of nations that includes Ghana, Niger, and Rwanda. Elsewhere, attitudes favoring family planning and resources for contraceptive delivery programs are at least becoming more prevalent. For the potential to be realized, programs will require sustained domestic and donor assistance, in the form of favorable political and policy support and funding.

6

Regional Analysis of Contraceptive Use

The preceding three chapters describe the main factors affecting contraceptive use in sub-Saharan Africa. In Chapter 3, several socioeconomic factors are shown to be associated with high fertility: low levels of female education and income per capita, rural residence, and high infant and child mortality. Although the associations between fertility and these socioeconomic characteristics are not always as strong as in other regions of the world, they do suggest that changes in these characteristics would have some effect on fertility, as in Botswana, Kenya, and Zimbabwe. We also suggest that changes in costs of living, due to economic reversals, may increase the acceptability of smaller family sizes in certain population subgroups, but the response to such changes is very much a country-specific matter.

In Chapter 4, we identify the aspects of African social structure that support high fertility norms, specifically, the importance attached to perpetuating the lineage, the linkage between number of children and access to resources, the use of child fostering to spread the costs and benefits of having numerous children, and the weak conjugal bond. Although these social characteristics are changing, it is clear that they have exerted considerable positive influence on historical fertility levels and have not disappeared today. In addition, the penetration of major religions (Christianity and Islam) has affected contraceptive use, primarily through female education and social organization, such as marriage patterns.

The contribution of family planning policies and programs to changes

170

in contraceptive use is discussed in Chapter 5. The changes in policy to promote family planning, as well as expansion of programs, have increased access to modern methods of contraception, fulfilling latent demand and possibly creating additional demand.

This chapter uses statistical analysis to examine the relative importance of those factors that can be measured by using World Fertility Survey (WFS) and Demographic and Health Survey (DHS) data. Whereas Chapter 2 highlights bivariate relationships based on individual-level data, this chapter examines these relationships using multivariate analysis and regional-level data. The factors described in earlier chapters—socioeconomic development, patterns of social organization, the influence of major religions (Christianity, Islam), and access to family planning services—clearly differ among regions within a given country.

Our analysis is based on the WFS and DHS data sets described in Chapter 2. The countries included are shown on a map in Figure 6-1, and a list of the weighted and unweighted sample sizes for each country is provided in Appendix B. The sample consists of 37 regions in the WFS data set, 55 regions in the DHS set, and 92 regions in the pooled (WFS and DHS) set. The full set of WFS and DHS data considered are shown in the appendices to this chapter.

We are limited by the variables collected under the two survey programs.[1] Accordingly, we focus on four variables that were shown to have a marked effect on patterns of reproduction in an earlier analysis by Lesthaeghe (1989b): two socioeconomic variables—the level of female schooling and the degree of urbanization—and two variables that reflect social organization—the extent of polygynous marriage and the proportion Muslim. Although by no means exhaustive measures of socioeconomic development and community/kinship relations, these four variables nonetheless capture important dimensions of the contextual variables discussed in earlier chapters. This current analysis confirms the relationships documented in the earlier analysis (Lesthaeghe, 1989b), which used a smaller, less diverse data set based primarily on the WFS. The WFS data were collected mainly in countries in West Africa.

Notably lacking in this analysis is a measure of the strength of the family planning supply environment.[2] Although national-level indicators

---

[1] It should be stressed that socioeconomic variables for which data was not collected under the WFS and DHS, such as income, are plausibly of importance in explaining differentials in contraceptive use.

[2] In addition, infant and child mortality were not included in the analysis. Because mortality may be influenced by high fertility or vice versa, we decided that it was not statistically sound to include mortality as an explanatory variable. We did explore this option, however, and found that mortality showed no significant independent effect on fertility, possibly because

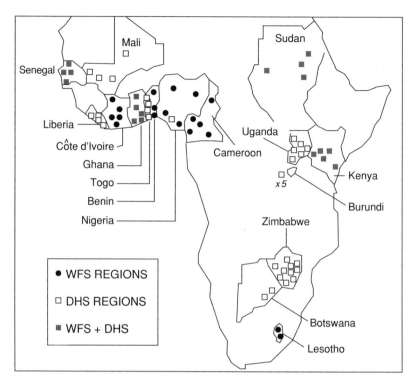

FIGURE 6-1   Location of countries and regions that participated in the World
Fertility Survey and Demographic and Health Survey programs.

are available to measure this dimension, there are no analogous measures at
the regional level that would reflect local differences in political commitment, access to services, variety of methods available, and related aspects
of the family planning supply environment. This major shortcoming should
be addressed in future research, especially in light of the evidence presented
in Chapter 5 on the progress in improving family planning services in Africa.[3]

female education influenced both contraceptive use and mortality. Although we highlight the
important positive association between mortality and fertility in Chapter 3, we cannot defini-
tively test mortality's relative effects on contraceptive use in this statistical analysis.

[3]The multivariate model described below was also tested with a national measure of family
planning effort (using scores developed by Mauldin and Ross, 1991). The t-statistic for the
positive coefficient was 1.93. There is too little variation in national-level scores to make this
an effective measure to explain regional differences. By introducing family planning effort
measured at the national level, we are probably underestimating its true effect. There is a great
likelihood that family planning has had a significant role to play in increasing contraceptive
use in sub-Saharan Africa, but its contribution is impossible to assess precisely.

In anticipation of the results of the multivariate analysis, which indicate the overriding importance of female education with respect to contraceptive use, we begin our regional analysis by focusing on the bivariate association of education with contraceptive practice.

FEMALE EDUCATION AND CONTRACEPTIVE PRACTICE

As we demonstrate in Chapters 2 and 3, education is positively associated with contraceptive use at the individual level and negatively associated with fertility at the national level. In our consideration of the relationship between female education and contraceptive practice, we examine not only modern contraceptive use, but also its precursors: ideal family size and knowledge of contraceptive use.

Ideal Family Size

Figure 6-2 depicts the relationship between the average length of schooling in the WFS and DHS regions and the percentage of married women with ideal family sizes not exceeding four children. One measure of association between two variables, the Pearson correlation coefficient, r, indicates the expected positive relationship ($r = .73$).[4] The percentage stating a preference for four or fewer children, here called "small ideal family size," commonly rises above 30 for regions with schooling averages of four years or more, and above 50 for several regions in Kenya and in urban centers of Botswana and Zimbabwe. By contrast, very few (about one-fifth) of the low-education regions reach the level of 30 percent stating small ideal family sizes. Furthermore, these tend to be national capitals—Khartoum, Lomé, Cotonou, Bamako—indicative perhaps of an effect of urban residence.

Areas with fewer than 10 percent of women stating small ideal family sizes have been concentrated predominantly in West Africa. Analysis of the WFS showed that such low percentages were observed in most of Côte d'Ivoire, Nigeria, and Cameroon. In Ghana and Benin, such low percentages were found in the northern regions. Also the WFS data for Senegal show percentages around 10 for regions other than Dakar and Thiès. The DHS data confirm the persistence of these low percentages of women with small ideal family size in West Africa. The 15 percent level is not ex-

---

[4]The Pearson correlation coefficient, r, is often used to measure the extent of a linear relationship between two variables. A positive r indicates that the slope of a regression line fit using data on the two variables is positive. (A negative r indicates that as one variable increases, the other decreases.) When r is statistically different from zero, it is determined that there is an association between the two variables.

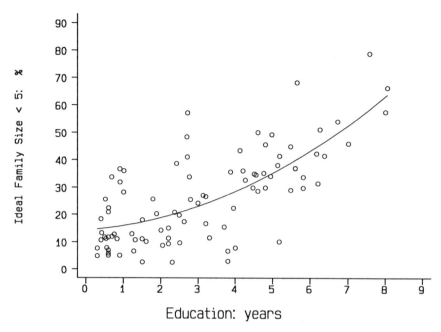

FIGURE 6-2 Relationship between percentage of currently married women ages 15-49 with ideal family sizes of four or fewer children and mean number of years of female education—WFS and DHS regions (r=.73). SOURCE: Demographic and Health Survey and World Fertility Survey reports.

ceeded in Northern and Upper Ghana; the Sinoe and Grand Gedeh regions of Liberia; the Mopti, Gao and Tombouctou, Kayes, and Koulikoro regions of Mali; in most of Senegal; in Ondo State (Nigeria); and in the Savanna region of Togo. The only regions outside West Africa with such low percentages are the Kordofan and Darfur provinces of Sudan.

Knowledge and Use of Modern Contraceptive Methods

Knowledge of modern methods of contraception is also strongly related to average female schooling levels in the pooled data set, as shown in Figure 6-3 (r = .77). At an educational average of less than four years, knowledge of at least one modern method among women in a union varies widely from close to 0 to almost 90 percent. Regions with schooling averages of more than four years generally exhibit knowledge levels of 50 percent or better.[5]

---

[5]Scatter plots relating average female schooling levels to urbanity (positive effect) and to the

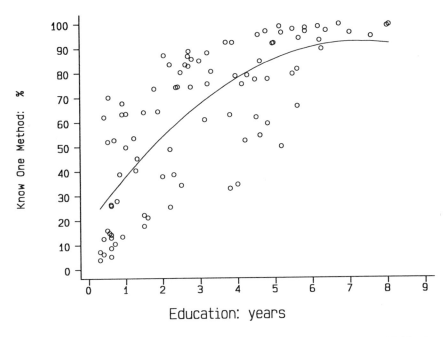

FIGURE 6-3 Relationship between percentage of married women ages 15-49 who know at least one method of contraception and mean number of years of female education—WFS and DHS regions ($r = .77$). SOURCE: Demographic and Health Survey and World Fertility Survey reports.

Figure 6-4 displays the relationship, in the pooled data set, between the use of modern methods and the knowledge of such methods. The relationship is strong ($r = .80$), but its pattern deviates markedly from linearity. Where the regional knowledge level is less than 80 percent, the use of modern methods remains less than 10 percent among women currently in a union. Only at very high levels of contraceptive knowledge is there a sharp increase in the use of such methods.

As indicated in Figure 6-3, knowledge levels of 90 percent or better emerge only in regions with female schooling averages of four years or more. As a consequence, one should expect levels of current use of modern contraception in excess of 15 percent to emerge only in regions with both high knowledge levels (80 percent or more) and high female educational levels (schooling averages of more than four years).

---

proportion Muslim or adhering to traditional religions (negative effect) also show strong relationships.

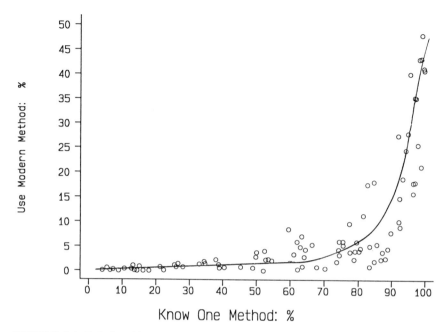

FIGURE 6-4 Relationship between percentage of married women ages 15-49 using modern methods of contraception and percentage of married women knowing of at least on modern method—WFS and DHS regions *(r = .80).* SOURCE: Demographic and Health Survey and World Fertility Survey reports.

This expectation is borne out in Figure 6-5, which shows the link between the percentage of users of modern methods and the regional female schooling averages in the WFS and DHS regions. Contraceptive prevalence greater than 10 percent is virtually never reached in regions with mean female education durations of less than four years. Beyond this schooling level, the scatter widens considerably and the average percentage of users rises much more rapidly.

An early inkling of increases in contraceptive use in the regions with more female education can be found among the WFS data for the late 1970s and early 1980s, as indicated by the circles in Figure 6-5. The additional information gathered by the DHS in the late 1980s, shown as triangles, further confirms this relationship.

It should be stressed, however, that the regions that score highly on both modern method use and female education stem largely from Zimbabwe and Botswana (see Figure 6-6, which graphs the same data points as Figure 6-5, but in this case, the circles represent regions of Zimbabwe and Botswana). Conversely, Islamic regions (more than 75 percent Islamic or traditional religions) contribute disproportionately to the set of WFS and DHS regions

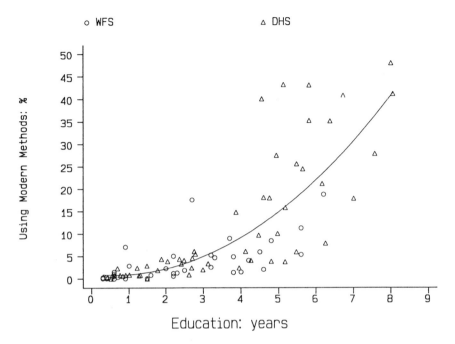

FIGURE 6-5 Relationship between percentage of married women ages 15-49 using modern methods of contraception and mean number of years of female education—WFS and DHS regions ($r = .80$). SOURCE: Demographic and Health Survey and World Fertility Survey reports.

characterized by the combination of low female schooling and low modern method usage (see Figure 6-7, circles).

The change in ideal family size and contraceptive knowledge and use can be demonstrated for the 1980s in countries that participated in both the WFS and the DHS, as shown in Table 6-1. In Kenya, knowledge levels were very high in 1978 (greater than 80 percent), and this knowledge base in combination with a rapid rise in the percentage of women preferring four or fewer children is reflected in substantial increases in users of modern methods between the two surveys. Knowledge levels in 1979-1980 were much more heterogeneous across regions in Ghana than in Kenya, and the increase in proportions with small ideal family sizes during the 1980s is more modest as well. Between the two surveys there was no change or even a decline in modern contraceptive use in Ghana. Hence, these two countries, both of which started after their independence with relatively high educational levels for women, have followed divergent paths with respect to family planning success.

Senegal and Northern Sudan are typical examples of Sahelian Islamic

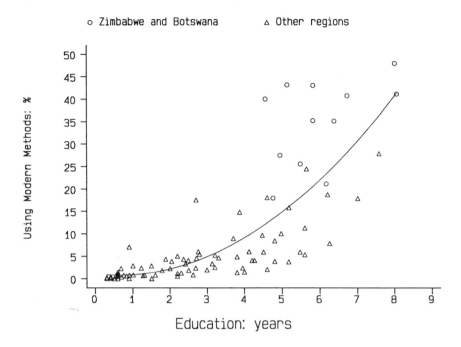

FIGURE 6-6 Relationship between percentage of married women ages 15-49 using modern methods and mean number of years of female education ($r = .80$). SOURCE: Demographic and Health Survey and World Fertility Survey reports.

societies with lower levels of female education. In both countries there was a noticeable increase during the 1980s in the knowledge of modern methods of contraception. Several areas, other than the capitals, now reach knowledge levels between 70 and 80 percent. Yet the proportion of women with small ideal family sizes has hardly changed, and the increase of modern contraceptive use remains insignificant. In the regions of northern Sudan, a decline in current use of modern methods may have occurred as well.

In summary, we find that:

• there is a strong relationship between the regional levels of female schooling and the proportion of women who have small ideal family sizes, who have knowledge of modern contraception, or who use a modern method (refer to Chapter 2 for individual-level confirmation);

• current use of modern methods increases above the 10-percent level only in regions that have a mean length of female schooling of four years or more; and

• these conditions have been met in Zimbabwe and Botswana, as well as several regions of Kenya. In these areas, there has been a corre-

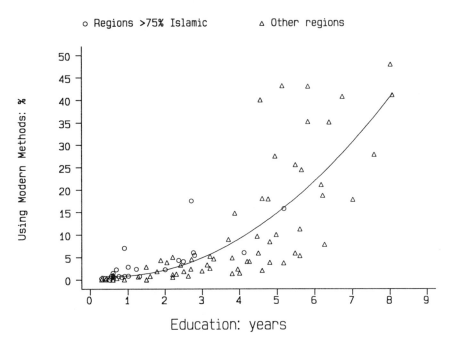

FIGURE 6-7 Relationship between percentage of married women ages 15-49 using modern mettods and mean number of years of education—WFS and DHS regions (*r* = .80). SOURCE: Demographic and Health Survey and World Fertility Survey reports.

sponding rise in actual contraceptive use. However, there are several areas in other countries with a mean length of female schooling of four years or more (e.g., Imbo province in Burundi, all regions in Ghana except the two northern ones, Montserrado in Liberia, Ondo State, Khartoum, and Kampala) in which current use has remained low or may have decreased in the last decade (Ghana and Sudan). This diversity of experience within regions with relatively high female schooling levels suggests that other variables may be equally or more important in influencing contraceptive use. All of the regions that would be expected to have a prevalence of modern methods of at least 10 percent and did not were located in countries with weak family planning programs, which suggests that contraceptive supply may be a factor.

MULTIVARIATE ANALYSIS OF
MODERN CONTRACEPTIVE USE

We now consider the relationship between female education and contraceptive practice at the regional level in a multivariate model. We present

TABLE 6-1 Comparison of Ideal Family Size, Modern Contraceptive Knowledge, and Modern Contraceptive Use for Women Currently in Union in Sub-Saharan Regions Included in Both WFS and DHS Surveys (percent)

Region and Date	Ideal Family Size ≤ 4		Know at Least One Modern Method		Use Modern Method	
	WFS	DHS	WFS	DHS	WFS	DHS
Kenya (1977-1978, 1988-1989)						
Nairobi	32	79	93	95	19	28
Central, Eastern	16	68	92	94	9	25
Rift Valley	12	50	81	85	5	18
Coast	15	36	83	92	5	15
Western, Nyanza	17	49	88	92	3	10
Ghana (1979-1980, 1988)						
Central, Western	27	33	76	79	5	4
Greater Accra, Eastern	37	51	81	90	11	8
Volta	35	46	62	78	6	4
Ashanti, Brong Ahafo	30	45	59	80	9	6
Northern, Upper	5	7	13	40	1	1
Senegal (1978, 1986)						
Central	11	11	13	70	0	1
Northeast	12	11	16	39	0	1
South	7	13	14	54	0	2
West (Dakar, Thiès)	14	26	38	86	2	6
Sudan (Northern, 1978-1979, 1989-1990)						
Central	37	20	63	80	7	4
Khartoum	41	41	82	96	18	16
Kordofan, Darfur	21	11	27	45	2	1
North, East	28	21	50	74	3	4

the results of multiple regressions applied first to the DHS data alone and then to the pooled WFS and DHS data (see Tables 6A-1 and 6A-2).

The least squares regression model for the pooled data is presented in Figure 6-8. (The results for the DHS data alone are similar to the results for the pooled data set.) In these models we consider four independent variables:

•   the average length of schooling for women ages 15-49,

•   the presence of a large and dominant urban area in a region (dummy variable),

•   the percentage of married women ages 15-49 that are in a polygynous union, and

•   the proportion of respondents that are Muslim or subscribe to traditonal religions.

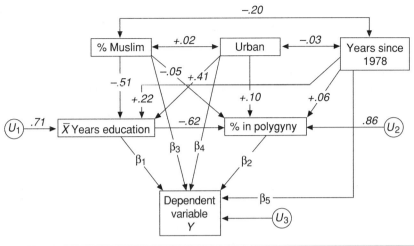

Dependent Variable y	β_1	β_2	β_3	β_4	β_5	R^2_{adj}	U_3
% Use Modern Method	+.65[a]	−.25[a]	+.12	−.06	0.16[b]	.62	.62
% Know 1+ Modern Method	+.54[a]	−.20[a]	−.03	−.04	0.29[a]	.64	.60
% Ideal Family Size ≤4	+.42[a]	−.24[a]	+.01	+.15[b]	+.34[a]	.61	.62
$\bar{x}$ Breastfeeding	−.60[a]	+.12	−.26[b]	−.15	+.19[b]	.38	.79
$\bar{x}$ Amenorrhea	−.68[a]	+.06	−.13	−.20[b]	+.29[a]	.54	.68
$\bar{x}$ Postpartum Abstinence	−.10	+.54[a]	−.36[a]	−.00	−.12	.32	.82
$\bar{x}$ Postpartum Nonsusceptible	−.54[a]	+.32[a]	−.33[a]	−.08	+.10	.43	.75

[a]Significant at 01.
[b]Significant at 05.

FIGURE 6-8 Regression model for various demographic dependent variables—WFS and DHS regions (n = 92).

In the regressions based on both the WFS and the DHS data, a calendar time variable (years since 1978) has also been introduced to allow for variation with respect to year of measurement. It should also be noted that the regions of Senegal, Kenya, northern Sudan, and Ghana contribute two data points in the pooled WFS and DHS sample. These measurements are approximately 10 years apart.

Relationships Among Background Variables

There are a number of relationships among these four background variables that have implications for the subsequent analysis.

Urbanity and the proportion Muslim have important but obviously opposite associations with the level of female education. These associations were found in both the DHS and the pooled regional samples: The effect of urbanity on education, measured by standardized regression (beta) coefficients, is +.47 and +.41, in the respective samples; by contrast, the effect of the proportion Muslim is −.49 and −.51, respectively.

When we tested the relationship of the proportion Muslim, urbanity, and female education to the percentage of married women in polygyny in both data sets, only the negative effect of female education was significant and large: beta coefficients are −.50 and −.62, respectively. Other factors, not specified in the model but subsumed in the residual variable U_2, exerted a major influence on the incidence of polygyny (effects of U_2 are .87 and .86). Polygyny is associated positively with other features of sub-Saharan culture and social organization (e.g., involvement of women in trade and survival of female secret societies or of institutionally structured economic and political networks for women; see Chapter 4). Also the negative association between polygyny and matrilineal systems of descent is another example of a historical connection that is not explicitly considered in the model. The polygyny variable can therefore be considered a proxy for a broader spectrum of features of social organization that is particularly relevant for the West African regions in our samples.

Relative Importance of These Background Variables in Contraceptive Practice

Of the four background variables included, level of education had by far the strongest effect (β_1) on modern contraceptive use in the two analyses (0.71 and 0.65). Next in influence was the percentage of women in polygyny, which was negatively related to modern contraceptive use (B_2). The two other background variables—urbanity and the proportion Muslim—influenced level of schooling, but had little or no direct effects on modern contraceptive use (although urbanity is significant in the individual-level analysis of contraceptive use in Chapter 2).

Similar patterns held when the knowledge of a modern method of contraception and small ideal family size (i.e., less than five children) were regressed on the background variables. The effect of female education is again strongest (+0.54 and +0.42, respectively). The effect of polygyny remains negative, as expected. The proportion Muslim has no effect after controlling for female education.. Urbanization (i.e., living in a major city) has a positive effect on smaller family size ideals, but not on the knowledge of at least one modern method.

Conclusions

These results for the pooled WFS and DHS sample are strikingly similar to the regression results of the WFS regional sample (Lesthaeghe, 1989b). However, there are no observations in either analysis for central Africa, or for regions that were in the past strongly affected by high levels of infecundity (e.g., Gabon, southern Sudan, northwest Zaire, and the Central African Republic).

In addition to this regression analysis, we also tested these relationships using LISREL models[6] applied to the two data sets (results not shown).[7] Those results confirmed the role of female education in the adoption of contraception. However, in the context of sub-Saharan Africa, it is essential to examine the dynamics of contraceptive use in the larger context of other birth spacing practices. In the next chapter we analyze the relative contribution of modern contraceptive use versus the traditional postpartum means of child spacing to changes in fertility.

---

[6]LISREL is a statistical package that allows for the construction of complex variables on the basis of highly correlated indicators. In this analysis, LISREL allowed for the simultaneous modeling of all the dependent variables presented in Figure 6-8 and gave a measure of the goodness of fit of the model. The results from the LISREL models are presented here to confirm the results of our simpler analysis.

[7]In the LISREL model, we assumed a causal linkage among a series of demographic variables including length of postpartum nonsusceptible period, small desired family size, knowledge of modern contraception, and current contraceptive use. The level of female education was then measured as the common component of the average female schooling duration and the percentage of illiterate women aged 15-49 in the regions. Finally, the percentage of users of modern contraception was complemented by a broader index of use-effectiveness (i.e., a weighted average of the method-specific use-effectiveness levels with the weights equal to the proportion of women using a given method; adapted from Bongaarts and Potter, 1983).

The two LISREL models were characterized by an excellent goodness of fit, uncorrelated residuals, and a strong similarity for the two data sets between the respective sets of standardized coefficients.

TABLE 6A-1   WFS Regional File—Part A

Region	Use Modern Method (%)	Contraceptive Use- Effectiveness Index	Married Who Know at Least 1 Modern Method (%)	Married Who Want ≤ 4 Children (%)
Benin				
Atacora, Borgou	0.6	2	5.4	5.9
Central, South	0.4	4	10.6	12.0
Cotonou	4.1	8	52.4	36.1
Cameroon				
Center-South, East	0.6	3	48.9	11.4
Littoral, Southwest	1.3	1	38.7	2.6
North	0.1	0	6.4	18.4
West, Northwest	0.1	1	22.3	2.7
Douala, Yaoundé	4.9	6	62.9	6.8
Côte d'Ivoire				
Abidjan	1.9	2	34.3	9.7
Rural forest	0.1	0	13.5	5.1
Rural savanna	0.1	0	4.0	4.9
Urban forest	1.2	2	25.5	9.4
Urban savanna	0.8	1	21.2	10.2
Ghana				
Central, Western	5.3	4	75.5	26.7
Greater Accra, Eastern	11.3	9	81.4	37.0
Volta	6.0	6	61.9	35.0
Ashanti, Brong Ahafo	8.5	6	59.4	29.9
Northern, Upper (East, Upper West)	1.1	1	13.1	5 .1
Kenya				
Nairobi	18.8	15	93.2	31.5
Central, Eastern	9.0	7	92.4	15.5
Rift Valley	4.7	5	80.6	11.6
Coast	5.1	4	83.4	15.1
Western, Nyanza	2.6	3	88.1	16.7
Lesotho				
Lowlands	5.4	6	66.4	37.1
Other (Foothills, Orange River Valley, Mountains)	2.1	3	54.5	28.7

Average Duration of Education (years)	Illiterate or Koranic Only (%)	Dummy Variable (1 = major urban, 0 = not urban)	Married in Polygamous Union (%)	Religion (%)		
				Muslim	Christian	Traditional
0.6	89	0	40.8	41	8	51
0.7	88	0	37.8	7	28	65
4.2	43	1	32.0	8	67	25
2.2	53	0	31.5	4	94	2
2.3	53	0	27.6	1	96	3
0.4	91	0	44.3	54	19	27
1.5	69	0	56.7	14	73	13
3.8	29	1	23.0	4	93	3
2.5	65	1	33.8	38	40	22
0.9	82	0	42.7	23	37	40
0.3	95	0	41.5	44	6	50
2.2	68	1	43.8	45	36	19
1.6	76	1	47.9	49	25	26
3.2	60	0	31.8	9	78	13
5.6	37	1	27.1	7	75	18
4.5	46	0	43.2	9	67	24
4.8	43	0	29.9	11	75	14
0.6	93	0	49.9	19	11	70
6.2	20	1	21.6	1	96	3
3.7	37	0	18.3	0	96	4
3.3	44	0	24.9	1	90	9
2.2	69	0	32.6	37	40	23
3.2	46	0	40.5	3	96	
5.6	4	0	8.4	0	86	14
4.6	11	0	8.7	0	78	22

TABLE 6A-1 WFS Regional File—Part A (*continued*)

Region	Use Modern Method (%)	Contraceptive Use-Effectiveness Index	Married Who Know at Least 1 Modern Method (%)	Married Who Want ≤ 4 Children (%)
Nigeria				
Northeast	0.0	0	8.9	11.7
Northwest	0.3	0	7.3	7.7
Southeast	1.4	1.2	32.9	3.0
Southwest	1.5	1.5	34.6	7.9
Senegal				
Central	0.4	0	12.7	10.7
Fleuve, Oriental	0.0	0	16.1	11.7
Casamance	0.0	0	14.3	7.0
Dakar, Thiès	2.3	2	37.9	14.3
Sudan (northern)				
Khartoum	17.6	13	82.7	41.1
North, east	2.9	3	49.8	28.2
Central	7.1	7	63.3	36.7
Kordofan, Darfur	1.5	2	26.5	20.9

Average Duration of Education (years)	Illiterate or Koranic Only (%)	Dummy Variable (1 = major urban, 0 = not urban)	Married in Polygamous Union (%)	Religion (%)		
				Muslim	Christian	Traditional
0.6	86.8	0	42.3	69	23	8
0.3	94.5	0	49.3	93	1	6
3.8	52.0	0	39.3	0	84	16
4.0	52.5	1	35.5	36	57	7
0.4	93	0	50.0	98	1	1
0.5	91	0	45.0	98	1	1
0.6	89	0	54.4	87	13	0
2.0	71	1	45.1	93	7	0
2.7	57	1	9.8	96	4	0
1.0	79	0	12.6	98	1	1
0.9	79	0	13.3	98	1	1
0.6	89	0	27.2	98	0	2

TABLE 6A-1 WFS Regional File—Part B

Region	Marriage Duration 10+ Years, with ≤ 1 Births (%)	Prevalence/Incidence Ratios				Age 15-19, Still Single (%)
		Postpartum Abstinence (months)	Postpartum Amenorrhea (months)	Breastfeeding (months)	Overall Nonsusceptible Period (months)	
Benin						
Atacora, Borgou	3.6	23	16	24	23	36.4
Central, South	1.9	17	13	21	18	53.8
Cotonou	2.2	11	9	17	13	82.9
Cameroon						
Center-South, East	8.9	15	13	18	17	60.8
Littoral, Southwest	7.5	18	12	19	19	54.0
North	11.8	14	14	20	17	19.4
West, Northwest	5.0	22	15	22	23	47.6
Douala, Yaoundé	9.5	12	9	16	14	68.5
Côte d'Ivoire						
Abidjan	10.3	14	11	18	16	43.9
Rural forest	9.2	16	13	22	18	37.6
Rural savanna	5.4	20	15	25	22	48.2
Urban forest	6.8	14	10	18	16	48.6
Urban savanna	13.0	15	11	18	17	54.6
Ghana						
Central, Western	0.9	7	12	15	13	61.0
Greater Accra, Eastern	4.4	9	12	17	13	78.2
Volta	3.2	17	15	22	20	78.6
Ashanti, Brong Ahafo	1.9	8	14	19	15	69.5
Northern, Upper (East, Upper West)	3.2	29	19	33	30	35.7

Kenya						
Nairobi	0.9	3	8	14	9	66.6
Central, Eastern	2.0	4	12	17	13	88.5
Rift Valley	1.5	6	11	17	12	69.9
Coast	7.8	4	15	20	15	46.3
Western, Nyanza	2.9	3	12	19	13	64.6
Lesotho[a]						
Lowlands	6.7	17	11	22	19	
Other (Foothills, Orange River Valley, Mountains)	7.0	19	11	22	20	
Nigeria						
Northeast	8.3	16.2	13.2	18.4	18.9	29.4
Northwest	9.0	18.9	16.5	22.6	22.9	17.3
Southeast	2.3	14.7	13.2	17.2	16.8	85.1
Southwest	3.0	19.7	13.2	24.4	20.6	81.9
Senegal						
Central	4.2	5	14	21	15	29.9
Fleuve, Oriental	5.4	6	13	19	14	28.3
Casamance	4.1	6	16	23	17	29.2
Dakar, Thiès	4.7	2	13	19	14	63.6
Sudan (northern)[a]						
Khartoum	3.9	3	9	17	10	
North, east	3.9	4	11	17	12	
Central	3.8	3	12	18	13	
Kordofan, Darfur	5.9	3	13	18	14	

[a]Only ever-married interviewed.

SOURCE: Data from Lesthaeghe (1989b) and WFS reports and data tapes.

TABLE 6A-2 DHS Regional File—Part A

Region	Use Modern Method (%)	Contraceptive Use- Effectiveness Index	Married Who Know at Least 1 Modern Method (%)	Married Who Want ≤ 4 Children (%)
Botswana				
Urban	40.8	40.1	99.7	54.1
Rural	27.5	27.2	91.9	34.1
Burundi[b]				
Central plateau	0.8	4.3	67.8	31.9
Imbo	6.1	10.4	75.4	43.4
Lowlands	0.0	2.0	52.0	25.6
Mumirwa	2.3	5.4	52.7	33.7
Mugamba	0.9	4.4	63.5	36.o
Ghana				
Central, Western	4.1	7.0	79.0	32.7
Greater Accra, Eastern	7.9	14.0	89.7	51.1
Volta	3.9	10.2	77.5	45.6
Ashanti, Brong Ahafo	6.0	8.8	79.5	44.9
Northern, Upper (East, Upper West)	0.7	6.7	40.4	6.7
Kenya				
Nairobi	27.9	30.4	94.8	78.8
Central, Eastern	24.5	33.1	94.1	68.2
Rift Valley	18.1	24.4	84.6	50.1
Coast	14.8	16.3	92.3	35.7
Western, Nyanza	10.1	12.o	92.1	49.3
Liberia				
Grand Gedeh	2.9	2.9	64.1	11.1
Montserrado	9.7	10.8	77.3	29.9
Sinoe	3.9	4.1	87.2	8.8
Rest of country	4.4	4.6	64.4	20.3
Mali				
Bamako	6.1	11.4	74.3	33.8
Kayes, Koulikoro	0.8	1.6	28.0	12.8
Mopti, Gao, Tombouctou	0.9	1.4	15.0	7.9
Sikasso, Segou	0.8	1.6	26.0	22.4
Nigeria				
Ondo State	3.8	5.1	50.0	10.2
Senegal				
Central	0.5	1.8	70.2	11.2
Northeast (Fleuve, Oriental)	0.6	1.1	38.9	11.1
South (Casamance)	2.4	2.6	53.5	13.0
West (Dakar, Thiès)	5.5	7.6	85.5	25.5

Average Duration of Education (years)	Illiterate or Koranic Only (%)	Dummy Variable (1 = major urban, 0 = not urban)	Married in Polygamous Union (%)	Religion (%)		
				Muslim	Christian	Traditional
6.72	10.2	1	a	0.0	36.6	63.4
4.94	25.5	0	a	0.0	29.2	70.8
0.91	62.4	0	8.2	b	b	b
4.12	46.5	1	24.5	b	b	b
0.52	73.1	0	20.7	b	b	b
0.69	70.1	0	12.1	b	b	b
1.01	65.3	0	6.8	b	b	b
4.26	58.3	0	27.0	7.3	82.9	9.7
6.25	39.4	1	27.0	8.1	80.5	11.5
4.80	50.6	0	43.8	4.4	59.4	36.2
5.47	46.2	0	30.2	8.4	75.6	16.0
1.27	87.6	0	48.3	28.3	18.7	52.9
7.57	9.3	1	15.5	6.6	88.4	4.9
5.64	21.3	0	14.5	0.3	98.5	1.2
4.60	34.0	0	19.8	0.7	91.4	8.0
3.87	41.5	0	34.1	34.7	46.0	19.3
4.97	31.8	0	33.2	1.1	97.7	1.3
1.49	73.8	0	55.5	6.4	66.5	27.0
4.47	47.5	1	25.8	16.6	61.5	22.0
2.04	68.2	0	35.6	1.2	82.9	15.9
1.88	70.7	0	40.7	14.8	48.7	36.6
2.76	58.2	1	32.7	95.8	4.2	0.0
0.76	88.7	0	50.4	92.0	2.8	5.2
0.56	89.7	0	42.4	94.3	3.9	1.9
0.61	89.6	0	45.4	91.7	0.9	7.5
5.17	40.5	0	46.1	13.4	84.7	1.9
0.54	92.5	0	49.1	98.2	1.8	0.0
0.83	88.3	0	47.1	98.6	1.4	0.0
1.22	82.7	0	51.7	91.1	7.9	1.0
2.79	65.2	1	41.1	93.3	6.6	0.1

TABLE 6A-2 DHS Regional File—Part A (*continued*)

Region	Use Modern Method (%)	Contraceptive Use-Effectiveness Index	Married Who Know at Least 1 Modern Method (%)	Married Who Want ≤ 4 Children (%)
Sudan (northern)				
Khartoum	15.8	18.8	96.3	41.4
North, east	4.4	5.7	74.2	20.8
Central	4.1	5.5	80.2	19.8
Kordofan, Darfur	0.8	1.3	45.3	10.8
Togo				
Central	1.9	4.1	73.6	25.7
Coastal (including Lomé)	4.6	11.5	88.8	57.2
Kara	3.3	9.6	74.4	38.7
Plateau	2.4	8.6	86.8	48.4
Savanna	0.3	0.7	62.1	13.3
Uganda				
West Nile	0.0	0.5	17.8	18.0
East	2.0	2.8	84.8	24.2
Central	2.4	3.7	78.7	22.4
West	3.4	5.3	61.0	27.1
Southwest	5.9	2.5	83.3	17.4
Kampala	17.9	21.4	96.3	46.0
Zimbabwe				
Bulawayo	41.2	41.5	99.5	66.3
Harare/Chitungwiza	48.0	48.6	99.0	57.6
Manicaland	25.6	28.7	97.7	29.0
Mashonaland Central	40.1	43.3	95.4	34.6
Mashonaland East (except Harare/Chitungwiza)	43.1	44.6	98.2	33.7
Mashonaland West	43.2	45.0	98.8	38.1
Masvingo	35.3	41.7	96.8	29.8
Matabeleland North (except Bulawayo)	18.0	23.1	96.9	35.2
Matabeleland South	21.2	24.8	98.7	42.3
Midlands	35.2	39.8	97.2	41.5

^aNot asked.
^bReligion not asked.

Average Duration of Education (years)	Illiterate or Koranic Only (%)	Dummy Variable (1 = major urban, 0 = not urban)	Married in Polygamous Union (%)	Religion (%)		
				Muslim	Christian	Traditional
5.18	33.4	1	13.5	94.5	5.5	0.0
2.36	61.3	0	14.0	97.5	2.5	0.0
2.49	62.7	0	15.1	99.2	0.7	0.1
1.31	78.9	0	32.1	99.7	0.3	0.0
1.78	77.8	0	60.9	46.4	20.5	33.0
2.71	62.3	1	52.5	5.7	40.1	54.1
2.41	66.0	0	52.8	12.0	32.2	55.7
2.69	58.0	0	46.8	6.6	59.8	33.5
0.42	94.9	0	53.9	14.9	4.8	80.4
1.50	77.6	0	33.1	24.2	75.8	0.0
2.99	58.0	0	42.0	17.2	81.8	1.0
3.95	39.0	0	31.3	13.6	86.1	0.3
3.13	45.5	0	39.0	1.2	98.1	0.7
2.62	44.4	0	27.4	3.8	95.3	0.9
7.00	13.1	1	34.3	14.2	85.4	0.4
8.05	6.6	1	7.5	0.0	77.6	22.4
8.00	4.9	1	12.7	0.0	84.6	15.4
5.48	19.0	0	20.2	0.0	66.0	34.0
4.55	32.6	0	22.1	0.0	67.0	33.0
5.81	19.5	0	14.1	0.0	64.1	35.9
5.13	25.9	0	12.2	0.0	64.3	35.7
5.81	15.3	0	18.3	0.0	56.9	43.1
4.76	30.7	0	28.1	0.0	65.1	34.9
6.16	11.0	0	11.5	0.0	56.9	43.1
6.37	14.9	0	20.4	0.0	70.4	29.6

TABLE 6A-2 DHS Regional File—Part B

Region	Marriage Duration 10+ Years, with ≤ 1 Births (%)	Prevalence/Incidence Ratios				
		Postpartum Abstinence (months)	Postpartum Amenorrhea (months)	Breastfeeding (months)	Overall Nonsusceptible Period (months)	Age 15-19, Still Single (%)
Botswana						
Urban	7.1	9.4	8.5	14.7	11.9	92.8
Rural	5.6	13.8	12.6	20.2	16.9	94.4
Burundi						
Central plateau	3.9	3.8	20.0	25.0	20.8	93.4
Imbo	6.1	5.1	13.5	18.5	14.8	89.3
Lowlands	4.6	2.8	19.2	23.7	19.9	87.5
Mumirwa	2.4	2.1	19.0	22.0	19.1	95.9
Mugamba	6.5	3.0	18.9	23.5	19.8	98.4
Ghana						
Central, Western	3.4	11.4	12.7	19.4	16.5	71.6
Greater Accra, Eastern	6.3	11.7	11.7	18.0	15.8	85.9
Volta	6.1	15.6	14.9	20.8	19.0	76.7
Ashanti, Brong Ahafo	4.3	10.2	14.0	20.1	16.6	68.3
Northern, Upper	2.8	26.9	20.2	26.6	27.9	60.6
Kenya						
Nairobi	6.0	6.3	9.1	19.9	11.5	71.1
Central, Eastern	2.7	7.0	9.9	19.8	12.4	86.6
Rift Valley	3.9	8.2	12.2	19.1	14.1	80.2
Coast	7.3	2.6	9.4	17.7	9.9	70.5
Western, Nyanza	3.6	3.7	11.6	19.5	12.6	76.0

Liberia						
Grand Gedeh	7.0	14.0	13.2	21.5	17.3	57.7
Montserrado	10.1	11.3	8.3	12.9	12.6	70.4
Sinoe	7.0	12.6	9.8	17.3	14.9	63.9
Rest of Country	9.6	13.9	12.2	18.1	16.2	61.6
Mali						
Bamako	11.2	5.1	10.8	19.3	12.6	25.0
Kayes, Koulikoro	9.6	7.6	16.6	21.9	17.8	17.1
Mopti, Gao,	6.9	6.6	16.2	21.7	18.2	40.2
Tombouctou						
Sikasso, Segou	6.6	7.1	14.9	21.7	16.1	21.4
Nigeria						
Ondo State	2.5	22.8	14.0	18.2	24.1	88.5
Senegal						
Central	8.9	4.1	17.9	19.6	18.1	44.3
Northeast (Fleuve, Oriental)	9.4	11.6	15.6	18.7	18.7	38.0
South (Casamance)	9.9	18.3	16.9	20.4	21.2	49.6
West (Dakar, Thiès)	9.1	6.1	14.1	17.4	16.0	76.9
Sudan (northern)[a]						
Khartoum	7.0	5.1	9.0	15.9	11.0	
North, East	6.0	5.8	12.9	19.8	14.4	
Central	4.8	4.1	14.5	20.4	15.2	
Kodofan, Darfur	4.9	5.3	16.7	20.6	17.7	
Togo						
Central	2.8	20.2	14.8	23.2	21.5	56.1
Coastal (including Lomé)	5.5	12.7	13.1	21.0	17.1	83.4
Kara	2.8	20.8	14.9	22.9	22.9	67.9
Plateau	3.6	18.2	12.6	22.4	20.2	72.8
Savanna	0.5	23.7	19.9	26.2	25.1	44.3

Continued

TABLE 6A-2 DHS Regional File—Part B (*continued*)

Region	Marriage Duration 10+ Years, with ≤ 1 Births (%)	Prevalence/Incidence Ratios				Age 15-19, Still Single (%)
		Postpartum Abstinence (months)	Postpartum Amenorrhea (months)	Breastfeeding (months)	Overall Nonsusceptible Period (months)	
Uganda						
West Nile	1.3	10.7	20.0	25.7	22.0	46.4
East	9.2	4.6	13.0	18.6	13.7	52.6
Central	11.1	3.6	11.1	16.7	12.1	50.8
West	1.5	2.6	11.9	17.9	12.5	53.3
Southwest	4.8	2.9	13.3	19.8	14.3	70.3
Kampala	6.3	6.4	8.8	14.9	11.4	73.2
Zimbabwe						
Bulawayo	7.0	5.5	9.4	15.1	11.2	88.8
Harare/Chitunwiza	4.5	4.8	9.3	15.5	11.5	84.3
Manicaland	4.0	6.6	9.9	17.7	11.6	74.2
Mashonaland Central	6.1	4.6	13.9	22.1	14.4	60.0
Mashonaland East (except Harare/ Chitungwiza)	4.8	5.3	10.5	17.0	12.8	81.5
Mashonaland West	5.7	4.6	10.7	15.9	11.9	77.4
Masvingo	4.8	5.3	11.1	17.2	12.9	81.9
Matabeleland North (except Bulawayo)	2.6	6.2	14.9	19.4	15.6	70.7
Matabeleland South	8.1	6.5	10.6	18.5	12.8	86.1
Midlands	5.9	4.1	11.4	19.1	12.3	86.5

*a*Only ever-married interviewed.

SOURCE: Demographic and Health Survey data tapes.

7

Contribution of Modern Contraceptive Use Relative to Postpartum Practices to Fertility Decline

This volume has focused on contraceptive use, not fertility per se. However, the keen interest among the population community in contraceptive prevalence in the higher use countries of Botswana, Kenya, and Zimbabwe stems from the possible implications for fertility decline in these and other countries.

In analyses of the variation in marital fertility in developing countries over the past two decades, contraceptive use has been the major determining factor in the majority of cases. Traditional postpartum practices (i.e., intermediate or proximate fertility variables including fecundity, lactational amenorrhea, and postpartum abstinence) have played a secondary role in other parts of the developing world (Bongaarts, 1978).

However, in Africa, postpartum nonsusceptibility has been shown to be a major determinant of variations in fertility levels (Bongaarts et al., 1984). Postpartum practices are closely related to cultural patterns and forms of social organization, particularly in Africa where regional differences with respect to these proximate determinants are very large (e.g., see Chapter 4; Caldwell, 1976; Page and Lesthaeghe, 1981). In light of the importance of these postpartum practices to fertility, an exclusive focus on contraceptive practice in the context of sub-Saharan Africa would be inappropriate (see Appendix A).

In this chapter, therefore, we address one final question: In Africa, what has been the relative importance of modern contraceptive use versus postpartum infecundability in inhibiting fertility?[1]

Central to this question is the theory of a two-phased fertility transition in Africa, which we review before proceeding to an analysis of the available data on a regional level.

THE TWO-PHASED FERTILITY TRANSITION

The basic premise of this transition theory is that fertility decline in sub-Saharan Africa will occur in two phases, a notion entertained by several authors writing about fertility transition in general (e.g., Kocher, 1973; Easterlin, 1983). These authors envision the possibility of an initial fertility rise (the first phase) occurring prior to a fertility decline (the second phase). This initial rise would stem from socioeconomic development factors affecting the levels of natural fertility and the supply of children. A decline in subfecundity or secondary sterility resulting from improved health care (Romaniuk, 1968; Retel-Laurentin, 1974; Frank, 1983a,b; Larsen, 1989), and the shortened durations of breastfeeding and postpartum abstinence are often strongly associated with increased female education and urbanization (cf. Olusanya, 1969; Caldwell and Caldwell, 1977; Nag, 1980; Romaniuk, 1980; Adegbola et al., 1981; Gaisie, 1981; Mosley et al., 1982; Lesthaeghe et al., 1983).[2] Moreover, the initial increase in the supply of children is further enhanced by increased infant and child survival.

With declining demand for children stimulated by some of the same socioeconomic changes, the second phase of the transition is set in motion. This phase is characterized by declining desired family size, increased knowledge of contraception, and subsequently increased use-effectiveness of fertility regulation. Reduced demand for children as a response to diminished child utility, increased costs of childrearing, and higher aspirations with respect to child quality are often associated with the same factors of socioeconomic development that produced the initial fertility rise (see Chapters 3 and 4).

In Africa, as in other parts of the world, female education is strongly linked with fertility (see Chapters 2 and 3). From Chapter 6 it is evident that education is the strongest of the four contextual variables tested in

---

[1]Because of the focus of this report on contraceptive use primarily among married women, we devote little attention to marriage patterns and their effects on fertility. For discussions of this topic, see Westoff, 1992; Jolly and Gribble, 1993; and the Working Group on the Social Dynamics of Adolescent Fertility, 1993.

[2]Although declines in the postpartum nonsusceptible period before the late 1970s are well documented, there is no study that systematically relates these declines to increases in fertility. However, it is the view of the working group that these declines, in addition to decreases in subfecundity, most likely led to increases in fertility.

determining modern contraceptive use. It is also associated with patterns of nuptiality and with postpartum practices in ways that are basic to African social organization, as discussed below.[3]

Regional Patterns of Nuptiality

The ages at entry into a regular sexual union vary widely across sub-Saharan African regions.[4] The proportions of single women aged 15-19 range from 10 to more than 90 percent. The corresponding singulate mean ages at marriage vary from about 16 to more than 21 years.

The main determinants of ages at entry into a sexual union are also well known (cf. Goldman and Pebley, 1989; Lesthaeghe et al., 1989a). First, there are a number of factors that are intimately linked to patterns of social organization. The incidence of polygyny is often singled out as a prime factor leading to early marriage for women, because polygyny presupposes a large age difference between the spouses and hence the combination of late marriage for men and early marriage for women. Lesthaeghe et al. (1992) examined the relationship between the incidence of polygyny and the age pattern of entry into a sexual union for women for the regions covered by the World Fertility Survey (WFS) and the Demographic and Health Survey (DHS). They found that highly polygynous societies can exhibit both early and fairly late marriage for women, provided the large age gap between spouses is maintained.

A second determinant of early marriage for women has been the Islamic influence on social organization. As argued by Goody (1973, 1976) and statistically supported by Lesthaeghe et al. (1989a), an early and more profound Islamization is associated with a preference for cousin-marriage (endogamy) and a tighter social control on women via early first marriage or fast remarriage following divorce or widowhood. Lesthaeghe et al. (1992) found that the Sahelian Islamic societies contributed quite heavily to the set

---

[3]The fourth proximate determinant, abortion, is not treated herein, given the dearth of reliable data on this topic. However, with possible exceptions in major urban areas among better-educated young women, abortion would appear to be fairly limited in African populations.

[4]Both the World Fertility Survey and the Demographic and Health Survey use a broad defnition of marriage and include women reported as "having a partner" as being in a regular sexual union. Occasional premarital sexual relations are not taken into account by the definition. The degree of tolerance of premarital sex varies considerably according to ethnic group and local custom. The norms range from a strong accentuation of premarital chastity to premarital sex and pregnancy being acceptable and occasionally desirable (Working Group on Social Dynamics of Adolescent Fertility, 1993).

of regions that had both a high incidence of polygyny and very low proportions single in the age group 15-19.

A third factor involved is matrilineal kinship organization. This factor
is generally associated with later marriage for women, largely because matrilineal
societies have less polygyny than neighboring patrilineal or bilateral ones
(cf. Lesthaeghe et al., 1988; Chapter 4).

Two additional factors have altered past practices: female schooling
and urbanization. Both tend to be associated positively with the proportion
of single women in the age group 15-19, either directly or through a negative effect on polygyny. Lesthaeghe et al. (1992) found that the vast majority of regions with average schooling durations of four years or more (or
with less than 50 percent illiterate women) have proportions of single women
15-19 in excess of 60 percent. At lower levels of education, however, there
was evidence of several confounding factors: polygyny, the proportion
Muslim, and the survival of traditional religions and syncretic churches.
These factors shape the positive relationship between female schooling levels and ages at entry into first union at the aggregate level.

Regional Patterns of Postpartum Infecundability

Postpartum infecundability potentially affects fertility in any society.
Yet it is of particular interest in sub-Saharan Africa because of the prolonged periods of breastfeeding and sexual abstinence, which lead to periods of postpartum nonsusceptibility that are much longer than in most parts
of the developing world. The relationship of these postpartum variables to
variations in fertility has been amply documented, as has the erosion of
these practices throughout Africa during the twentieth century (Bongaarts,
1981; Caldwell and Caldwell, 1981; Ferry, 1981; Gaisie, 1981; Lesthaeghe
et al., 1981; Schoenmaeckers et al., 1981).

Table 7-1 presents data on the postpartum measures, as well as average
length of schooling of women, for the countries and regions for which both
WFS and DHS data are available. Clearly, there has been little further
erosion of these means of child spacing between the survey dates for these
regions. Even so, with regard to breastfeeding, the sub-Saharan populations
examined here still have relatively long durations in comparison with many
other regions of the world. For example, regions with aggregate schooling
levels of five or more years have an average duration of breastfeeding of
about 17 months, with none dipping below one year.

The length of lactational amenorrhea in the regions at the time of the
DHS varies between 9 and 20 months, and the mean duration for the regions
with higher levels of schooling is still on the order of 11 months. The
period of postpartum abstinence is considerably shorter than that of lactational amenorrhea in three of the four countries shown in Table 7-1; it

varies in duration from an average of three months to as long as 27 months (e.g., Upper and Northern regions of Ghana).

The outcome variable that directly matters for fertility is the length of the overall postpartum period of nonsusceptibility (PPNS). It is defined for each individual as the longest of either the duration of lactational amenorrhea or the length of postpartum abstinence. The "abstinence bonus," the difference between the mean length of the overall PPNS and the mean duration of lactational amenorrhea (Lesthaeghe, 1989b), is about three months when the average duration of postpartum abstinence equals that of lactational amenorrhea. However, the abstinence bonus rises rapidly if the mean of abstinence becomes larger than the mean of amenorrhea. Abstinence bonuses of the order of five to ten months were common in the WFS regions of Côte d'Ivoire, Benin, Ghana, Nigeria, and Cameroon. In the DHS regions, abstinence bonuses of four to ten months are found in Liberia, Togo, and Ondo State (Nigeria).

In short, the fragmentary evidence for a small subset of regions supports the thesis that the traditional mechanisms of child spacing may have remained fairly intact at the durations observed during the late 1970s. Therefore, gains in contraceptive use would have become the primary source of change in marital fertility during the 1980s. It is, however, still necessary to stress the conditional nature of this statement because the presumed absence of a further downward trend in the postpartum variables requires documentation for many other regions of Africa as well.

Notwithstanding the evidence of "no further erosion" in the 1980s, female education has been one of the prime factors involved in the shortening of birth intervals in sub-Saharan Africa during at least the last three decades, as demonstrated by a number of individual-level analyses (e.g., Olusanya, 1971; Caldwell and Caldwell, 1977; Page and Lesthaeghe, 1981; Mosley et al., 1982; Gaisie, 1984; Locoh, 1984; Tambashe, 1984; Mpiti and Kalule-Sabiti, 1985). Thus, increased schooling levels for women have been partially responsible for the initial fertility increase during the first phase of the transition.

At the regional level, similar negative relationships to education are found within the WFS and DHS samples. This holds for all postpartum variables, although we graph in Figure 7-1 the relationship for only one of the four: the length of the postpartum nonsusceptible period.

Role of Education in the Two-Phased Transition

The intricate link between education and the two-phased transition appeared in Cochrane's (1979, 1983) analysis of cross-sectional data gathered at the individual level in a variety of countries. As discussed in Chapter 3, Cochrane found that monotonically increasing relations of fertility with education

TABLE 7-1 Comparison of Mean Durations of Postpartum Variables in Sub-Saharan Regions Covered by Both the WFS and the DHS

Regions and Dates	Breastfeeding (months)		Postpartum Amenorrhea (months)		Postpartum Abstinence (months)		Overall Postpartum Nonsusceptible Period (months)		Average Length of Schooling (years)	
	WFS	DHS	WFS	DHS	WFS	DHS	WFS	DHS	WFS	DHS
Kenya										
Nairobi	14	20	8	9	3	6	9	12	6.2	7.8
Central, Eastern	17	20	12	10	4	7	13	12	3.7	5.6
Rift Valley	17	19	11	12	6	8	12	14	3.3	4.6
Coast	20	18	15	9	4	3	15	10	2.2	3.9
Western, Nyanza	19	20	12	12	3	4	13	13	3.2	5.0
Ghana										
Central, Western	15	19	12	13	7	11	13	17	3.2	4.3
Greater Accra, Eastern	17	18	12	12	9	12	13	16	5.6	6.3
Volta	22	21	15	15	17	16	20	19	4.5	4.8
Ashanti, Brong Ahafo	19	20	14	14	8	10	15	17	4.8	5.5
Northern, Upper	33	27	19	20	29	27	30	28	0.6	1.3

Senegal										
Central	21	20	(14)	18	(5)	4	(15)	18	0.4	0.5
Northeast	19	19	(13)	16	(6)	11	(14)	19	0.5	0.8
South	23	20	(16)	17	(6)	18	(17)	21	0.6	1.2
West (Dakar, Thiès)	19	17	(13)	14	(2)	6	(14)	16	2.0	2.8
Sudan (northern)										
Central	18	20	12	15	3	4	13	15	0.9	2.5
Khartoum	17	16	9	9	3	5	10	11	2.7	5.2
Kordofan, Darfur	18	21	13	17	3	5	14	18	0.6	1.3
North, East	17	20	11	13	4	6	12	14	1.0	2.4

NOTE: Durations of postpartum abstinence (and hence also durations of postpartum nonsusceptibility) for Senegal were not measured in the WFS. The results presented here are based on evidence from other surveys by Cantrelle and Ferry, and Anderson et al. (see Lesthaeghe et al., 1989b:136 for details). Similarly, the durations of lactational amenorrhea for Senegal were estimated from the WFS results for the length of breastfeeding. All other mean durations are estimated as prevalence-incidence ratios for births for the three years prior to the survey.

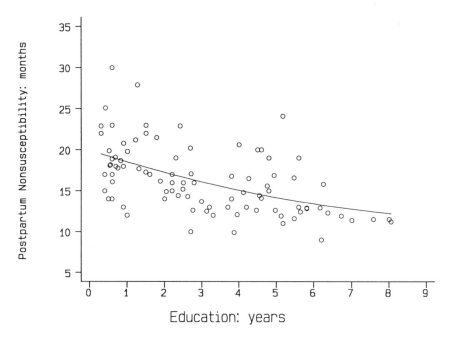

FIGURE 7-1   Relationship between the length of postpartum nonsusceptibility in months and the mean number of years of female education—WFS and DHS regions ($r = .53$). SOURCE: Demographic and Health Survey and World Fertility Survey reports.

or inverted U-shaped relations were typical for areas in which female education acted more strongly in favor of increased natural fertility and reduced child spacing than in favor of enhanced contraception. The cross-sectional effect of education on fertility is more negative at later than at earlier points in time, and more likely to be found in countries that have higher levels of urbanization, per capita income, and daily caloric intake (Cochrane, 1983).

These conclusions were largely borne out for sub-Saharan Africa in the contextual analysis of female education performed by Lesthaeghe et al. (1989a) for regions covered by the WFS. Through the calculation of the Bongaarts (1983) proximate determinants indices, these authors attempted to measure the effects of the overall nonsusceptible period and contraceptive use on fertility. These indices were calculated for different educational groups within various age groups for each of the 33 WFS regions (Nigeria excluded). Overall child spacing was viewed as being negatively affected by education in these cross sections if the better-educated women (five or more years of schooling) did not offset the effect of reduced overall post-partum nonsusceptibility by increased contraception and would, therefore—other things being equal—have higher marital fertility than illiterate women. The same contrast was also examined for women with a few years of schooling (one to four years) compared to illiterate women. The conclusions of this study, which pertain predominantly to the late 1970s and capture many regions in western Africa during the first phase of the transition, can be summarized as follows: In areas where female education was low to begin with and Islam predominated, child spacing was reduced most by increases in education. Conversely, in less-Islamic regions, increased use of contraception was found to offset the effects of decreased postpartum nonsusceptibility.

Hence, in the late 1970s, female education operated both as an individual and as a contextual variable, and the balance between child spacing via lactational amenorrhea and postpartum abstinence on the one hand and contraception on the other was conducive toward a positive fertility-education relationship in areas with the lowest scores for female education. However, one might expect that eventually as overall levels of education and contraceptive use increase, a negative relationship would hold. These findings for the late 1970s are in line with the general argument advanced by Caldwell (1980) that mass education, especially when it incorporates women, is capable of triggering fertility transitions in developing countries. The effects, as indicated by WFS data, would begin to emerge once most women receive partial or full primary education and when illiteracy among them has been considerably reduced. Mass education, however, affects all components of reproduction, including those that initially produce an increase in the potential supply of children. Similarly, mass education is an equally forceful agent in the reduction of infant and childhood mortality and may therefore account for much of the statistical relationship found between the pace of the early-life mortality reduction and declining fertility.

CONTRACEPTION, NONSUSCEPTIBILITY, AND FERTILITY DECLINE

We return to the question of the relative contribution of contraceptive use versus postpartum nonsusceptibility to fertility change. Specifically, using WFS and DHS regional data, we examine the association of female education with the combined effects of postpartum nonsusceptibility and contraception and with the trade-off between the two fertility-inhibiting factors.

We first convert the mean length of the period of postpartum nonsusceptibility and the proportions of women using contraception to the Bongaarts indices of nonsusceptibility (C_i) and of contraception (C_c) (see Bongaarts and Potter, 1983). The index C_i is defined as[5]

$$C_i = 20/(18.5 + \text{PPNS}).$$

The index of contraception is defined as

$$C_c = 1 - (1.08ue)$$

where u is the proportion of users among women aged 15-49 in a sexual union and e is the method-specific use-effectiveness.[6]

The two indices C_i and C_c indicate, respectively, what fraction of the total fecundity rate (TF), or the fertility level observed in the absence of these proximate determinants, remains after allowing for the fertility-reducing effects of postpartum nonsusceptibility and contraception (given no change in the other proximate determinants of fertility). Because C_i and C_c generally affect fertility only within sexual union, the total marital fertility rate (TMFR) can be written as

$$\text{TMFR} = \text{TF} \cdot C_i \cdot C_c$$

or, after taking logarithms to put the equation in an additive form,

$$\log \text{TMFR} = \log \text{TF} + \log C_i + \log C_c .$$

Because C_i and C_c range in value from 0 to 1, their logarithms have negative values. In the present application, we ignore the value of TF and adopt a *ceteris paribus* clause with respect to the total fecundity rate across the regions. It should, however, be noted that levels of infecundity higher than normal have a major negative effect on TF. In the sample of regions used here, the central African zone of high levels of infecundity is not represented.

The joint degree of fertility reduction stemming from postpartum nonsusceptibility and contraception can be represented as $C_i C_c$ or (log C_i +

---

[5]If no breastfeeding and postpartum abstinence are practiced, the birth interval equals about 18.5 months, including waiting time to conception, time lost due to fetal loss, and gestation, plus 1.5 months for minimal postpartum amenorrhea. The index C_i is a simple ratio between such a minimal birth interval of 20 months and an interval prolonged by the observed period of postpartum nonsusceptibility.

[6]In our computations, e is set at 0.60 for the less efficient methods and at 0.97 for the more efficient ones. The coefficient 1.08 represents an adjustment for the fact that some couples do not use contraception if they know or believe that they are infecund.

log C_c). Because we are adding two negative values in the latter expression, the degree of fertility reduction increases as the sum reaches larger negative values. The joint effect will be denoted as S:

$$S = 1,000(\log C_i + \log C_c) .$$

Alternatively, we also wish to determine to what extent the modern form of contraception is overtaking the child spacing via postpartum nonsusceptibility. We therefore define the difference D as

$$D = 1,000(\log C_i - \log C_c) .$$

As D approaches zero, contraception is catching up with the effect of postpartum infecundability, and when D reaches positive values, the fertility-reducing effect of contraception outweighs that of lactational amenorrhea and postpartum abstinence.

The plot of S versus D is presented in Figure 7-2. The curvilinear

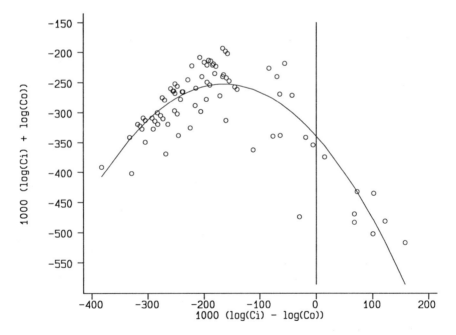

FIGURE 7-2 Relationship between the total degree of fertility reduction (S = vertical axis) and the difference between the share of postpartum nonsusceptibility and of contraception (D = horizontal axis)—WFS and DHS regions ($r = .86$). SOURCE: Demographic and Health Survey and World Fertility Survey reports.

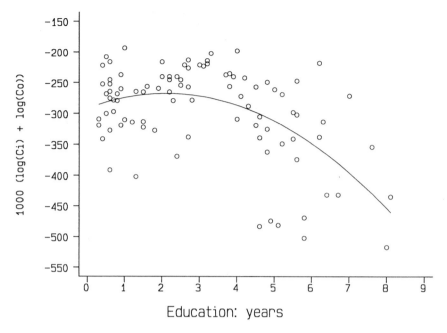

FIGURE 7-3 Relationship between the joint fertility-reducing effects of postpartum nonsusceptibility and contraception, and the average length of female education— WFS and DHS regions ($r = .54$). SOURCE: Demographic and Health Survey and World Fertility Survey reports.

relationship clearly indicates that a relatively high degree of fertility reduction can be achieved via the exclusive action of lactational amenorrhea and long periods of postpartum abstinence (regions to the left in the figure). When periods of postpartum infecundability are shortened without adequate compensation through contraception, the overall degree of fertility reduction obviously weakens (regions at the center of the figure). The second phase of the transition is observed in areas where modern contraception increases and produces again higher levels of overall fertility reduction (regions immediately to the left of zero in the figure). In the present sample of regions, there are only nine cases in which the effect of contraception is greater than that of postpartum nonsusceptibility (positive values of D). These regions are located in Zimbabwe (7), Botswana (1), and Kenya (1). However, a few urban areas are close to this demarcation line: Khartoum, Kampala, and Nairobi. The same also holds for rural Botswana, the remainder of Zimbabwe, and several other regions in Kenya.

The relationships between female education and S and D, respectively, are shown in Figures 7-3 and 7-4. The relationship to the overall degree of fertility reduction (S) is weakest because high degrees of fertility reduction

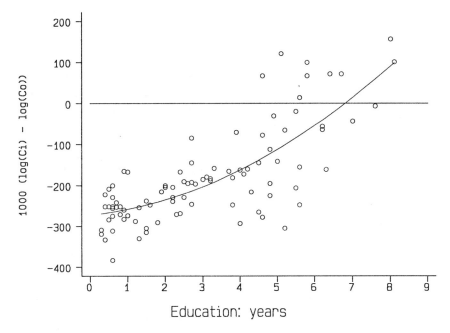

FIGURE 7-4 Relationship between the growing impact of fertility reduction via contraception over postpartum nonsusceptibility, and the average length of female schooling—WFS and DHS regions ($r = .77$). SOURCE: Demographic and Health Survey and World Fertility Survey reports.

can be obtained via either the traditionally long period of nonsusceptibility or modern contraception. The relationship of female education to D is stronger because the two components of D work in opposite ways in relation to female education. Clearly, the importance of contraception relative to postpartum nonsusceptibility increases with education. However, it should be noted again that the scatter widens considerably for regions with average female schooling levels of four years or more. Western African regions with better schooling levels have lower degrees of compensation via modern contraception, whereas the eastern and southern African regions with similar schooling levels are reaching or crossing the break-even point (i.e., $D = 0$).

THE UNCERTAIN FUTURE

The momentum of increased contraceptive use and the spread of contraception to other regions depend on a number of conditions. First, the demand for children must be declining as a consequence of diminished child utility or increased costs of children. Rising aspirations with respect to child quality and rising educational costs could trigger a fertility decline (see Chapters 3 and 4). Secondly, efficient forms of contraception must be available at affordable prices (see Chapter 5).

If, by contrast, there are a contraction of job opportunities, a breakdown of the schooling system, and a growing scarcity of family planning supplies and services, other scenarios may well develop. During the last decade, many sub-Saharan countries experienced declining foreign earnings, which have led to actual declines in primary school enrollment figures, although there is a continuing increase in the enrollment ratio of women relative to men (see Chapter 3). The engine of the demographic transition process, identified in this chapter as increased female education, has stalled in some regions. If in addition, the availability of family planning supplies and services declines, the original notion of a "crisis-led" fertility transition might be abandoned as couples are not able to meet their fertility goals.

CONCLUSION

It should be reiterated that the WFS and DHS samples of regions are not representative for the whole of sub-Saharan Africa. As a consequence, the results of the present study should be interpreted with care.

The main points derived from the analyses can be summarized as follows:

•   In the majority of regions studied, fertility is still controlled predominantly through prolonged periods of postpartum nonsusceptibility. Only in a minority of regions in three countries (Zimbabwe, Botswana, Kenya) is there a comparable effect stemming from contraceptive use.

•   In countries having comparable data over time, there are no traces of a further decline in the components of the nonsusceptible period during the 1980s. Under such circumstances, rises in contraceptive use would carry their full effect.

•   Western African regions still benefit from a considerable postpartum abstinence bonus, but continue to score low on contraceptive knowledge, small ideal family size, and actual contraceptive use.

•   Female education is particularly strongly associated with reduced duration of postpartum nonsusceptibility and increased use of contraception. These relationships are, however, curvilinear. As noted in Chapter 6, contraceptive use greater than 10 to 15 percent emerges only in regions with average female schooling durations of four years or better. Furthermore, the scatter widens considerably beyond this educational threshold. Among areas with higher levels of female education, there is a marked contrast with respect to contraceptive use between regions in Zimbabwe,

Botswana, and Kenya with high levels of use and other regions in the sample with much lower levels.

•   Given recent economic reversals and associated curtailments or stagnation of per capita expenditures on social services, especially education (see Chapter 3), the future is quite uncertain with respect to the prospects for both further increases in female education and improved family planning services.

8

Conclusions

In this concluding chapter, we first return to the question motivating this report: Is sub-Saharan Africa on the brink of a contraceptive revolution that signals the onset of fertility decline? We then consider the research needed to answer outstanding questions.

FINDINGS

Although there is considerable uncertainty about Africa as a whole, the evidence on balance points to an undeniable trend in Zimbabwe, Botswana, and Kenya. The changes observed in these three countries over the past decade indicate that selected parts of Africa have joined other regions of the developing world in a contraceptive revolution.

However, in the vast majority of countries within Africa,[1] the prevalence of use of modern methods of contraception is less than 6 percent, placing them squarely in the "emergent" category with regard to family planning programs (Destler et al., 1990). In these countries, postpartum nonsusceptibility due to lactational amenorrhea and sexual abstinence is more dominant than modern contraception in restraining fertility.

---

[1] One can make this statement not only for countries that have had a major demographic survey, but also for those that have not, given that in the majority of the remaining countries there has been little family planning program activity.

A number of factors are associated with the increased use of modern contraception. Female education is clearly an important determinant of contraceptive use at the individual, regional, and national level (see Chapters 2, 3, and 6). In this sense, Africa follows a pattern common to other regions of the developing world, although the changes in contraceptive use associated with changes in female schooling are not as large as in much of Latin America. As demonstrated in Chapter 6, current use of modern methods increases above the 10 percent level only in regions that have a mean length of female schooling of four years or more. No doubt in part because of the greater educational opportunities available in urban than in rural areas, urbanity was shown to directly and positively affect contraceptive use at the individual level and negatively affect fertility at the national level (see Chapters 2 and 3). At the regional level, urbanization was shown to influence the average level of schooling, but otherwise had no direct effect on contraceptive use (see Chapter 6).

The percentage of women in a polygynous union, a proxy for features of social organization that promote high fertility, was also negatively related to contraceptive use at the regional level. The proportion Muslim indirectly reduced contraceptive use by influencing the average level of schooling.

Although significant progress has been made in reducing infant and child mortality in Africa, the three higher-use countries are clearly distinctive with respect to mortality levels and trends. In our view, steady increases in contraceptive use resulting in fertility decline in other countries of Africa are doubtful without continued improvements in mortality. Mortality decline has provided parents with greater assurance that their children will survive to adulthood, thus reducing the need to have additional children as insurance against this threat or as compensation for the actual loss of one or more children. Such improvements in mortality may prove difficult in countries experiencing economic difficulties and cuts in the provision of health services.

In addition to these factors associated with contraceptive use, the strength of family planning programs is central to the prospects for fertility decline. Evidence reviewed in Chapter 5 demonstrates that family planning programs in Botswana, Kenya, and Zimbabwe are the most well developed in Sub-Saharan Africa. As shown in Chapter 6, certain regions that would be expected to have a prevalence of modern method use of at least 10 percent (based on levels of female education) did not, and all these were located in countries with weak family planning programs. Whereas much of the earlier demographic literature focused on the socioeconomic factors affecting fertility, there has been a growing awareness during the past decade of the important role of the family planning supply environment with respect to meeting the needs of couples motivated to delay or limit births.

In the sub-Saharan African countries that have achieved at least moderate success in family planning, the public sector provided the national coverage of services that resulted in increases in national contraceptive use. However, it is clear from Chapter 5 that private family planning associations have played a pioneering role in legitimizing the use of family planning and implementing many of the early services.

Assuming that the use of modern methods continues to increase in the three higher use countries (and begins to take hold in others), we suspect that Africa will follow the pattern of other developing countries in terms of diversification of method mix. The oral pill is the most widely used contraceptive according to the World Fertility Survey (WFS) and Demographic and Health Survey (DHS) studies conducted in Africa to date (see Chapter 2). Yet the experience of other developing regions suggests that method mix will expand as overall prevalence increases.[2] Indeed, the 4 to 5 percent prevalence of female sterilization found in Botswana and Kenya suggests that even this method—once thought to be totally unacceptable in cultures that placed such a high value on fertility—is gaining in acceptance. Given anecdotal evidence as to the popularity of Depo-Provera (the three-month injection) in those countries where it has been introduced, increased availability of this method would be expected to result in greater diversification of the method mix.

Remarkable as the increases in contraceptive use have been in the countries with higher prevalence, it is important to keep in perspective the fact that in demographic terms, these three countries represent less than 7 percent of the population of sub-Saharan Africa. Moreover, even these countries have attained only a moderate level of use in terms of family planning program evolution. If one excludes Mauritius and South Africa (as we have done in this report, except in passing, based on their atypical socioeconomic levels and ethnic compositions), the two African countries (Liberia and northern Sudan) that follow these three countries in terms of contraceptive prevalence have a modern use rate of only 5.5 percent.

Our analysis indicates that several factors will be influential in determining future contraceptive prevalence levels. Although impressive progress was made during the decade of the 1980s in terms of population policy and family planning program implementation, it is our view that the continued

---

[2]The majority of developing countries in Asia and Latin America with a contraceptive prevalence of at least 30 percent are not single-method countries (Rutenberg et al., 1991). Historically, as prevalence increases, users demand methods for both spacing (satisfied by reversible methods) and limiting (satisfied by long-term or permanent methods), and method mix is in turn diversified. Moreover, with the U.S. Food and Drug Administration approval of Depo-Provera and NORPLANT[R], the range of methods available in sub-Saharan Africa should be greater in the 1990s than in the 1980s.

development of strong family planning programs will be needed to meet the demand for family limitation and offer an alternative to high fertility. The evidence presented in Chapter 5, although qualitative in nature, indicates that the three countries that have achieved modern prevalence rates of more than 15 percent have had the best-developed family planning programs. The development of programs in Africa will be helped undoubtably by sustained government commitment. Recent statements from more than 50 African ministers at the Third African Population Conference in Dakar, Senegal, attest to the growing support for family planning (United Nations Population Fund, 1992).

The mechanisms used to deliver family planning services in Africa in the coming years are likely to resemble those now in use both in Africa and in other regions of the developing world: clinic-based facilities, community-based distribution, and social marketing. However, the patterns of social organization in Africa may provide a unique opportunity to involve local organizations and community networks (women's groups, networks of traders, etc.) in legitimizing the concept of family planning and disseminating information on the methods. In addition, given that men have a dominant role in fertility decision making, programs in Africa may derive particular benefit from targeting interventions to this subgroup.

In view of economic difficulties in some African countries, donor support for family planning is likely to remain crucial in the coming years. Even where the political will exists, governments stretched thin with providing basic services to growing populations will find it difficult to implement effective family planning programs without continued donor support. Whereas in the past, Africa had been somewhat neglected (relative to Asia and Latin America) by international donors to population activities, this situation shifted dramatically during the 1980s, when Africa became a priority for numerous organizations. The external investment in family planning in the 1980s contributed to the increases in contraceptive use in Botswana, Kenya, and Zimbabwe, and it may begin to affect prevalence rates in the 1990s in other countries that have intensified their program efforts (e.g., Niger, Rwanda).

Changes in African social structure will certainly affect the future demand for children. As shown in Chapter 4, social factors at the community and household levels (particularly the value attached to perpetuation of the lineage, which has served as an organizing cultural principle in many areas of Africa) have exerted pressure on couples to have large families. In many ways, these factors explain "why Africa is different" with regard to the fertility transition. Yet these social structures are not immutable, and changes in the nature of kinship support and of spousal relations would be expected to influence attitudes toward the value of family planning.

There is consensus in the literature that pro-natalist social factors are being undermined progressively by economic development and perhaps, in some areas, by economic crisis. Thus, the degree to which African social organization will limit fertility decline in the future is unclear. For example, there are indications of growing conjugal closeness and shared decision making, possibly resulting from changes in childrearing costs and educational aspirations. Land scarcity due to high population density and rising educational costs in some areas may increase the perceived benefits of fewer children. As discussed in Chapter 3, deteriorating economic conditions in some countries may decrease the prevalence of child fostering as families seek to care for their immediate kin and avoid the costs associated with caring for children of relatives. These same conditions may also increase the likelihood of resource pooling and joint decision making as families strive to meet the sustenance and educational needs of their children.

What is clear from our review of African social structure is that there is great variation in how it affects the demand for children. Although scattered qualitative evidence indicates that social factors are changing in such a way that might lead to lower fertility desires, there is an insufficient body of knowledge to predict the direction of change for most of Africa. Many of the changing factors we have emphasized are more important in urban areas and among the educated—populations that have expressed a desire for family limitation. Although the high-fertility rationale persists in many areas, the examples of Zimbabwe, Botswana, and Kenya demonstrate that parts of sub-Saharan Africa are receptive to contraceptive use. However, dramatic increases in prevalence may not be imminent for other areas, although we believe that contraceptive use will take hold eventually. Because of the variation in cultural and socioeconomic structures across Africa, we expect increases in contraceptive use to be uneven; increase is initially more likely in areas that are urban, with educated populations, and with access to social services.

There are several factors that may curtail the spread of contraceptive use in Africa. First, although there are few hard data to substantiate the point, preliminary reports from countries ravaged by acquired immune deficiency syndrome (AIDS) suggest that this epidemic may change perceptions regarding mortality. In an effort to ensure the survival of sufficient numbers of children and to maintain continuity of the lineage, women may seek to have as many children as soon as possible. Under such circumstances, contraceptive use would be counterproductive. However, educational programs to increase condom use to prevent the spread of AIDS may have the opposite effect on use.

Second, a few African countries are experiencing extreme political and social unrest. Civil war and famine have devastated regions of Angola, Ethiopia, Liberia, Mozambique, Somalia, Sudan, Uganda, and Zaire. Under conditions that threaten survival on a daily basis and severely disrupt access to health, family planning, and other services, there is no reason to expect more widespread use of contraception.

Third, further increases in contraceptive use are dependent on continued improvements in female education and the returns to schooling. As discussed in Chapter 3, the willingness of parents to accept the quantity-quality trade-off (having fewer children but investing more heavily in their schooling) is dependent on their perceptions that increased schooling will in fact result in greater economic benefits to both the child and the family in later life. However, studies in selected countries demonstrate that the quality of education has deteriorated, which decreases the return that can be expected on such an investment. The return is also heavily dependent on the supply and demand for labor by educational level. Thus, the evidence for a quantity-quality demographic transition is decidedly mixed, and continued progress in terms of female education cannot be taken for granted.

RESEARCH GAPS

There are a number of areas in which further research would greatly assist in understanding of the dynamics of contraceptive use in sub-Saharan Africa. We present these topics in an order that mirrors the chapters in this volume.

Levels and Trends in Contraceptive Use—
Contraceptive Discontinuation

There is little reliable information on the average duration of contraceptive use (i.e., once an acceptor begins a period of contraceptive use, how long does she use the original method or, if switching occurs, any method). As mentioned in Chapter 2, such information can be obtained from two different sources: program records or population-based surveys. In many countries, service statistics—if collected at all—are unreliable. Even if carefully recorded, data based on service statistics suffer from the problems of sample selectivity and loss to follow-up. Because of these limitations, there is a preference for obtaining continuation data from population-based surveys. The DHS questionnaire for high-prevalence countries contains an instrument for obtaining retrospective data with which to calculate continuation rates. But to date, none of the African DHS have employed this questionnaire, given their relatively low levels of prevalence. A more widespread use of these questions in African countries that have at least 15 to 20 percent prevalence of modern contraceptive methods would provide some needed information on discontinuation.

Socioeconomic Context

Effects of Economic Downturns

There are competing hypotheses as to the effects of economic hardship on contraceptive use. On one hand, it has been argued that low levels of socioeconomic development (which are generally accompanied by low levels of female education, high infant mortality, and large percentages of the population living in rural areas) work to sustain the demand for a large number of children. On the other, it has been hypothesized that the current economic crisis in many parts of Africa may cause Africans to respond by altering their attitudes regarding family size and increasing their receptivity to family planning. The theories underlying these competing positions are discussed in detail in Chapter 3, but there has been very little empirical work on the effects of economic downturns.[3]

Effects of Child Mortality and AIDS on Demand for Children and Attitudes Toward Family Planning

It is generally accepted that high levels of child mortality tend to sustain the demand for a large number of children among parents seeking to insure themselves against possible future loss or compensation for deaths that have already occurred. The populations of countries ravaged by the AIDS epidemic are now painfully aware that children born to mothers infected with the human immunodeficiency virus (HIV) may be infected themselves. Whereas medical specialists advise against pregnancy for women who are infected with HIV (to avoid hastening the onset of symptoms), this advice may be meaningless to women who measure their own personal worth by their contribution to continuing the lineage. More data of a qualitative nature are needed to understand the motives of women in this situation and how AIDS affects their attitudes toward family planning.

Costs of Investments in Children, Including Education

Given the importance of the quantity-quality trade-off to the question of impending fertility decline in Africa, it is surprising that there are not more data on the actual costs of investments in children in the African context. The few studies presented in this report suggest that in certain

---

[3]An exception is the report of the Working Group on the Effects of Economic and Social Reversals (1993), which estimates the effects of economic reversals on child mortality, marriage, and fertility, with special attention to first and second births, in seven African countries.

settings (e.g., Kenya), men have begun to entertain the prospect of fewer children because of the increased costs of schooling. However, these studies have tended to be qualitative in nature, such that the results are limited in geographical scope and do not produce quantitative estimates of investment per child. To investigate this issue more rigorously, it is essential to have better data on the actual costs of schooling in different countries, as well as the perceptions of the costs and benefits of investing in children's education.

Female Education, Income, and Contraceptive Use

Although improvements in female education are associated with increased contraceptive use, the research that has led to this finding generally lacks controls for income, which may distort the relationship. Because increases in female education most likely result in higher incomes (and both are associated with lower fertility), it is important to distinguish which of these changes is primary in driving lower fertility. Income has not been included in most studies because of the difficulty of measuring it. The one study we found that does control for income suggests that female education is significantly associated with decreased fertility regardless of the effect of income on fertility (see Chapter 3). Further work in this area would be most useful if it included such information.

Community/Kinship/Household

Extent of Nucleation of the Family and Child Fostering

There is need for further research on the extent of joint decision making between spouses. The premise of the weak conjugal bond needs to be revisited in light of urban life-styles, exposure to western ideas via the mass media, and changing economic circumstances. Because of the heterogeneity of sub-Saharan Africa, these factors may result in different responses. In some areas there may be greater pooling of resources and conjugal closeness (see Chapter 4) and in other areas the family structure may not depart from a lineage orientation. Moreover, the effects of these factors on child fostering may be mixed. Such varied responses will have a profound effect on the future fertility desires of different African populations.

Quantification of Kinship Factors

Given the importance of kinship in influencing the demand for children, it would be useful to devise means for integrating kinship factors into quantitative data analysis. Such efforts would clarify the relative effects of social organization and socioeconomic factors on the demand for births.

Local Social Organization and the Diffusion of Family Planning

Chapter 4 highlighted the potential role of local social networks in the provision of information and the legitimization of contraception. There is a need for further research on the possible contributions of these organizations.

Population Policies and Program Implementation—
Service Availability at the Regional Level

Not only in Africa but also in other parts of the developing world, attempts to evaluate and quantify the family planning supply environment have been limited to date. Although some information is available on the national level, there is a need for subnational data that indicate not only the quantitative but also the qualitative aspects of service delivery. Without these data, it is impossible to assess the effect of family planning programs on changes in contraceptive use.

This list of research gaps is by no means exhaustive. However, it includes those items that would have been most beneficial to improving our analysis of the factors affecting contraceptive use in sub-Saharan Africa.

Regardless of the limitations of our study, a central conclusion remains: We believe that although the social supports for high fertility have not disappeared, Zimbabwe, Botswana, and Kenya demonstrate that increases in contraceptive use can occur in sub-Saharan Africa. We believe that future fertility decline is likely in these three and other countries assuming provision of family planning services, improvements in child mortality, and progress in female education.

Appendix A

Adapting the Easterlin-Crimmins Synthesis Model to Sub-Saharan Conditions

This appendix explores whether the Easterlin and Crimmins (1985) synthesis model of reproductive decisions provides an appropriate framework for the study of contraceptive use in Africa. The synthesis perspective centers attention on an individual couple of reproductive age. What is at issue is the number of children the couple expects to bear if no contraception is employed, compared with the number of births that are wanted or demanded. If the potential supply of births exceeds the quantity demanded, there exists a motivation for contraceptive use. Thus, the model draws together three essential elements: reproductive capacity, the demand for reproductive outcomes, and the principal means—contraception—by which couples bring actual reproductive outcomes into agreement with their reproductive desires.

Socioeconomic determinants enter the model via the concept of demand, which encompasses factors such as the risks of child mortality and the access to and costs of contraceptive methods.[1] Although the Easterlin-Crimmins model is usually taken to be a model of lifetime fertility or of the behavior of ending or limiting reproduction, and their socioeconomic deter-

---

[1]Easterlin and Crimmins (1985) introduce a second concept of demand, having to do with the desired number of births in the absence of mortality risk, that assumes away all monetary, time, or psychic costs of contraception. As discussed in Montgomery (1987), this hypothetical or notional concept of demand plays no essential part in the synthesis model. Hence, the concept of demand employed in the material that follows is conventional, in that mortality risks and contraceptive costs are hypothesized to affect the desired number of births.

minants, the model can be used equally well to understand the demand for spacing births. As discussed below, the spacing-limiting distinction has to do with the length of the decision period envisioned in the synthesis model. Potential supply and demand may be compared over a period as short as the monthly reproductive cycle or as long as the reproductive span itself. In addition to its connections to birth spacing and limiting, the length of decision periods is also an issue in the model's treatment of proximate determinants other than contraception.

In effect, the synthesis perspective divides the full range of proximate determinants of fertility (e.g., contraception, involvement in sexual union, postpartum nonsusceptibility, and induced abortion) into three mutually exclusive groups. First, there are the *exogenous* proximate determinants such as individual fecundability, which set constraints on reproductive capacity. By exogenous we mean those determinants that are not under the control of the couple during the decision period under consideration. This category of determinants defines the couple's potential supply of births. The second group of proximate determinants comprises the effective and less effective methods of contraception; these are clearly *endogenous* in being, at least in part, the means by which the couple puts into effect its reproductive demands.[2] In the third category of determinants fall those behaviors that cannot be neatly classified as either exogenous or endogenous in nature. One could include breastfeeding intensity and duration in this third category, together with postpartum sexual abstinence, participation in a reproductive union, and spousal separation. The degree of exogeneity displayed by such behaviors will depend on the length of the decision period in question and on the specific character of the economic, social, and cultural organization.

By distinguishing among categories of proximate determinants, directing attention to the category of contraceptive use, and providing an organizing framework that shows how reproductive constraints and demands are expressed in contraceptive use, the synthesis perspective has much to recommend it. Its usefulness in this regard was recognized by an earlier National Research Council report on determinants of fertility in developing countries (Bulatao and Lee, 1983).

---

[2]At this point we should remark on the place of induced abortion in the conceptual framework developed below. It seems that by all accounts, the psychic and access costs of abortion in sub-Saharan Africa are of such a magnitude that it is rarely employed in marriage, although recent evidence indicates that abortion is increasing (Coeytaux, 1988). We regard these costs as being grouped with other factors that implicitly determine the demand for contraception. There is little need to single out the costs of abortion as a distinct motivation for contraception, unless (1) these costs, or components of the costs, can be measured; and either (2) the costs vary significantly across socioeconomic or demographic groups; or (3) the costs are expected to change in the future, perhaps as a result of policy.

In what follows we make a few brief comments, primarily of a theoretical nature, on the elements of the analytic framework as applied to Africa. The bulk of the discussion concerns the relations between the concepts of supply and demand and their connections to contraceptive use, these factors being grouped in the lowermost portion of Figure 1-1. The ambiguities in these concepts are revealed perhaps more clearly in an application to sub-Saharan Africa than they are in other settings, and we attempt to clarify the issues as much as possible.

DEMAND FOR BIRTHS

As envisioned in the framework of Figure 1-1, the concept of demand for births incorporates demands both for spacing births and for limiting them. The distinction between spacing and limiting motivations is of course very important with respect to the longer-run implications of method use. However, apart from sterilization, use of a contraceptive method does not in itself give evidence as to the relative weight of the spacing and limiting motives.

Rather, birth spacing is accommodated in the Easterlin-Crimmins synthesis by the consideration of a relatively short decision period, wherein an individual attaches utility rankings to various probabilities of conception within the period in question. A person with a strong motivation to delay the next birth would assign a utility penalty to behavioral choices that entail high probabilities of conception; so too would a person with a strong motivation to avert the next birth altogether. The birth spacer may be motivated by concern for child survival, the birth averter by a desire to limit family size; but each is engaged in behavior that has a contraceptive effect. The differences in these underlying motivations would emerge in the subsequent sequence of decision periods, as the utility penalty associated with conception progressively declines for birth spacers while (presumably) remaining constant for birth averters.

To put it differently, the spacing-limiting distinction has to do, in one respect, with the length of the decision period to which the analytic model is applied and, in another, with the linkages among such decision periods over the reproductive life span. We do not propose to address here the theoretical issues associated with birth spacing and limiting. A full treatment would require an explicitly dynamic decision framework with due allowance for uncertainty and for the interplay over the reproductive span between reproductive outcomes and contraceptive-related choices.[3] Rather,

---

[3]For exploratory work in this area, see the volume edited by Tsui and Herbertson (1989); one article in the collection, Montgomery (1989), sets out the dynamic theory as applied to contraceptive use.

the framework of Figure 1-1 is drawn so as to give equal theoretical standing to spacing and limiting motives for contraceptive use, and to suggest further that in sub-Saharan Africa, there need be no neat line of division separating them.

Along with the intertemporal aspect of demand, the interpersonal aspect must also be recognized. We argue in Chapters 3 and 4 that a reproductive decision framework appropriate to sub-Saharan Africa must admit the possibility of separate interests on the part of the male and the female in a reproductive pair. It follows that the concept of demand must itself be individual specific. Thus, in assigning utility rankings to decision options regarding method use, a woman would take into consideration her own present and expected future resources, resources from her husband on which she can expect to rely in the future, the possibility of future marital dissolution or the entry of new wives into the union, and so on. The husband would have his own calculations in these matters, which would not necessarily yield rankings in agreement with those of his wife.

Indeed, once the reproductive pair is split in this fashion, a gap is introduced between individual demands and contraceptive behavior. Whose demands and utility rankings are actually expressed in contraceptive use? The use of certain methods, including most of the coitus-dependent methods, requires a measure of cooperation between spouses or, at minimum, an acquiescence on the part of one spouse. Other methods can be employed unilaterally and even surreptitiously, without requiring the knowledge of one's spouse. In some socioeconomic circumstances where one might expect husband-wife conflicts, it might prove useful to distinguish among contraceptive methods according to the degree of spouse cooperation they entail.

SUPPLY OF BIRTHS

As indicated above, the supply of births that influences decisions about contraceptive use is affected by proximate determinants that are clearly exogenous, such as individual fecundability; those that can be treated as exogenous only in the short run, such as spouse separation; and possibly determinants such as breastfeeding and postpartum abstinence, whose exogeneity is in doubt.

However, there is considerable empirical evidence that marriage, marital dissolution, spouse separation, breastfeeding, and postpartum abstinence are correlated with the same socioeconomic factors (e.g., urbanization and female education) that influence contraceptive use.

Moreover, in a number of African societies (Page and Lesthaeghe, 1981) the motivation for breastfeeding and abstinence is explicitly understood in contraceptive terms: as the traditional African means of spacing births.

(The spacing motive has to do with the health of the child and the mother, but this is not the important point.) How then can these behaviors be viewed as exogenous determinants of contraceptive use? A related question must be raised about the appropriateness of including women who are breastfeeding or postpartum abstinent in calculations of contraceptive prevalence.

From the analytic point of view, it would be awkward to group postpartum behaviors such as breastfeeding, which is tied in a physiological sense to a previous birth, with contraceptive methods that in principle can be adopted at any point in the reproductive span. One simply does not take up breastfeeding six months into a birth interval; the prevalence of breastfeeding is therefore bound up with the incidence of births in a way that the prevalence of the pill or the intrauterine device (IUD) is not.

The case of postpartum sexual abstinence is less clear-cut because, unlike breastfeeding, abstinence could well be adopted midway in a birth interval. Here we must argue that the psychic costs associated with a given spell of abstinence are lower if the spell begins at the event of birth, rather than at some later point in the birth interval. This argument returns to the African emphasis given to birth spacing and the social sanctions that surround weaning and the resumption of sexual relations (Caldwell and Caldwell, 1981). From this perspective, abstinence can be viewed as a postpartum behavior somewhat akin to breastfeeding, although its link to the previous birth is behavioral and social in origin rather than physiological.

The analytic awkwardness associated with treating breastfeeding and postpartum abstinence on an equal footing with contraceptive methods consists in both the *interpretation* and the *implications* of contraceptive prevalence rates. Consider a prevalence calculation in which the base comprises all nonpregnant women and nonuse is distinguished from use of various contraceptive methods. If we decide to group breastfeeding and abstinence with other conventional contraceptive measures, we must at the same time recognize their highly distinctive patterns of adoption and discontinuation, and for breastfeeding, a contraceptive failure rate that is strongly dependent on duration.[4]

To be correctly interpreted, contraceptive prevalence rates that incorporate breastfeeding and abstinence would have to be calculated by holding constant the duration since last birth. Consider a comparison of distribu-

---

[4]It has been hypothesized that the contraceptive effect of breastfeeding could be maintained indefinitely if feeding were to be sustained at maximum intensity. But the usual pattern is for breastfeeding to decline in intensity as food supplements are introduced into the infant's diet, and this process may be accelerated by the physiological strain or fatigue on the part of the mother associated with long durations of full breastfeeding. Hence, it is safe to assume that the use-effectiveness of breastfeeding, as it were, will tend to erode with duration since last birth.

tions of nonuse and use by method among nonpregnant women at two durations, d and $d + 1$, since last birth. In moving from duration d to duration $d + 1$, one would expect to see a systematic reduction in the percentage breastfeeding and postpartum abstinent, and a systematic inflation in the sum of nonuse and use of conventional methods. One would then have to devise corrections to the prevalence rates that would net out such systematic patterns, in order for more interesting behavioral regularities to be discerned in the data.

Moreover, owing to the systematic decline in the contraceptive failure rate of breastfeeding with duration since birth, the greater the duration d is, the larger is the fraction of women breastfeeding and not pregnant at d who then conceive and are removed from consideration at duration $d + 1$. So far, as we are aware, no other conventional means of contraception displays such a pronounced duration dependence in its failure rate. When contraceptive methods are defined so as to include breastfeeding therefore, the implications of a given method mix for the degree of contraceptive protection will depend on the duration since last birth.

The second part of the rationale for treating breastfeeding and postpartum abstinence differently from contraceptive use has to do with the contribution to understanding and to policy of statistical analyses based on a synthesis framework. The concern is a general one, perhaps most readily evident here in respect to postpartum behaviors, but also of relevance in marriage, spouse separation, and other choice-related behavior having an influence on the risks of conception. The issue can be framed in the following way: In what sense, if any, will analyses of contraceptive use defined as *conditional* on the status of other proximate determinants, tend to mislead?

The central issue is that of statistical exogeneity, selectivity bias, and the importance of unmeasured variables.[5] Perhaps a simple representation

---

[5] Economic demographers have given great emphasis to the concept of statistical exogeneity, as is evident in Schultz's (1986) critique of the Easterlin synthesis. It should be recognized that the key issue is in fact of a statistical nature, rather than being an issue of the appropriate theory.

The concept of *conditional* demand functions, wherein the demand for one good is expressed as being conditional on demands for other goods, is well accepted in economic theory. The analogy here would be to the demand for contraception conditional on breastfeeding status or conditional on the status of other proximate determinants. But economists have also recognized the difficulties in statistical applications of conditional demand theory, given that the theoretically appropriate conditional demand functions will typically include a number of variables that are not subject to empirical measurement. Thus, an empirical application of conditional demands will be vulnerable to the charge of selectivity bias arising from omitted variables.

This contrast in perspectives is evident in the exchange between Easterlin (1986) and of method use and postpartum abstinence can help to illuminate. Let C_i denote the use of a contraceptive method by individual i and let A_i indicate postpartum abstinence on the part of this individual. A set of variables X_i encompasses all measurable exogenous socioeconomic determinants of contraceptive use, including program-related measures of contraceptive access and costs. In any empirical application, important components of the determinants of use will doubtless go unmeasured, and these unobserved influences are summarized in the variable ε_i, the value of which will vary across individuals. We assume that X_i and ε_i are uncorrelated.[6]

If both contraceptive use, C_i, and postpartum abstinence, A_i, are viewed as endogenous, a linear statistical representation[7] of the determinants of C_i and A_i could be set out as follows:

$$C_i = X_i'\beta_C + \varepsilon_i + v_i$$

$$A_i = X_i'\beta_A + \alpha\,\varepsilon_i + u_i,$$

where the unmeasured background factors ε_i exert an influence on both method use and postpartum abstinence. (We accommodate any additional unmeasured influences on abstinence in the disturbance terms v_i and u_i, which can be taken to be uncorrelated with ε_i.) Because X_i and (ε_i and v_i) are uncorrelated, we have

$$E[C_i|X_i] = X_i'\beta_C,$$

and the coefficients β_C of the contraceptive use equation can be consistently estimated by conventional methods.

Consider now the alternative approach in which the equation for contraceptive use C_i is estimated as *conditional* on abstinence status A_i. For instance, the contraceptive use equation could be estimated on the subsample of women who are not postpartum abstinent, which we may represent as $A_i = 0$. Then in the subsample,

---

Schultz (1986) concerning empirical applications of the synthesis model. Easterlin defends his empirical specification of the model in terms of conditional demand theory (although he does not use this language), whereas Schultz attacks the specification primarily on statistical grounds.

[6]That is, X_i is exogenous from the statistical point of view.

[7]We use a linear regression representation only to illustrate the key issues; clearly it is not the most appropriate framework for qualitative variables such as contraceptive method choice.

$$E[C_i | X_i, A_i = 0] \quad = \quad X_i' \beta_C + E[\varepsilon_i | A_i = 0]$$

$$= \quad X_i' \beta_C + E[\varepsilon_i | \varepsilon_i = (-1/\alpha)(X_i' \beta_A + u_i)]$$

$$\neq \quad X_i' \beta_C.$$

In short, when a common unmeasured variable ε_i enters both the contraception and the abstinence equations, the influence of socioeconomic and program determinants of demand X_i cannot be consistently determined *in general* through the conditional approach. The degree of bias inherent in this approach is an empirical matter, and it would be very difficult to know, a priori, whether the bias would be small enough to ignore for policy or other purposes.

The conditional approach can be defended in two ways. First, one could argue that ε_i does not in fact appear in the abstinence equation (i.e., $\alpha = 0$), which amounts to an assertion that unobserved characteristics affecting abstinence do not have any influence on method use—a strong assertion indeed given the documented associations between the *observed* socioeconomic factors X_i and abstinence. Second, one could assert that when the data are grouped according to specific socioeconomic or cultural criteria, so little individual-specific variation remains in ε_i that it is, in effect, absorbed into the constant terms of the regression equations, which is the essence of the argument that proceeds from the assertion that postpartum abstinence and breastfeeding are "culturally determined," to the conclusion that one can examine contraceptive use on a conditional basis.[8]

We wish to underscore this point: To justify using the conditional approach, one or the other of these arguments must be applied to each of the other proximate determinants, including marital status and spouse separation.

These analytic and statistical complications surrounding the synthesis framework are not beyond resolution, but to address the issues in full in this report would carry us into new and possibly controversial terrain with regard to methodology. In addition, we believe that the payoff in terms of lessons for policy could be small. For both physiological and behavioral reasons, breastfeeding and postpartum abstinence are necessarily limited behaviors. No conceivable policy could hope to extend the duration of breastfeeding or abstinence much beyond three years, and even reaching three years would be doubtful in the case of abstinence, whereas policies in sub-Saharan Africa could well encourage durations of modern contraceptive

---

[8] The group-specific nature of ε_i would then be captured in dummy variables indicating region, ethnicity, and the like.

use of this length or longer. With regard to the other proximate determinants such as marital status, it seems unlikely that program interventions directed to contraceptive use could have important spillover influences on selection into marriage.

To sum up, our approach in this volume proceeds as follows: Our judgment is that marital status is probably not sufficiently endogenous to cause concern. Thus, we calculate measures of contraceptive prevalence for currently married women. Breastfeeding and abstinence are treated as potentially endogenous; we do not calculate contraceptive prevalence measures conditional on breastfeeding and abstinence status. But neither do we merge breastfeeding and abstinence with other contraceptive methods. Our attention is restricted to modern method use.

This focus on a subset of the endogenous variables may well be adequate for an exploration of contraceptive use, but given the possibilities for substitution between breastfeeding/abstinence and modern contraceptive methods, it could yield misleading predictions about fertility. This issue is discussed in Chapters 2 and 7 in connection with the two-phased fertility transition in Africa.

Appendix B

Sample Sizes for the WFS and DHS Regional Files

Country	Survey	Sample Size Weighted	Unweighted	Region
Benin	WFS	Self-weighting	1,091	Atacora, Borgou
			2,426	Central, South
			501	Cotonou
Botswana	DHS	1,316	2,258	Urban
		3,052	2,110	Rural
Burundi	DHS	2,251	1,984	Central plateau
		307	757	Imbo
		559	487	Lowlands (depressions)
		469	408	Mumirwa
		384	334	Mugamba
Cameroon	WFS	1,624	2,336	Center-South, East
		1,100	998	Littoral, Southwest
		2,651	1,848	North
		1,835	1,447	West, Northwest
		917	1,487	Yaoundé, Douala
Côte d'Ivoire	WFS	Self-weighting	1,092	Abidjan
			2,341	Rural forest
			1,113	Rural savanna
			740	Urban forest
			475	Urban savanna

Country	Survey	Sample Size Weighted	Unweighted	Region
Ghana	DHS	Self-weighting	856	Central, Western
			1,301	Greater Accra, Eastern
			500	Volta
			1,323	Ashanti, Brong Ahafo
			508	Northern, Upper
	WFS	Self-weighting	921	Central, Western
			1,740	Greater Accra, Eastern
			599	Volta
			1,959	Ashanti, Brong Ahafo
			906	Northern, Upper (East and West)
Kenya	DHS	554	859	Nairobi
		2,389	2,179	Central, Eastern
		1,519	1,100	Rift Valley
		498	720	Coast
		2,189	2,292	Nyanza, Western
	WFS	434	700	Nairobi
		2,624	2,605	Central, Eastern
		1,479	1,506	Rift Valley
		680	648	Coast
		2,856	2,621	Western, Nyanza
Lesotho	WFS	1,457	1,483	Lowlands
		1,929	1,903	Other (Foothills, Orange River Valley, Mountains)
Liberia	DHS	293	920	Grand Gedeh
		1,459	1,060	Montserrado
		150	834	Sinoe
		3,337	2,425	Remainder
Mali	DHS	290	503	Bamako
		961	830	Kayes, Koulikoro
		703	650	Mopti, Gao, Tombouctou
		1,246	1,217	Sikasso, Segou
Nigeria	DHS	Self-weighting	4,213	Ondo State
	WFS	2,343	2,069	Northeast
		2,221	2,290	Northwest
		3,139	2,806	Southeast
		2,027	2,562	Southwest

		Sample Size		
Country	Survey	Weighted	Unweighted	Region
Senegal	DHS	Self-weighting	1,528	Central
			641	Northeast (Fleuve, Oriental)
			573	South (Casamance)
			1,673	West (Dakar, Thiès)
	WFS	Self-weighting	1,551	Central
			648	Fleuve, Oriental
			544	Casamance
			1,242	Dakar, Thiès
Sudan (northern)	DHS	Self-weighting	1,249	Khartoum
			1,061	North, East
			1,599	Central
			1,951	Kordofan, Darfur
	WFS	404	580	Khartoum
		716	749	North, East
		898	807	Central
		1,096	979	Kordofan, Darfur
Togo	DHS	Self-weighting	306	Central
			1,501	Coastal (includes Lomé)
			409	Kara
			767	Plateau
			377	Savanna
Uganda	DHS	265	161	West Nile
		1,304	865	East
		1,177	1,392	Central
		273	166	West
		1,415	1,619	Southwest
		296	527	Kampala
Zimbabwe	DHS	Self-weighting	379	Bulawayo
			345	Harare/Chitungwiza
			527	Manicaland
			288	Mashonaland Central
			543	Mashonaland East (except Harare/Chitungwiza)
			495	Mashonaland West
			497	Masvingo
			189	Matabeleland North (except Bulawayo)
			282	Matabeleland South
			656	Midlands

References

Abu, K.
  1983   The separateness of spouses: Conjugal resources in an Ashanti town. Pp. 156-168
          in C. Oppong, ed., *Female and Male in West Africa*. London: George Allen and
          Unwin.

Adegbola, O., H.J. Page, and R. Lesthaeghe
  1981   Child-spacing and fertility in Lagos. Pp. 147-180 in H.J. Page and R. Lesthaeghe,
          eds., *Child-Spacing in Tropical Africa - Traditions and Change*. London: Aca-
          demic Press.

Adegbola, O., G. Jinadu, M. Montgomery, and F. Oyekanmi
  1991   The effects of structural adjustment on fertility and child schooling in Nigeria.
          Unpublished manuscript. Department of Economics, State University of New
          York at Stony Brook.

Ainsworth, M.
  1990   Socioeconomic determinants of fertility in Côte d'Ivoire. Unpublished paper.
          Africa Technical Department, The World Bank, Washington, D.C.
  1991   Economic aspects of child fostering in Côte d'Ivoire. Unpublished manuscript.
          Africa Technical Department, The World Bank, Washington, D.C.

Allen, S., J. Tice, P. Van de Perre, A. Serufilira, E. Hudes, F. Nsengumuremyi, J. Bogaerts, C.
Lindan, and S. Hulley
  1992   Effect of serotesting with counselling on condom use and seroconversion among
          HIV discordant couples in Africa. *British Medical Journal* 304:1605-1609.

Arhin, K.
  1983   The political and military roles of Akan women. Pp. 91-98 in C. Oppong, ed.,
          Female and Male in West Africa. London: George Allen and Unwin.

Armar, A.A.
  1975   Ghana. Pp. 283-286 in W.B. Watson and R.J. Lapham, eds., Family Planning
          Programs: World Review 1974. *Studies in Family Planning* 6:283-286.

Asante-Darko, N., and S. van der Geest
    1983   Male chauvinism: Men and women in Ghanaian highlife songs. Pp. 242-255 in C.
            Oppong, ed., *Female and Male in West Africa*. London: George Allen and Unwin.
Baird, V., G. O'Sullivan, and F. Yao
    1990   Togo Assessment: March 19-April 6, 1990. Contract No. USAID/DPE-3051-Z-
            00-8034-00. The Futures Group/SOMARC, Washington D.C.
Baker, J., and S. Khasiani
    1992   Induced abortion in Kenya: Case histories. *Studies in Family Planning* 23(1):34-
            44.
Baum, S., K. Dopkowski, W.G. Duncan, and P. Gardiner
    1974   The World Fertility Survey inventory: Major fertility and related surveys con-
            ducted in Africa, 1960-73. *WFS Occasional Paper*, No. 4. Voorburg, Netherlands:
            International Statistical Institute.
Becker, G., and H. Lewis
    1973   On the interaction between the quantity and quality of children. *Journal of Politi-
            cal Economy* 81(2)Part II:S279-288.
Benneh, G., J.S. Nabila, and J.B. Gyepi-Garbrah
    1989   *Twenty Years of Population Policy in Ghana*. Accra: Population Impact Program.
Bertrand, J.T., and J.E. Brown
    1992   Family planning success in two cities in Zaire. *World Bank Working Paper*.
            Washington, D.C.: The World Bank.
Bertrand, J.T., N. Mangani, and M. Mansilu
    1984   The acceptability of household distribution of contraceptives in Zaire. *Interna-
            tional Family Planning Perspectives* 10(1):21-26.
Bertrand, J.T., N. Mangani, M. Mansilu, and E. Landry
    1985   Factors influencing the use of traditional versus modern family planning methods
            in Bas Zaire. *Studies in Family Planning* 16(6): 332-342.
Bertrand, J., N. Mathu, J. Dwyer, M. Thuo, and G. Wambwa
    1989   Attitudes toward voluntary surgical contraception in four districts of Kenya. *Stud-
            ies in Family Planning* 20(5):281-288.
Bertrand, J.T., M.E. McBride, N. Mangani, N.C. Bacghman, and K. Mombela
    1993   Community-based distribution in Zaire: The PRODEF experience. *International
            Family Planning Perspectives*, in press.
Black, T.R., and P.D. Harvey
    1976   A report on a contraceptive social marketing experiment in rural Kenya. *Studies
            in Family Planning* 7(4):101-107.
Blanc, A., and C. Lloyd
    1990   Women's childrearing strategies in relation to fertility and employment in Ghana.
            Working Paper No. 16. New York: The Population Council.
Bledsoe, C.
    1989   The cultural meaning of AIDS and condoms for stable heterosexual relations in
            Africa: Recent evidence from local print media. Paper presented at the Seminar
            on Population Policy in Sub-Saharan Africa: Drawing on International Experi-
            ence, sponsored by the IUSSP, Committee on Population and Policy, with the
            collaboration of Dept. of Demographie de l'Université de Kinshasa, Kinshasa,
            Zaire, Feb 27-March 2.
    1990a   The politics of AIDS, condoms, and heterosexual relations in Africa: Recent
            evidence from the local print media. Pp. 197-224 in W.P. Handwerker, ed., *Births
            and Power: Social Change and the Politics of Reproduction*. Boulder, Colo.:
            Westview Press.

1990b   Transformations in sub-Saharan African marriage and fertility. *Annals, AAPSS*
         510:115-125.
In   The politics of polygyny in Mende education and child fosterage transactions. In
press   B. Miller, ed., *Sex and Gender Hierarchies*. Cambridge: Cambridge University
         Press.
Bledsoe, C., and U. Isiugo-Abanihe
1989   Strategies of child-fosterage among Mende grannies in Sierra Leone. Pp. 442-474
         in R. Lesthaeghe, ed., *Reproduction and Social Organization in Sub-Saharan Af-
         rica*. Berkeley: University of California Press.
Bleek, W.
1987   Family and family planning in southern Ghana. Pp. 138-153 in C. Oppong, ed.,
         Sex Roles, Population and Development in West Africa. Portsmouth, N.H.: Heinemann.
Boissiere, M., J. Knight, and R. Sabot
1985   Earnings, schooling, ability and cognitive skills. *American Economic Review* 75(5):1016-
         1030.
Bongaarts, J.
1978   A framework for analyzing the proximate determinants of fertility. *Population
         and Development Review* 4(1):105-132.
1981   The impact on fertility of traditional and changing child-spacing practices. In H.J.
         Page and R. Lesthaeghe, eds., *Child Spacing in Tropical Africa: Traditions and
         Change*. London: Academic Press.
1991   Do reproductive intentions matter?   Pp. 223-248 in *Demographic and Health
         Surveys World Conference, Proceedings*, Vol. 1. Columbia, Md.: Institute for
         Resource Development/Macro International, Inc.
Bongaarts, J., and R. Potter
1983   *Fertility, Biology, and Behavior: An Analysis of the Proximate Determinants*.
         New York: Academic Press.
Bongaarts, J., O. Frank, and R. Lesthaeghe
1984   The proximate determinants of fertility in Sub-Saharan Africa. *Population and
         Development Review* 10(3):511-537.
Bongaarts, J., W.P. Mauldin, and J.F. Phillips
1990   The demographic impact of family planning programs. *Studies in Family Plan-
         ning* 21(6):299-310.
Boserup, E.
1970   *Women's Role in Economic Development*. London: George Allen and Unwin.
1985   Economic and demographic interrelationships in sub-Saharan Africa. *Population
         and Development Review* 11(3):383-397.
Botswana
1989   *Demographic and Health Survey*. (L. Lesetedi, G. Mompati, P. Khulumani, G.
         Lesetedi, and N. Rutenberg, eds.) Gaborone: Central Statistics Office and Family
         Health Division; and Columbia, Md.: Institute for Resource Development/Macro
         Systems, Inc.
Brain, J.
1976   Less than second-class: Women in rural settlement schemes in Tanzania. Pp.
         265-282 in N. Hafkin and E. Bay, eds., *Women in Africa: Studies in Social and
         Economic Change*. Stanford, Calif.: Stanford University Press.
Brydon, L.
1983   Avatime women and men, 1900-80. Pp. 320-329 in C. Oppong, ed., *Female and
         Male in West Africa*. London: George Allen and Unwin.
Bulatao, R., and R. Lee, eds.
1983   *Determinants of Fertility in Developing Countries*. New York: Academic Press.

Caldwell, J.C.
1976   *The Socio-economic Explanation of High Fertility.* Canberra: Australian National University.
1980   Mass education as a determinant of the timing of fertility decline. *Population and Development Review* 6(2):225-255.
1982   Mass education as a determinant of fertility decline. Chapter 10 in J. Caldwell, *Theory of Fertility Decline.* London: Academic Press.
1991   Population trends and determinants: Is Africa different? Unpublished paper. Health Transition Centre, Australian National University, Canberra.

Caldwell, J.C., and P. Caldwell
1977   The role of marital sexual abstinence in determining fertility: A case study of the Yoruba in Nigeria. *Population Studies* 31(2):193-217.
1981   The function of child-spacing in traditional societies and the direction of change. Pp. 73-92 in H. Page and R. Lesthaeghe, eds., *Child-Spacing in Tropical Africa: Traditions and Change.* London: Academic Press.
1987   The cultural context of high fertility in sub-Saharan Africa. *Population and Development Review* 13(3):409-437.
1988   Is the Asian family planning program model suited to Africa? *Studies in Family Planning* 19(1):19-28.
1990   Cultural forces tending to sustain high fertility. Pp. 199-214 in G. Acsadi, G. Johnson-Acsadi, and R. Bulatao, eds., *Population Growth and Reproduction in Sub-Saharan Africa.* Washington, D.C.: The World Bank.

Caldwell, J., P. Caldwell, and P. Quiggan
1989   The social context of AIDS in sub-Saharan Africa. *Population and Development Review* 15(2):185-234.

Caldwell, J., I. Orubuloye, and P. Caldwell
1991   The destabilization of the traditional Yoruba sexual system. *Population and Development Review* 17(2):229-262.
1992   Africa's new kind of fertility transition. *Health Transition Working Paper*, No. 13. Canberra, Australia: Health Transition Centre, Australian National University.

Castadot, R.G., I. Sivin, P. Reyes, J.O. Alers, M. Chapple, and J. Russel
1975   The international postpartum program: Eight years of experience. *Reports on Population/Family Planning* 18:1-53.

Center for Population and Family Health
1989   *Lagos Market-Based Family Planning Projects: Final Report.* New York: School of Public Health, Columbia University.
1990a   *Accra Market Operations Research Project: Final Report.* New York: School of Public Health, Columbia University.
1990b   *Ibadan Market-Based Health and Family Planning Project: Final Report.* New York: School of Public Health, Columbia University.
1990c   *Ilorin Market-Based Distribution Project: Final Report.* New York: School of Public Health, Columbia University.

Chibalonza, K., C. Chirhamolekwa, and J. Bertrand
1989   Attitudes toward tubal ligation among acceptors, potential candidates, and husbands in Zaire. *Studies in Family Planning* 20(5):273-280.

Cochrane, S.H.
1979   *Fertility and Education: What Do We Really Know?* Baltimore, Md.: Johns Hopkins University Press.
1983   Effects of education and urbanization on fertility. Pp. 587-625 in R.A. Bulatao and R.D. Lee, eds., *Determinants of Fertility in Developing Countries*, Vol. 2. New York: Academic Press.

Cochrane, S., and S. Farid
1990   Socioeconomic differentials in fertility and their explanation. Pp. 215-233 in G. Acsadi, G. Johnson-Acsadi, and R. Bulatao, eds., *Population Growth and Reproduction in Sub-Saharan Africa*. Washington, D.C.: The World Bank.

Coeytaux, F.M.
1988   Induced abortion in sub-Saharan Africa: What we do and do not know. *Studies in Family Planning* 19(3):186-190.

Columbia University, Center for Population and Family Health
1987   *Proceedings of the Conference on Community Based and Alternative Distribution Systems in Africa, Harare, Zimbabwe, Nov. 3-7, 1986*. New York: Columbia University.
1990   *Final Report: Bouafle Community Health Project*. New York: Columbia University.

Committee on Population
1991   *Measuring the Influence of Accessibility of Family Planning Services In Developing Countries: Summary of an Expert Meeting*. Commission on Behavioral and Social Sciences and Education, National Research Council. Washington, D.C.: National Academy Press.

Cornelius, R.
1992   Analysis of UNFPA funding trends for Africa, memo to Duff G. Gillespie. Office of Population, U.S. Agency for International Development, Washington, D.C.

Cornia, G., and F. Stewart
1987   Country experience with adjustment. Pp. 105-130 in G. Cornia, R. Jolly and F. Stewart, eds., *Adjustment with a Human Face*. New York: Oxford University Press.

Cross, A.
1990   1991 Comparative Analysis of Family Planning Statistics. Demographic and Health Surveys, Presentation, November 1, 1990.

DeBoer, C.N., and M. McNiel
1989   Hospital outreach community based health care: The case of Chogoria. *Social Science and Medicine* 28(10):1007-1017.

DeLancey, V.
1990   Socioeconomic consequences of high fertility for the family. Pp. 115-130 in G. Acsadi, G. Johnson-Acsadi and R. Bulatao, eds., *Population Growth and Reproduction in Sub-Saharan Africa*. Washington, D.C.: The World Bank.

Destler, H., D. Liberi, J. Smith, and J. Stover
1990   Family planning: Preparing for the twenty-first century: Principles for family planning service delivery in the nineties. Family Planning Services Division, Office of Population, U.S. Agency for International Development, Washington, D.C.

de Sweemer, C.C.
1975   Nigeria. Pp. 291-293 in W.B. Watson and R.J. Lapham, eds., Family Planning Programs: World Review 1974. *Studies in Family Planning* 6:291-293.

di Domenico, C., L. de Cola, and J. Leishman
1987   Urban Yoruba mothers at home and at work. Pp. 118-132 in C. Oppong, ed., *Sex Roles, Population and Development in West Africa*. Portsmouth, N.H.: Heinemann.

Dinan, C.
1983   Sugar daddies and gold-diggers: The white-collar single women in Accra. Pp. 344-366 in C. Oppong, ed., *Female and Male in West Africa*. London: George Allen and Unwin.

Direction de la Santé Familiale and Population Communication Services
1989   *Household Survey of Family Planning Knowledge, Attitudes and Practices in Niamey,*

Maradi and Zinder. Niamey, Niger: Ministère de la Santé Publique et Affaires Sociales; Baltimore, Md.: Johns Hopkins University.

DK-Tyagi International
1992   *1991 Contraceptive Social Marketing Statistics*. Washington, D.C.

Donaldson, P.J., and A.O. Tsui
1990   The international family planning movement. *Population Bulletin* 45(3):1-45.

Eades, J.
1980   *The Yoruba Today*. Cambridge: Cambridge University Press.

Easterlin, R.A.
1983   Modernization and fertility—A critical essay. Pp. 562-586 in R.A. Bulatao and R.D. Lee, eds., *Determinants of Fertility in Developing Countries*, Vol. 2. New York: Academic Press.
1986   Economic preconceptions and demographic research. *Population and Development Review* 12(3):517-528.

Easterlin, R., and E. Crimmins
1985   *The Fertility Revolution*. Chicago: University of Chicago Press.

Economic Commission for Africa
1984   *Kilimanjaro Plan of Action*. Second African Population Conference, Arusha, Tanzania, January 9-13.

Emmanuel, S.
1988   Politiques et programmes de population dans le monde et au Rwanda. Pp. 5-11 in *Famille, Santé, Développement*. Kigali, Rwanda: Office National de la Population.

Etienne, M.
1983   Gender relations and conjugality among the Baule. Pp. 303-319 in C. Oppong, ed., *Female and Male in West Africa*. London: George Allen and Unwin.

Evans-Pritchard, E.E
1940   *The Nuer: A Description of the Modes of Livelihood and Political Institutions of a Nilotic People*. Oxford: Clarendon.

Fapohunda, E.R.
1987   Urban women's roles and Nigerian government development strategies. Pp. 203-212 in C. Oppong, ed., *Sex Roles, Population and Development in West Africa*. Portsmouth, N.H.: Heinemann.
1988   The nonpooling household: A challenge to theory. Pp. 143-154 in D. Dwyer and J. Bruce, eds., *A Home Divided: Women and Income in the Third World*. Stanford, Calif.: Stanford University Press.

Fapohunda, E., and M. Todaro
1988   Family structure, implicit contracts, and the demand for children in Southern Nigeria. *Population and Development Review* 14(4):571-594.

Farah, A.A., and D. Lauro
1988   *Final Report: Sudan Community Based Distribution Family Health Project*. New York: Columbia University Center for Population and Family Health.

Faruqee, R., and R. Gulhati
1983   Rapid population growth in sub-Saharan Africa: Issues and policies. *World Bank Staff Working Papers*, No. 559. Washington, D.C.: The World Bank.

Ferry, B.
1981   *Breastfeeding*. World Fertility Survey Comparative Study No. 13. Voorburg, Netherlands: International Statistical Institute.

Finkle, J., and B. Crane
1975   The politics of Bucharest: Population, development, and the new international order. *Population and Development Review* 1(1):87-114.

Ford Foundation
    1990   *1990 Annual Report*. New York.

Fortes, M.
    1945   *The Dynamics of Clanship Among the Tallensi, Being the First Part of an Analysis of the Social Structure of a Trans-Volta Tribe*. London: Oxford University Press.
    1949   *The Web of Kinship Among the Tallensi: The Second Part of an Analysis of the Social Structure of a Trans-Volta Tribe*. London: Oxford University Press.

Frank, O.
    1983a   Infertility in sub-Saharan Africa: Estimates and implications. *Population and Development Review* 9(1):137-144.
    1983b   Infertility in sub-Saharan Africa. *Working Paper of the Center for Policy Studies*, No. 97. New York: The Population Council.
    1987   The demand for fertility control in sub-Saharan Africa. *Studies in Family Planning* 18(4):181-201.
    1988   The childbearing family in sub-Saharan Africa: Structure, fertility, and the future. Paper prepared for the joint Population Council/International Center for Research on Women Seminar Series on the Determinants and Consequences of Female Headed Households.

Frank, O., and G. McNicoll
    1987   An interpretation of fertility and population policy in Kenya. *Population and Development Review* 13(2):209-244.

Freedman, R.
    1987   The contribution of social science research to population policy and family planning program effectiveness. *Studies in Family Planning* 18(2):57-105.

Futures Group
    1988a   Options for Population Policy. Prepared for the Development Policy Seminar of the African Development Bank, October. Washington, D.C.
    1988b   *Materials for Preparing National Population Policies for African Countries*, Vol. 1. Washington, D.C.: The Futures Group.

Gaisie, S.K.
    1981   Child-spacing patterns and fertility differentials in Ghana. Pp. 237-253 in H.J. Page and R. Lesthaeghe, eds., *Child-Spacing in Tropical Africa—Traditions and Change*. London: Academic Press.
    1984   The proximate determinants of fertility in Ghana. *WFS Scientific Reports*, No. 53. Voorburg, Netherlands: International Statistical Institute.

Gauthier, H., and G.F. Brown
    1975a   Francophone countries. Pp. 297-300 in W.B. Watson and R.J. Lapham, eds., Family Planning Programs: World Review 1974. *Studies in Family Planning* 6(8).
    1975b   Anglophone countries. Pp. 293-297 in W.B. Watson and J. Lapham, eds., Family Planning Programs: World Review, 1974. *Studies in Family Planning* 6(8).

Gelbard, A., N. McGirr, and M. Brockerhoff
    1988   The availability of data to assess family planning programs in sub-Saharan Africa. Paper presented at the Population Association of America Annual Meeting, New Orleans, La.

Ghana
    1989   *Demographic and Health Survey*. Accra: Ghana Statistical Service; Columbia, Md.: Institute for Resource Development/Macro Systems, Inc.

Ghana Registered Midwives Association and Columbia University Center for Population and Family Health
    1988   *Operations Research Project Final Report: Ghana Registered Midwives Association Family Planning Programme*. Accra and New York.

Glewwe, P.
    1991   Schooling, skills and the returns to government investment in education. *Living Standards Measurement Study Working Paper*, No. 76. Washington, D.C.: The World Bank
Goldman, N., and M. Montgomery
    1990   Fecundability and husband's age. *Social Biology* 36(3-4):146-166.
Goldman, N., and A. Pebley
    1989   The demography of polygyny in sub-Saharan Africa. Pp. 212-237 in R. Lesthaeghe, ed., *Reproduction and Social Organization in Sub-Saharan Africa*. Berkeley, Calif.: University of California Press.
Goliber, T.J.
    1989   Africa's expanding population: Old problems, new policies. *Population Bulletin* 44(3):1-48.
Goody, E.
    1982   *Parenthood and Social Reproduction: Fostering and Occupational Roles in West Africa*. Cambridge: Cambridge University Press.
Goody, J.
    1973   Polygyny, economy and the role of women. In J. Goody, ed., *The Character of Kinship*. Cambridge: Cambridge University Press.
    1976   *Production and Reproduction—A Comparative Study of the Domestic Domain*. Cambridge: Cambridge University Press.
    1990   Futures of the family in rural Africa. *Population and Development Review*. Supplement to Vol. 15: *Rural Development and Population: Institutions and Policy* 119-144.
Gribble, J., ed.
    1992   *AIDS in Sub-Saharan Africa: Summary of a Planning Meeting*. Committee on Population, National Research Council. Washington, D.C.: National Academy Press.
Gugler, J.
    1981   The second sex in town. Pp. 169-184 in F. Steady, ed., *The Black Woman Cross-Culturally*. Cambridge: Schenkman.
Guyer, J.
    1981   Household and community in African studies. *African Studies Review* 24(2-3):87-137.
    1988a   Dynamic approaches to domestic budgeting: Cases and methods from Africa. Pp. 155-172 in D. Dwyer and J. Bruce, eds., *A Home Divided: Women and Income in the Third World*. Stanford, Calif.: Stanford University Press.
    1988b   Changing nuptiality in a Nigerian community: Observations from the field. Paper presented in the seminar on Nuptiality in Sub-Saharan Africa, International Union for the Scientific Study of Population, Paris, November.
Hagan, G.
    1983   Marriage, divorce and polygyny in Winneba. Pp. 192-203 in C. Oppong, ed., *Female and Male in West Africa*. London: George Allen and Unwin.
Hammerslough, C.R.
    1991a   Women's groups and contraceptive use in rural Kenya. IUSSP seminar on the course of the fertility transition in sub-Saharan Africa, Harare, Nov. 19-22.
    1991b   Proximity to contraceptive services and fertility transition in rural Kenya. Pp. 1287-1304 in *Demographic and Health Surveys World Conference Proceedings*, Vol. II. Columbia, Md.: Institute for Resource Development/Macro International, Inc.
Hansen, S.
    1990   Absorbing a rapidly growing labor force. Pp. 60-73 in G. Acsadi, G. Johnson-

Acsadi, and R. Bulatao, eds., *Population Growth and Reproduction in Sub-Saharan Africa*. Washington, D.C.: The World Bank.

Heckel, N.I.

1986 Population laws and policies in sub-Saharan Africa, 1975-1985. *International Family Planning Perspectives* 12(4):122-124

1990 *Innovations in Population Law and Policy in Sub-Saharan Africa: 1975-1985*. Working Paper #27. New York: Columbia University, Center for Population and Family Health.

Henn, J.

1984 Women in the rural economy: Past, present and future. Pp. 1-18 in M. Hay and S. Stichter, eds., *African Women South of the Sahara*. London: Longman.

Hicks, N.

1991 Expenditure reductions in developing countries revisited. *Journal of International Development* 3(1):29-37.

Hicks, N., and A. Kubisch

1984 Recent experience in cutting government expenditures. *Finance and Development* 21:37-39.

Hill, A.G., and C. Bledsoe

1992 Local cultural interpretations of Western contraceptive technology in rural Gambia. Abstract submitted to the 1993 International Union for the Scientific Study of Population General Conference, Montreal.

Hill, A.L.L.

1990 Population conditions in mainland sub-Saharan Africa. Pp. 3-28 in G. Acsadi, G. Johnson-Acsadi, and R. Bulatao, eds., *Population Growth and Reproduction in Sub-Saharan Africa*. Washington, D.C.: The World Bank.

1991a Infant and child mortality: Levels, trends, and data deficiencies. Pp. 37-74 in R. Feachem and D. Jamison, eds., *Disease and Mortality in Sub-Saharan Africa*. New York: Oxford University Press for The World Bank.

1991b Trends in childhood mortality in sub-Saharan Africa in the 1970s and 1980s. Africa Technical Department, Population, Health and Nutrition Division, The World Bank, Washington, D.C.

1993 Trends in childhood mortality. In K. Foote, K. Hill, and L. Martin, eds., *Demographic Change in Sub-Saharan Africa*. Panel on Population Dynamics of Sub-Saharan Africa, Committee on Population, National Research Council. Washington, D.C.: National Academy Press.

Huber, S.C., and P.D. Harvey

1989 Family planning programmes in ten developing countries: Cost effectiveness by mode of service delivery. *Journal of Biosocial Sciences* 21:267-277.

Hyden, G.

1990 Local governance and economic-demographic transition in rural Africa. *Population and Development Review*. Supplement to Vol. 15: *Rural Development and Population: Institutions and Policy* 193-211.

International Planned Parenthood Federation

1990 *Annual Report, 1989-1990*. London.

Isaac, B., and S. Conrad

1982 Child fosterage among the Mende of Upper Bambara chiefdom, Sierra Leone: Rural-urban and occupational comparisons. *Ethnology* 21(3):243-258.

Johns Hopkins University Population Information Program

1983 Family planning programs: Sources of population and family planning assistance. *Population Reports* 11(1):621-655.

Jolly, C., and J. Gribble

1993 The proximate determinants of fertility. In K. Foote, K. Hill, and L. Martin, eds.,

Demographic Change in Sub-Saharan Africa. Panel on Population Dynamics of Sub-Saharan Africa, Committee on Population, National Research Council. Washington, D.C.: National Academy Press.

Karambizi, J., and G. O'Sullivan
   1989   Trip Report: Rwanda Assessment, Aug. 21-Sept. 2, 1989. Contract No. USAID/ DPE-3051-Z-8034-00. Washington, D.C.: The Futures Group/Social Marketing for Change.

Karanja, W.
   1987   "Outside wives" and "inside wives" in Nigeria: A study of changing perceptions in marriage. Pp. 247-262 in D. Parkin and D. Nyamwaya, eds., *Transformations of African Marriage.* Manchester: Manchester University Press.

Keller, A., P. Severyns, A. Khan, and N. Dodd
   1989   Toward family planning in the 1990's: A review and assessment. *International Family Planning Perspectives* 15(4):127-135,159.

Kelley, A., and C. Nobbe
   1990   Kenya at the demographic turning point? Hypotheses and a proposed research agenda. *World Bank Discussion Paper,* No. 107. Washington D.C.: The World Bank.

Kendall, M.
   1979   The World Fertility Survey: Current status and findings. *Population Reports* Series M(3):73-102.

Kenya
   1980   *Kenya Fertility Survey, First Report,* Vol. 1. Nairobi: Ministry of Economic Planning and Development, Central Bureau of Statistics.
   1989   *Demographic and Health Survey.* Nairobi: National Council for Population and Development, Ministry of Home Affairs and National Heritage; Columbia, Md.: Institute for Resource Development/Macro Systems, Inc.

Knodel, J., A. Chamratrithirong, and N. Debavalya
   1987   *Thailand's Reproductive Revolution: Rapid Fertility Decline in a Third-World Setting.* Madison: University of Wisconsin Press.

Knodel, J., N. Havanon, and W. Sittitra
   1990   Family size and the education of children in the context of rapid fertility decline. *Population and Development Review* 16(1):31-62.

Knowles, J., and R. Anker
   1981   An analysis of income transfers in a developing country: The case of Kenya. *Journal of Development Economics* 8(2):205-226.

Kocher, J.E.
   1973   *Rural Development, Income Distribution and Fertility Decline.* New York: The Population Council.

Kritz, M., and D. Gurak
   1991   Women's economic independence and fertility among the Yoruba. Paper presented to the DHS World Conference, Washington D.C., August.

Kroeber, A.L.
   1938   Basic and secondary patterns of social structure. *Journal of the Royal Anthropological Institute* 68:299-309.

Krystall, A.
   1975   Kenya. Pp. 286-288 in W.B. Watson and R.J. Lapham, eds., Family Planning Programs: World Review, 1974. *Studies in Family Planning* 6(8):286-288

Kuper, A.
   1982a   Lineage theory: A critical retrospect. *Annual Review of Anthropology* 11:71-95.
   1982b   *Wives for Cattle: Bridewealth and Marriage in Southern Africa.* London: Routledge and Kegan Paul.

Ladipo, P.
1987   Women in a maize storage co-operative in Nigeria. Pp. 101-117 in C. Oppong, ed., *Sex Roles, Population and Development in West Africa*. Portsmouth, N.H.: Heinemann.

Lande, R.E., and J.S. Geller
1991   Paying for family planning. *Population Reports* 39:7.

Lapham, R.J., and W.P. Mauldin
1984   Family planning program effort and birthrate decline in developing countries. *International Family Planning Perspectives* 10(4):109-118.

1985   Contraceptive prevalence: The influence of organized family planning programs. *Studies in Family Planning* 16(3):117-137.

Larsen, U.
1989   A comparative study of the levels and the differentials of sterility in Cameroon, Kenya and Sudan. Pp. 167-211 in R. Lesthaeghe, ed., *Reproduction and Social Organization in Sub-Saharan Africa*. Berkeley: University of California Press.

Lesthaeghe, R.
1989a   Social organization, economic crises, and the future of fertility control in Africa. Pp. 475-505 in R. Lesthaeghe, ed., *Reproduction and Social Organization in Sub-Saharan Africa*. Berkeley: University of California Press.

1989b   Production and reproduction in sub-Saharan Africa: An overview of organizing principles. Pp. 13-59 in R. Lesthaeghe, ed., *Reproduction and Social Organization in Sub-Saharan Africa*. Berkeley: University of California Press.

1989c   Introduction. Pp. 1-12 in R. Lesthaeghe, ed., *Reproduction and Social Organization in Sub-Saharan Africa*. Berkeley: University of California Press.

Lesthaeghe, R., C. Vanderhoeft, S. Becker, and M. Kibet
1983   Individual and contextual effects of female education on the Kenya marital fertility transition. *IPD-Working Paper 83-9*. Vrije Universiteit Brussel, Belgium.

Lesthaeghe, R., G. Kaufmann, D. Meekers, and J. Surkyn
1988   Age at marriage, polygyny and postpartum abstinence—A macro-level analysis of sub-Saharan societies. Rockefeller Foundation workshop on "Status of Women and Fertility," Bellagio, June 6-10.

Lesthaeghe, R., G. Kaufmann, and D. Meekers
1989a   The nuptiality regimes in sub-Saharan Africa. Pp. 238-337 in R. Lesthaeghe, ed., *Reproduction and Social Organization in Sub-Saharan Africa*. Berkeley: University of California Press.

Lesthaeghe, R., C. Vanderhoeft, S. Gaisie, and G. Delaine
1989b   Regional variation in components of child-spacing: The role of women's education. Pp. 122-166 in R. Lesthaeghe, ed., *Reproduction and Social Organization in Sub-Saharan Africa*. Berkeley: University of California Press.

Lesthaeghe, R., C. Verleye, and C. Jolly
1992   Female education and factors affecting fertility in sub-Saharan Africa. *IPD-Working Paper 1992-2*. Interuniversity Programme in Demography, Belgium.

Lewis, B.
1976   The limitations of group action among entrepreneurs: The market women of Abidjan, Ivory Coast. Pp. 135-156 in N. Hafkin and E. Bay, eds., *Women in Africa: Studies in Social and Economic Change*. Stanford, Calif.: Stanford University Press.

Lewis, J.
1978   Small farmer credit and the village production unit in rural Mali. *African Studies Review* 21(3):29-48.

Lewis, M.A.
1985   Pricing and cost recovery experience in family planning programs. *World Bank*

Staff Working Papers No. 684, Population and Development Series No. 9. Washington, D.C.: The World Bank.

Lightbourne, R.E.
  1980   Urban-rural differentials in contraceptive use. *WFS Comparative Studies*, No. 10. Voorburg, Netherlands: International Statistical Institute.

Lloyd, P.C.
  1971   The elite. In P.C. Lloyd, A.L. Mabogunje, and B. Awe, eds., *The City of Ibadan.* Cambridge: Cambridge University Press.

Lloyd, C., and A. Brandon
  1991   Women's roles in maintaining households: Poverty and gender inequality in Ghana. Research paper prepared for the joint Population Council/International Center for Research on Women project on "Family Structure, Female Headship and Poverty." The Population Council, New York.

Lloyd, C., and S. Desai
  1991   Children's living arrangements in developing countries. *Working Paper No. 31.* New York: The Population Council.

Lloyd, C., and S. Ivanov
  1988   The effects of improved child survival on family planning practice and fertility. *Studies in Family Planning* 19(3):141-161.

Locoh, T.
  1984   *Fécondité et Famille en Afrique de l'Ouest—Le Togo Méridional Contemporain.* Cahier de l'INED, nr. 107. Paris: Presses Universitaires de France.
  1991   The socio-economic context of contraceptive utilization in sub-Saharan Africa. Background paper prepared for Working Group on Factors Affecting Contraceptive Use, Committee on Population, National Research Council.

London, K.A., J. Cushing, S.O. Rutstein, J. Cleland, J.E. Anderson, L. Morris, and S.H. More
  1985   Fertility and family planning surveys: An update. *Population Reports* Series M(8).

Lucas, D.
  1991   Mass education and fertility decline: Implications for Southern Africa. Paper presented to the Seminar on "The Course of Fertility Transition in Sub-Saharan Africa," sponsored by the IUSSP Committee on Comparative Analysis of Fertility and the University of Zimbabwe, Harare, November 19-22.

Makinwa-Adebusoye, P.
  1991   Changes in the costs and benefits of children to their parents: The changing cost of educating children. Paper presented to the Seminar on "The Course of Fertility Transition in Sub-Saharan Africa," sponsored by the IUSSP Committee on Comparative Analysis of Fertility and the University of Zimbabwe, Harare, November 19-22.

Mali
  1989   *Enquête Démographique et de Santé.* (B. Traoré, M. Konaté, and C. Stanton, eds.) Bamako: Centre d'Etudes et de Recherches sur la Population pour le Développement, Institut du Sahel; and Columbia, Md.: Institute for Resource Development/Westinghouse.

Mauldin, W.P., and J.A. Ross
  1991   Family planning programs: Efforts and results, 1982-1989. *Studies in Family Planning* 22(6):350-367.

Mauldin, W.P., and S.J. Segal
  1986   *Prevalence of Contraceptive Use in Developing Countries: A Chart Book.* New York: The Rockefeller Foundation.
  1988   Prevalence of contraceptive use: Trends and issues. *Studies in Family Planning* 19(6):335-353.

Mauldin, W.P., N. Choucri, F. Notestein, and M. Teitelbaum
    1974   A report on Bucharest. *Studies in Family Planning* 5(12):357-395.
Mauritius Ministry of Health, University of Mauritius, and Centers for Disease Control
    1992   *1991 Mauritius Contraceptive Prevalence Survey: Preliminary Report.* Atlanta,
            Ga.: Centers for Disease Control, U.S. Department of Health and Human Ser-
            vices.
May, J.F., M. Mukamanzi, and M. Vekemans
    1990   Family planning in Rwanda: Status and practice. *Studies in Family Planning*
            21(1):20-32.
McGinn, T.
    1990   Accelerated family planning acceptance in Rwanda: Results of an OR project.
            Paper presented at the 17th Annual Meeting of the American Public Health Asso-
            ciation, Chicago, October 22-26.
McGinn, T., A. Bamba, and M. Balma
    1989a   Male knowledge, use and attitudes regarding family planning in Burkina Faso.
            International Family Planning Perspectives 15(3):84-87.
McGinn, T., P. Sebgo, T. Fenn, and A. Bamba
    1989b   Family planning in Burkina Faso: Results of a survey. *Studies in Family Plan-
            ning* 20(6):325-331.
McNamara, R., T. McGinn, D. Lauro, and J. Ross
    1990   Family Planning Programs in Sub-Saharan Africa: Case Studies from Ghana,
            Rwanda and the Sudan. Review prepared for the World Bank. Columbia Univer-
            sity Center for Population and Family Health, New York.
Messina, M.
    1992   Background paper prepared for Working Group on Factors Affecting Contracep-
            tive Use, Committee on Population, National Research Council, Washington, D.C.
Montgomery, M.
    1987   A new look at the Easterlin "synthesis" model. *Demography* 24(4):481-496.
    1989   Dynamic behavioural models of contraceptive use. Supplement to Vol. 11: *Dy-
            namics of Contraceptive Use. Journal of Biosocial Sciences* 17-40.
Montgomery, M., and A. Kouame
    1992   The quantity-quality tradeoff in Côte d'Ivoire. Work in progress, Department of
            Economics, State University of New York, Stony Brook.
Mony-Lobe, M., D. Nichols, I. Zekeng, J. Salla, and L. Kaptue
    1989   The use of condoms by prostitutes in Yaoundé, Cameroon. Abstract WDP 8.7. *V
            International Conference on AIDs Abstract Vol.,* Montreal, June 4-9.
Mosley, W.H., C.H. Werner, and S. Becker
    1982   The dynamics of birth-spacing and marital fertility in Kenya. *World Fertility
            Survey Scientific Reports*, No. 30. Voorburg, Netherlands: International Statisti-
            cal Institute.
Mott, F., and S. Mott
    1985   Household fertility decisions in West Africa: A comparison of male and female
            survey results. *Studies in Family Planning* 16(2): 88-99.
Mpiti, A.M., and I. Kalule-Sabiti
    1985   The proximate determinants of fertility in Lesotho. *WFS-Scientific Reports*, No.
            78. Voorburg, Netherlands: International Statistical Institute.
Munachonga, M.
    1988   Income allocation and marriage options in urban Zambia. Pp. 173-194 in D.
            Dwyer and J. Bruce, eds., *A Home Divided: Women and Income in the Third
            World.* Stanford, Calif.: Stanford University Press.
Musagara, M., M.J. Wawer, N.K. Sewankambo, and S. Musgrave
    1991   Family planning and birth regulation in communities affected by AIDS in rural

Uganda. International Conference on the Bio-Psycho-Social Aspects of HIV Infection. Amsterdam, September.

Mueller, E., and K. Short
1983   Effects of income and wealth on the demand for children. Pp. 590-642 in R. Bulatao and R. Lee, eds., *Determinants of Fertility in Developing Countries*, Vol. 1. New York: Academic Press.

Nabila, J.S.
1986   The Ghana National Family Planning Programme and National Development. Pp. 1-6 in *National Conference on Population and National Reconstruction 1986*. Vol. II: Contributed Papers. Legon: University of Ghana.

Nag, M.
1980   How modernization can also increase fertility. *Current Anthropology* 21(2):27-36.

Ngubane, H.
1987   The consequences for women of marriage payments in a society with patrilineal descent. Pp. 173-182 in D. Parkin and D. Nyamwaya, eds., *Transformations of African Marriage*. Manchester: Manchester University Press.

Nichols, D., O.A. Ladipo, J. Paxman, and E.O. Otolorin
1986   Sexual behavior, contraceptive practice and reproductive health among Nigerian adolescents. *Studies in Family Planning* 17(2):100-106.

Nigeria
1992   *Demographic and Health Survey*. Lagos: Federal Office of Statistics; Columbia, Md.: Institute for Resource Development/Macro International, Inc.

Nigeria (Ondo State)
1989   *Demographic and Health Survey*. Ondo State, Nigeria: Medical/Preventive Health Division of the Ministry of Health, Akure; Columbia, Md.: Institute for Resource Development/Macro Systems, Inc.

Nortman, D.L.
1981   *Population and Family Planning Programs: A Compendium of Data Through 1981*. Eleventh edition. New York: The Population Council.

Obbo, C.
1987   The old and the new in East African elite marriages. Pp. 263-282 in D. Parkin and D. Nyamwaya, eds., *Transformations of African Marriage*. Manchester: Manchester University Press.

Okali, C.
1983   Kinship and cocoa farming in Ghana. Pp. 169-178 in C. Oppong, ed., *Female and Male in West Africa*. London: George Allen and Unwin.

Okojie, C.
1991   Micro-consequences of high fertility in Nigeria: Pilot study. Research report prepared for the Population Council. Department of Economics and Statistics, University of Benin.

Okonjo, K.
1983   Sex roles in Nigerian politics. Pp. 211-222 in C. Oppong, ed., *Female and Male in West Africa*. London: George Allen and Unwin.

Olusanya, P.O.
1969   Modernization and the level of fertility in western Nigeria. In *Proceedings of the International Population Conference*. Liège: International Union for the Scientific Study of Population.
1971   Nigeria: Cultural barriers to family planning among the Yorubas. *Studies in Family Planning* 37:13-16.

Oppong, C.
1987a   Introduction to Part III. Pp. 133-137 in C. Oppong, ed., *Sex Roles, Population and Development in West Africa*. Portsmouth, N.H.: Heinemann.

1987b   Responsible fatherhood and birth planning. Pp. 165-178 in C. Oppong, ed., *Sex Roles, Population and Development in West Africa*. Portsmouth, N.H.: Heinemann.

Page, H.J.
1989   Childrearing versus childbearing: Coresidence of mother and child in sub-Saharan Africa. Pp. 401-441 in R. Lesthaeghe, ed., *Reproduction and Social Organization in Sub-Saharan Africa*. Berkeley: University of California Press.

Page, H.J., and A.J. Coale
1972   Fertility and child mortality south of the Sahara. Pp. 51-67 in S.H. Ominde and C. Ejiogu, eds., *Population Growth and Economic Development in Africa*. London: Heinemann.

Page, H.J., and R. Lesthaeghe, eds.
1981   *Child-Spacing in Tropical Africa: Traditions and Change*. London: Academic Press.

Paulme, D.
1963   Introduction. Pp. 1-16 in D. Paulme, ed., *Women of Tropical Africa*. Berkeley: University of California Press.

Pinstrup-Andersen, P., M. Jaramillo, and F. Stewart
1987   The impact on government expenditure. Pp. 73-89 in G. Cornia, R. Jolly, and F. Stewart, eds., *Adjustment with a Human Face*. New York: Oxford University Press.

Piotrow, P.T.
1973   *World Population Crisis: The United States Response*. New York: Praeger Publishers.

Pittin, R.
1987   Documentation of women's work in Nigeria. Pp. 25-44 in C. Oppong, ed., *Sex Roles, Population and Development in West Africa*. Portsmouth, N.H.: Heinemann.

Plummer, F., M. Braddick, W. Cameron, J. Ndinya-Achola, J. Kreiss, M. Bosire, A. Ronald, and E. Ngugi
1988   Durability of changed sexual behavior in Nairobi prostitutes: Increasing use of condoms. Abstract 5141 *IV International Conference on AIDS, Abstract*, Vol. 1. Stockholm, June.

Population Council
1989   *Annual Report 1989*. New York.

Population Crisis Committee
1990   Report on progress towards population stabilization. *Briefing Paper No. 23*. Washington, D.C.
1991   *Access to Affordable Contraception: 1991 Report on World Progress Towards Population Stabilization*. Washington, D.C.: Population Crisis Committee.

Population Reference Bureau
1990   Options Database. Prepared for the Futures Group, Washington, D.C.
1992   *World Population Data Sheet*. Washington, D.C.: The Population Reference Bureau.

Preston, S.
1975   Health programs and population growth. *Population and Development Review* 1(2):189-199.

Preston, S., ed.
1978   *The Effects of Infant and Child Mortality on Fertility*. New York: Academic Press.

Reinke, W.
1985   The Danfa, Lampang and Narangwal projects: A comparative review. Pp. 43-50 in M.J. Wawer, S. Huffman, D. Cebula, and R. Osborn, eds., *Health and Family*

Planning in Community Based Distribution Projects. Boulder, Colo.: Westview Press.

Rempel, H., and R. Lobdell
1978   The role of urban-to-rural remittances in rural development. *Journal of Development Studies* (April).

Retel-Laurentin, A.
1974   Sub-fertility in black Africa. Pp. 69-80 in B.K. Adadevoh, ed., *Subfertility and Infertility in Africa.* Ibadan: The Claxton Press.

Robertson, C.
1976   Ga women and socioeconomic change in Accra, Ghana. Pp. 111-133 in N. Hafkin and E. Bay, eds., *Women in Africa: Studies in Social and Economic Change.* Stanford, Calif.: Stanford University Press.

Robinson, W.
1992   Kenya enters the fertility transition. *Population Studies* 46(4):445-457.

Romaniuk, A.
1968   Infertility in tropical Africa. Pp. 214-224 in J.C. Caldwell and C. Okonjo, eds., *The Populations of Tropical Africa.* London: Longmann.
1980   Increase in natural fertility during the early stages of modernization—Evidence from an African case study: Zaire. *Population Studies* 34(2):293-310.

Ross, J.A.
1986   Family planning pilot projects in Africa: Review and synthesis. *Working Paper Series, Center for Population and Family Health.* New York: Columbia University.

Ross, J.A., M. Rich, J. Molzan, and M. Pensak
1988   *Family Planning and Child Survival: 100 Developing Countries.* New York: Columbia University Center for Population and Family Health.

Roudi, N.
1991   Population policies for Africa: A 1991 scorecard. *International Planned Parenthood Federation/People Wallchart.* London: International Planned Parenthood Federation.

Rutenberg, N., M. Ayad, L.H. Ochoa, and M. Wilkinson
1991   *Knowledge and Use of Contraception.* DHS Comparative Studies, 6. Columbia, Md: Institute for Resource Development/Macro International.

Rutstein, S.O., L. Morris, and R. Blackburn
1992   The reproductive revolution: New survey findings. *Population Reports* Series M(11):1-44.

Sala-Diakanda, M.
1980   *Approche Ethnique des Phénoménes Démographiques: le cas du Zaïre.* Louvain: Cabay Couvain-la-Neuve.

Sanjek, R.
1983   Female and male domestic cycles in urban Africa: The Adabraka case. Pp. 330-343 in C. Oppong, ed., *Female and Male in West Africa.* London: George Allen and Unwin.

Sathar, Z.A., and V.C. Chidambaram
1984   Differentials in contraceptive use. *WFS Comparative Studies*, No. 36. Voorburg, Netherlands: International Statistical Institute.

Schildkrout, E.
1983   Dependence and autonomy: The economic activities of secluded Hausa women in Kano. Pp. 107-126 in C. Oppong, ed., *Female and Male in West Africa.* London: George Allen and Unwin.

Schoenmaeckers, R., I.H. Shah, R. Lesthaeghe, and O. Tambashe
1981   The child-spacing tradition and the postpartum taboo in tropical Africa. Pp. 25-72

in H.J. Page and R. Lesthaeghe, eds., *Child-Spacing in Tropical Africa—Traditions and Change.* London: Academic Press.

Schultz, T.P.

1986 Review of R. Easterlin and E. Crimmins *The Fertility Revolution. Population and Development Review* 12(1):127-140.

1987 School expenditures and enrollments, 1960-80: The effects of income, prices and population growth. Pp. 413-478 in D. Johnson and R. Lee, eds., *Population Growth and Economic Development: Issues and Evidence.* Madison: University of Wisconsin Press.

Senegal, Ministry of Health, and U.S. Agency for International Development

1982 End of Project Evaluation of the Sine Saloum Rural Health Services Development Project. (July) Dakar.

Serwadda, D., M.J. Wawer, S. Musgrave, J. Konde-Lule, J. Ndumu, and W. Naamara

1989 An assessment of AIDS related knowledge, attitudes and practices (KAP) in Rakai District, Uganda. Abstract MGO 14, *V International Conference on AIDS, Abstract*, Vol. 2. Montreal, June 4-9.

Serwadda, D., S. Musgrave, M.J. Wawer, M. Musagara, J. Konde-Lule, and N. Sewankambo

1990 HIV-1 risk factors in a randomly selected population in rural Rakai District, Uganda. Abstract FC 100, *VI International Conference on AIDS, Abstract*, Vol. 2. San Francisco, June 20-24.

Smith, D.P., E. Carrasco, and P. McDonald

1984 Marriage dissolution and remarriage. *WFS Comparative Studies*, No. 34. Voorburg, Netherlands: International Statistical Institute.

Stark, O., and R. Lucas

1988 Migration, remittances and the family. *Economic Development and Cultural Change* 36(3):465-482.

Steady, F.

1976 Protestant women's associations in Freetown, Sierra Leone. Pp. 213-237 in N. Hafkin and E. Bay, eds., *Women in Africa: Studies in Social and Economic Change.* Stanford, Calif.: Stanford University Press.

1981 The black woman cross-culturally: An overview. Pp. 7-42 in F. Steady, ed., *The Black Woman Cross-Culturally.* Cambridge: Schenkman.

1987 Polygamy and the household economy in a fishing village in Sierra Leone. Pp. 211-232 in D. Parkin and D. Nyamwaya, eds., *Transformations of African Marriage.* Manchester: Manchester University Press.

Strobel, M.

1976 From lelemama to lobbying: Women's associations in Mombasa, Kenya. Pp. 183-211 in N. Hafkin and E. Bay, eds. *Women in Africa: Studies in Social and Economic Change.* Stanford, Calif.: Stanford University Press.

Sudarkasa, N.

1981 Female employment and family organization in West Africa. Pp. 49-64 in F. Steady, ed., *The Black Woman Cross-Culturally.* Cambridge: Schenkman.

Suitters, F.

1973 *Be Brave and Angry: Chronicles of the International Planned Parenthood Federation.* London: International Planned Parenthood Federation.

Tambashe, O.

1984 Niveaux et corrélats de la fécondité à Kinshasa. Ph.D. dissertation. Interuniversity Programme in Demography, Vrije Universiteit Brussel, Belgium.

Tambashe, O., and D. Shapiro

1991 *Employment, Education, and Fertility Behavior: Evidence From Kinshasa.* Substantive report prepared for The Rockefeller Foundation, Research Program on

Population Policies and Programs in Sub-Saharan Africa under Grants RF 88078#54 and RF 89092#74. Kinshasa, Zaire: Département de Démographie, Université de Kinshasa.

Taylor, H.C.
   1979   Maternal and child health/family planning programs, introductory remarks. Technical Workshop Proceedings. October 3-November 2. The Population Council, New York.

Taylor, H.C., Jr., and B. Berelson
   1971   Comprehensive family planning based on maternal/child health services: A feasibility study for a world program. *Studies in Family Planning* 2(2):21-54.

Trias, M.
   1980   Some considerations on the integration of family planning programs. *Forum* December:35.

Tsui, A., and M. Herbertson, eds.
   1989   *Dynamics of Contraceptive Use*, Supplement to Vol. 11, *Journal of Biosocial Sciences*.

Uganda
   1989   *Demographic and Health Survey.* (E. Kaijuka, E. Kaija, A. Cross, and E. Loaiza, eds.) Entebbe: Ministry of Health and Ministry of Planning and Economic Development; Columbia, Md.: Institute for Resource Development/Macro Systems, Inc.

United Nations
   1989a   Levels and trends of contraceptive use as assessed in 1988. *Population Studies.* No. 110 ST/ESA/SER.A110. New York.
   1989b   *Trends in Population Policy.* Population Series No. 114. Department of International Economic and Social Affairs ST/ESA/SER.A/114. New York.
   1993   *United Nations 1993 Monitoring Report.* New York.

United Nations Educational, Scientific and Cultural Organization
   1990   *UNESCO Statistical Yearbook.* New York: United Nations.

United Nations Population Fund
   1979   On integration of family planning with rural development. Pp. 2-3 and 14-26 in *Policy Development Studies*, Vol. 1. New York.
   1983   *Africa: Population Profiles #20.* New York.
   1991   *United Nations Population Fund, Global Population Assistance Report 1982-1989.* New York.
   1992   *United Nations Population Fund, Global Population Assistance Report, 1982-1990.* New York.

University College Hospital, State Health Council, and the Columbia University Center for Population and Family Health
   1986   *Oyo State Health and Family Planning Community-Based Distribution Project, Final Report.* Ibadan, Nigeria: University of Ibadan and Oyo State Ministry of Health; New York: Columbia University.

U.S. Agency for International Development
   1990   Overview of A.I.D. Population Assistance, Fiscal Year 1989. Office of Population. Washington, D.C.
   1991   Overview of A.I.D. Population Assistance. Fiscal Year 1990.

Vandemoortele, J.
   1991   Labour market informalisation in sub-Saharan Africa. Pp. 81-114 in G. Standing and V. Tokman, eds., *Towards Social Adjustment: Labour Market Issues in Structural Adjustment.* Geneva: International Labour Office.

Vellenga, D.D.
   1971   Attempts to change the marriage laws in Ghana and the Ivory Coast. In P. Foster

and A.R. Zolberg, eds., *Ghana and the Ivory Coast: Perspectives on Modernization*. Chicago: University of Chicago Press.

Vercruijsse, E.

1983   Fishmongers, big dealers and fishermen: Co-operation and conflict between the sexes in Ghanaian canoe fishing. Pp. 179-191 in C. Oppong, ed., *Female and Male in West Africa*. London: George Allen and Unwin.

Warren, C.W., J.T. Johnson, G. Gule, E. Hlophe, and D. Kraushaar

1992   The determinants of fertility in Swaziland. *Population Studies* 46:5-17.

Warwick, D.P.

1982   *Bitter Pills: Population Policies and Their Implementation in Eight Developing Countries*. Cambridge: Cambridge University Press.

Watkins, S.

1991   More lessons from the past: Women's informal networks and fertility decline. Paper presented to the IUSSP Committee on Comparative Analysis of Fertility and the University of Zimbabwe Seminar on "The Course of Fertility Transition in Sub-Saharan Africa," Harare, Zimbabwe, November 19-22.

Wawer, M.J., L. Gaffikin, V. Ravao, H. Maidouka, and K. Traore

1990   Results of a contraceptive prevalence survey in Niamey, Niger. *International Family Planning Perspectives* 16(3):90-96

Wawer, M.J., D. Serwadda, S.D. Musgrave, J.K. Konde-Lule, M. Musagara, and N.K. Sewankambo

1991a   Dynamics of the spread of HIV-1 infection in a rural district of Uganda. *British Medical Journal* 303:1303-1306.

Wawer, M.J., McNamara, R., McGinn, T., and D. Lauro

1991b   Family planning operations research in Africa: Reviewing a decade of experience. *Studies in Family Planning* 22(5):279-293.

Webb, G., O.A. Ladipo, and R. McNamara

1991   Qualitative methods in operations research on contraceptive distribution systems: A case study for Nigeria. *Social Science and Medicine* 33(3):321-326.

Westoff, C.F.

1990   Reproductive preferences and fertility rates. *International Family Planning Perspectives* 16(3):84-89.

1991   Reproductive preferences: A comparative view. *DHS Comparative Studies*, No. 3. Columbia, Md.: Institute for Resource Development.

1992   *Age at Marriage, Age at First Birth, and Fertility in Africa*. World Bank Technical Paper No. 169. Washington, D.C.: The World Bank.

Westoff, C.F., and L.H. Ochoa

1991   Unmet need and the demand for family planning. *DHS Comparative Studies*, No. 5. Columbia, Md.: Institute for Resource Development.

Wilkinson, M.I., N. Abderrahim, and W. Njogu

1991   Availability and use of contraception: A comparative analysis. Pp. 1255-1272 in *Demographic and Health Surveys World Conference Proceedings*, Vol. II. Columbia, Md.: Institute for Resource Development/Macro International, Inc.

Willis, R.

1973   A new approach to the economic theory of fertility behavior. *Journal of Political Economy* 81(2)Part II:S14-64.

Wipper, A.

1984   Women's voluntary associations. Pp. 69-86 in M. Hay and S. Stichter, eds., *African Women South of the Sahara*. London: Longman.

Working Group on Demographic Effects of Economic and Social Reversals

1993   *Demographic Effects of Economic Reversals in Sub-Saharan Africa*. Panel on

Population Dynamics of Sub-Saharan Africa, Committee on Population, National Research Council. Washington, D.C.: National Academy Press.

Working Group on the Health Consequences of Contraceptive Use and Controlled Fertility

1989   *Contraception and Reproduction: Health Consequences for Women and Children in the Developing World.* Committee on Population, Commission on Behavioral and Social Sciences and Education, National Research Council. Washington D.C.: National Academy Press.

Working Group on Kenya

1993   *Population Dynamics of Kenya.* W. Brass and C.L. Jolly, eds. Panel on Population Dynamics of Sub-Saharan Africa, Committee on Population, National Research Council. Washington, D.C.: National Academy Press.

Working Group on Social Dynamics of Adolescent Fertility

1993   *Social Dynamics of Adolescent Fertility in Sub-Saharan Africa.* C.H. Bledsoe and B.H. Cohen, eds. Panel on the Population Dynamics of Sub-Saharan Africa, Committee on Population, National Research Council. Washington, D.C.: National Academy Press.

World Bank

1980   *Kenya: Population and Development. A World Bank Country Study.* Washington, D.C.

1982   *Zimbabwe Population, Health and Nutrition Sector Review,* Vol. I. Washington, D.C.

1984   *World Development Report 1984.* New York: Oxford University Press.

1985   *Population Change and Economic Development.* Oxford: Oxford University Press.

1986   *Population Growth and Policies in Sub-Saharan Africa.* Washington, D.C.

1988   *Education in Sub-Saharan Africa: Policies for Adjustment, Revitalization, and Expansion.* Washington, D.C.

1989   *Report of the Africa Region Task Force on Population.* FY90-92, Vol. I. Washington, D.C.

1990a   *African Economic and Financial Data* (on diskette.) Washington, D.C.

1990b   *1990 World Development Report.* Washington, D.C.

1990c   Structural adjustment and poverty: A conceptual, empirical and policy framework. *Social Dimensions of Adjustment Unit, Africa Region.* Report No. 8393-AFR. Washington, D.C.

1991   *1991 World Development Indicators* (on diskette). Washington, D.C.

1992   World Bank assistance in population. Discussion note for the Expert Group Meeting on Family Planning, Health and Family Well-being for the International Conference on Population and Development, 1994. Bangalore, October 26-30.

1993   Data sheets from the office of the Senior Population Advisor to the World Bank. Washington, D.C.

Zimbabwe

1989   *Zimbabwe Demographic and Health Survey.* Harare: Central Statistical Office, Ministry of Finance, Economic Planning, and Development; Columbia, Md.: Institute for Resource Development/Macro Systems, Inc.

Zimbabwe National Family Planning Council

1985   *Zimbabwe Reproductive Health Survey 1984.* Columbia, Md.: Westinghouse Public Applied Systems.